D1429035

FIFTY YEARS
OF THE
AMERICAN NOVEL

FIFTY YEARS

OF THE

AMERICAN NOVEL

A CHRISTIAN APPRAISAL

EDITED BY

HAROLD C. GARDINER, S. J.

CHARLES SCRIBNER'S SONS, NEW YORK

CHARLES SCRIBNER'S SONS, LTD., LONDON

1952

CHRISTO REGI

ET

CONSERVIS EJUS

EUM

UT ARTES EXPRIMANT

Foreword

One famous rhetorical device much favored by the Ciceronian school was called *praeteritio*. It was a convenient means of castigating an opponent while pretending simply to have nothing to say about him. "I shall pass over the fact," Cicero would declaim, "that Milo has done such and such a nefarious deed"—the deed of course being specified in the alleged display of reticence.

It was suggested to me that this foreword might employ some such device, not, of course, as a means of castigation, but rather as a convenient summary of much American literary history not covered in the succeeding essays. It might, indeed, have provided a fine opportunity to explain precisely why prominent and even influential American writers have not found their place in this symposium on fifty years of the American novel.

I am afraid that many students will lament, and probably with good reason, the omission of such novelists as Henry James, Hamlin Garland, Booth Tarkington, Jack London and Frank Norris, and Sherwood Anderson. Some of these omissions can be explained, I hope, if not justified, because of the rather arbitrary limits set. Authors whose main body of work antedated 1900 were simply ruled out. This may seem to be high-handed indeed, particularly in view of the noteworthy current revival of interest in Henry James. But I believe that James is without doubt a nineteenth-century writer. Moreover, it can be convincingly maintained that he is least in need of a "Christian appraisal." This proposition finds support in the fact that James is very sympathetically criticized by such eminently Christian critics as Chesterton (in *The Common Man*) and Graham Greene (in *The Lost Childhood*). That this view is controverted in one of the studies that follow is but another evidence of the Christian *in dubiis, libertas* of which I shall speak at length later. Finally, a rather thorough, if oblique, criticism of James will be found in three of the following critiques.

I would have inclined personally to include a study of Booth Tarkington, for I believe that he, like John Marquand, has never received from critics the just estimate he deserves as a commentator on the American middle-class scene. Booth Tarkington is perhaps still waiting as perceptive a critic to rescue him from critical snobbery as John Marquand finds in this book.

The omission of Sherwood Anderson is perhaps more puzzling, particularly in view of the two excellent critical studies of him that have appeared recently, the one by James Schevill (the University of Denver Press), the other by Irving Howe (Sloane Associates: *American Men of Letters* Series). Anderson had, if I may quote from a review by C. Carroll Hollis, "uncanny intuitive perceptions of the loneliness of the sensitive person amid the conforming pressures of the small town," and in this he is certainly the peer of Sinclair Lewis. Further, he towers over Lewis because "his love for his characters is that of great charity and his language is that of Twain's native idiom faithfully and sensitively refined."

Anderson's influence, however, has not been wide or deep. We will hear Thomas Wolfe later acknowledging a debt to him and at the same time pointing out rather cannily that the Anderson after *Winesburg, Ohio,* was largely a spent force. Perhaps that happened because, as Mr. Hollis says: "It was only when, in rejecting the past, he attempted to correct that bewilderment by offering assorted psychological, physiological and sociological panaceas that he lost his art in becoming a prophet."

At any rate, Anderson (and others of equal stature) was not simply overlooked. It may be that a brief account of how this volume grew (I hope in not too Topsy-like a fashion) will serve to exonerate the editor from the charge of snubbing some of the great figures among American novelists.

Once the idea of this study was conceived, I set about a bit of questionnaire work. My first field of inquiry, obviously enough, was among my confreres in universities (mainly Catholic and Jesuit) throughout the country. I sent a double list of names, one of novelists who might deserve treatment, the second of critics who might do the best job of evaluation on the individual novelists. The result was really astonishing when one recalls the usual fate of questionnaires. Some universities, indeed, were so cooperative that they called a special meeting of the English faculty to discuss the questionnaire and to send in corporate suggestions. Twenty-seven colleges and universities gave me, in this fashion, most needed and heart-warming cooperation, and in addition some seventy-five individuals—book reviewers, critics, publishers—added to the wealth of guidance that I so keenly desired. The novelists chosen for consideration in this volume were voted for in this communal fashion. The critics, too, who spread their wares before you in the following pages were chosen because they had most frequently been mentioned for their competence on a particular novelist.

In these many senses, therefore, I believe it can be maintained in all modesty that this volume is truly representative of Catholic literary scholarship. It is catholic too, in another sense. Not one of the critics was instructed by the editor on what he was to say, no common approach was outlined save that indicated in the sub-title of the book, namely, that each critic was to give—as indeed he would have given without suggestion—a "Christian appraisal." Accordingly, the reader will find in these pages some diversity of opinion. There is no "party line." Many a reader will probably be surprised to see that critics who are Catholics have some kind things to say of James Joyce—a symptom of the wide but unflabby tolerance that marks all the subsequent studies. Critics will be discovered criticizing other critics. And this, I believe, is all to the good. If such freedom of judgment and diversity of opinion baffle non-Catholic readers who harbor the sneaking suspicion that all Catholics must say the same thing about everything (being but poor, intellectually-regimented souls), or if they puzzle fellow Catholics who believe it highly desirable that all Catholics agree on all things, permit me to recall a famous dictum. It is attributed to St. Augustine. Even if the great Bishop of Hippo, himself a towering literary figure, never said it, it is the type of thing to which he would agree with a heartfelt "bravo!" The immortal phrase is: *in neces-saris, unitas; in dubiis, libertas; in omnibus, caritas.* The *necessaria* refers to the dogmas of Christian faith and the imperatives of Christian morality. In this there must be unity. The *dubia* admits discussable areas—for our purposes here they include matters of literary taste and opinion—and there liberty dominates; the *omnia* is *all* things—whether those on which agreement is necessary or those wherein diversity of opinion has its place. In all, charity must be the soul that informs all.

One final word as to the moral assessment of the novelists. It will be found, I believe, that each critic does precisely that. He weighs the extent to which his author comes to grips with the life of man in action, and that is inevitably to involve man in the sphere of morals. But no one of the critics directly answers the question some are sure to raise: "Should I or should I not read this particular author?" This is a question to be answered from the data of one's experience—providing, of course, that a higher spiritual authority to which one owes fealty has not exercised a just restriction. A criticism, then, is not necessarily a recommendation; neither is it necessarily a warning. It is an evaluation of such a nature that the prospective reader is able to divine whether the particular author, with *his* subject-matter and *his* treatment, can prudently be read without danger of jeopardizing a greater good. For no novelist *has* to be read; but spiritual integrity does *have* to be preserved. I have gone into this question more thoroughly in *Tenets for Readers and Reviewers* (The America Press, 1947).

The critiques that follow have been written in the spirit of that charity I have mentioned above. If they are read in the same spirit I firmly believe that this modest corporate essay of Catholic scholarshsip will, if I may end on a brilliantly original phrase, have served its purpose.

The most deeply appreciated help has already been men-tioned—that, namely, of my confreres in the literary field. Space does not allow me to name them all nor would their modesty permit it. I must, however, single out some whose interest has been most heartening. Dr. Francis X. Connolly of Fordham University has been very patient in hearing me try to talk myself into clarity and most prolific in offering fruitful suggestions. Father William I. Bundschuh, S.J., of the University of Detroit, provided me with an extremely detailed bibliography. I have to offer sincere apologies to Father Bundschuh for not having included his bibliographical survey; my publisher and I agreed that this volume should not take on too formidable an appearance with a great deal of scholarly apparatus.

I am indebted to Mrs. Theodore Dreiser for permission to quote from Mr. Dreiser's *The Financier, The Titan, The Genius* and *The Bulwark;* to Houghton Mifflin Company for the passage from John Dos Passos' *Manhattan Transfer;* to Little, Brown & Company for the passages from John P. Marquand's *Point of No Return, H. M. Pulham, Esq., B. F.'s Daughter, So Little Time, The Late George Apley* and *Wickford Point;* to Harper & Brothers for the passage from Thomas Wolfe's *The Web and the Rock;* to Rinehart & Company for the passage from Norman Mailer's *The Naked and The Dead;* to Harcourt, Brace & Company for the passage from Robert Penn Warren's *All the King's Men;* to Random House for the passages from William Faulkner's *The Sound and the Fury, As I Lay Dying, Absalom! Absalom!, Wild Palms, Go Down Moses, Intruder in the Dust,* and to the same firm for a passage from Robert Penn Warren's *World Enough and Time;* to Charles Scribner's Sons for the passage from F. Scott Fitzgerald's *The Great Gatsby* and for quotations from Thomas Wolfe's *Letters to His Mother, Look Homeward, Angel* and *Of Time and the River;* to Viking Press for the quotation from *The Portable Faulkner,* edited by Malcolm Cowley; to Sheed & Ward, Inc., for quotations from *The Meaning of Man,* by Jean Mouroux, as well as for quotations from *A Companion to the Summa,* by Walter Farrell, O.P.; to the Vanguard Press for quotations from James T. Farrell's *The Young Manhood of Studs Lonigan, Judgment Day, A World I Never Made, Bernard Clare, The Road Between,* and *The Short Stories of James T. Farrell,* and to

FOREWORD

The Catholic World for permission to use passages from Michael F. Moloney's article, "Half-Faiths in Modern Fiction," August, 1950.

My thanks are due, too, to Miss Mary J. Hubbard not only for the unglamorous labor of typing and checking references, but also for a lively interest in the work-in-progress. For all, the very best I can do to give thanks is to hope that the wish expressed in the dedication will be effective.

Campion House   HAROLD C. GARDINER, S.J.
New York City   June 6, 1951

Contents

CONTENTS

FIFTY YEARS
OF THE
AMERICAN NOVEL

A Christian Appraisal:

The Point of It

HAROLD C. GARDINER, S. J.

OVER A quarter of a century ago, in the inaugural issue of
the New York *Herald Tribune Book Review,* the newly appointed editor, Stuart P. Sherman, laid down a critical platform which was remarkable then for its good sense, lucidity
and richness "in the presence of some of the recent attenua-
tions of critical theory," and which now, it seems, needs recalling and a more specific restatement. Mr. Sherman then
took his stand foursquare against many critics whose slogans
were much in vogue and whose theories were widely put into
practice. "Disinterestedness," was the catchword of the day,
and what it summarized was a philosophy that left the ideal
critic "standing not inside all human interests, at the center,
but outside all human interests, buzzing in a moral vacuum,
where judgment, which Brunetière called 'one of the four
ends of man,' is impossible." Criticism, in other words, was
condemned to the unmuscular and weak-willed exercise of
merely narrating "what had happened," of coming to the
work to be criticized "without preconception or ulterior purpose."

1

This is not the place to recount all the witty broadsides Mr. Sherman leveled at such a theory, nor all the steps by which he reached the opposite viewpoint. His cardinal thought, however, is quite pertinent to this introduction to a series of "Christian appraisals" of the major American novelists during the past half-century. For Mr. Sherman summarized his opposition to the "disinterested" school of criticism in this key sentence: "We value our critics in proportion to the soundness and the abundance of their preconceptions and in proportion to the adequacy of their ulterior purposes."

This is the thought which I believe needs restatement and a more specific refinement. And it is a thought which I feel will be seen illustrated in the studies that follow this signpost introduction. A signpost, you know, need not be a work of art. It would perhaps be more delightful and refreshing for the human spirit if all our road markers were from the brushes of a Da Vinci or a Rembrandt rather than from the stencils of Highway Departments, but even so they really would not do much better the job of pointing out the right direction to the questing traveler. So, if this introduction turns out (to the surprise of all hands) to be a work of art in its own right, so much the more thanks to the heavenly patrons of the pen; if not, it may still serve to point out the road trod by all the intrepid travelers who follow in these pages.

The contributors to this symposium are all professed Christians, in fact they are all Catholics. As such, it seems to me, they are all committed to endorse Mr. Sherman's manifesto, at least the terms of it that are referred to above. For the Christian critic, precisely because he is a Christian, is indeed committed to preconceptions and engaged in criticism for ulterior purposes.

What is the basic preconception? It is an intellectual conviction that is *pre* in the sense that it is an antecedent to literary judgments and necessarily charts, at least in a wide and general direction, the course of those judgments. And it is a basic preconception because it has to do with a basic question: what is the nature of man? "What is man," the

Psalmist pondered many human centuries ago, "that Thou shouldst be mindful of him, or the son of man, that Thou shouldst visit him?" And down through the ages, and in all the pages of the world's literature, that question recurs hauntingly again and again.

But the Christian critic's preconception is that the question did actually, at a definite point in history, get a complete answer. The question no longer echoes in a void. There came One who gave the answer, and it was not an answer made by word of mouth alone. It was made in living fact and we call that fact the life and the redemptive death of Jesus Christ. The Christian critic will come to his work equipped with an awareness of this answer.

What, then, *is* the nature of man? Some years ago, Fr. Jean Mouroux meditated the Christian answer in some wonderful passages in his *The Meaning of Man*. They respond far better than I could, so I would like to give you his thought:

> Man is a mystery first because he is a kind of limit or horizon between two worlds. He is immersed in the flesh, but constituted by the spirit; occupied with matter, but drawn toward God; growing in time, but already breathing the air of eternity; a being of nature and of the world, but also transcending the universe in virtue of his liberty and capacity for union with God . . . But if man is twofold he is also one; [he is] susceptible of a full unity and, on the other hand, of a full disaggregation; [he] has to acquire a significance of his own, and is tossed about meanwhile in all the whirlpools of the flesh and the world. We live out this drama, we suffer from it and bleed, but remain for the most part inwardly withdrawn from it because without acute sense of it. On the day when, by some flash of intellectual enlightenment, or some effort at spiritual progress, we come to realize what we really are, we are seized with a kind of shiver . . . Man then is radically a "mystery" that refuses to be "degraded into a problem."

It is the critic's function to rub together the sometimes too-dry sticks of the reader's attention and interest and so generate that "flash of intellectual enlightenment." Indeed, the critic may be a sort of catalytic agent in the "effort at spiritual progress," as we shall see later. But permit Fr. Mouroux to continue setting our sights straight and high:

> This first mystery leads to a second . . . because man is fallen and redeemed. . . . At this stage the mystery of man lies in the dynamic co-existence, so to call it, of these two forces which dispute the human being between them by disputing his love and his liberty . . . The entire person, soul and body, instincts and passions, love and intelligence; and, around the person as well as within him, the world of things, the world of men, the world of invisible spirits—all that is one immense field of battle . . . Man's mystery is here deepened in both directions. It is more opaque, more carnal, more terrible—and at the same time more luminous, more spiritual and more joyous than we could ever have dared to think (pp. 268-271).

This is a statement more eloquent, perhaps, than most of us could achieve, but thereby the richer in its delineation of the concept of the nature of man which the Christian critic brings to his evaluation of literature. Certainly no such critic will be cabined and confined in the scope of his thinking about man's nature by the blindness of those who, to paraphrase Fr. Mouroux, miss man's misery because they miss his greatness. A realization of both is an essential tool in the trade of the Christian critic. And tools, it must be remembered, exist prior to the work to which they are put.

To repeat, this preconception is a conviction held with reason. It is not a prejudice, for the critic has all the reasons in the world (and an utterly incontrovertible reason from beyond this world) for holding it. Literature may, indeed, shed further light on this concept as well as be illumined by it, but the realization of man as fundamentally a religious being comes prior to the study of man as literature reveals him.

One of the most fundamental statements that can be made about man is that he is a created being. If that truth is unknown—and much more if it is denied—man remains an insoluble riddle. And from this springs what is a basic human longing, deeper even than love, deeper than self-preservation. It is man's sense of incompleteness—in other words his realization, however mute, however confused, of his creaturehood, of the fact that he is dependent, or, in terms of scholastic philosophy, that he is a *contingent* being. That contingency will never—not even in all the stretches of eternity—be transmuted into non-contingency (for that would be to have man become God), but it will be—how shall it be said?—buoyed up by, plunged into, absorbed, without diminution of personality, by the being of God in the intuitive knowledge of the Beatific Vision where our incompleteness shall become whole in Him.

This thought has, of course, been expressed many times over in the pages of the world's literature that have confronted the mystery of man, but perhaps no one has ever phrased it with such manly poignancy as St. Augustine in his famous phrase: "Thou hast made us for Thyself, O God, and our hearts are restless till they rest in Thee."

This deep yearning of the human soul for completeness betrays itself in many guises, but perhaps it is revealed nowhere more strikingly than in the terms we use to describe those most profound and intimate human experiences which are the acts of love by which we seek union with another, be it a fellow human in the physical act of love or God in the mysterious depths of the soul. To express the apex of both loves we use the same word—ecstasy. And what does that mean save a "standing out" of one's self, a losing of one's self (though the self is therein most truly found), a getting away from the narrow and so often boring circle of self into the "otherness" of another.

The infirm man by the roadside, then, cried out in terms wider and wiser than he knew when he petitioned the passing Christ: "Lord, make me whole!" That is the yearning, at the core, of all the world's literature. "Let me look at man," cry the writers, "and I will see how he can be made whole. Perhaps I won't even be able to do that; perhaps all I will be

5

able to do is to see what keeps him incomplete. If even I can catch his cry for completeness and cry back that I understand —though I know no answers—perhaps that sympathy may, of itself, add a little to his sense of completeness." Ellen Glasgow, for example, seems to have been expressing such a thought when she said that she was trying in her novels to alleviate somewhat the unhappiness of the world, the general suffering, not by articulating a moral in her stories, but "by asking the questions humanity cannot ask of itself."

From all this it would seem to follow—and I think it does —that literature is essentially religious. *Essentially,* I say; not in the sense that it is formalized, systematized, made sectarian. If man's nature be religious antecedently to being social or economic, and if literature be a study, through the imagination and the emotions, of the nature of man, then literature, of *its* nature, is religious in bent. If I may be bold enough to quote myself (always a flattering foible), I would like to repeat what I have written in *Tenets for Readers and Reviewers:*

. . . if the dim path of my labored reasoning has at last broken somewhat into sunlight, what we have to conclude is that all great literature is, therefore, a religious literature. Can this be?

I think there is no doubt whatever of the greatest works of literature. Dante, Shakespeare, Milton, Racine— these are all religious writers, throwing the light of eternal truths on the scenes, the incidents they choose to illuminate. But what of the vast mass of the great but lesser works? Is *Huckleberry Finn* religious? Does the question cause a smile?

Well, perhaps it should, but there is a real sense in which such a classic *is* religious. Perhaps the best way I have at hand of expressing what I mean is to recall a remark that Hilaire Belloc, I think it was, once made in one of his essays. All the worthwhile books he had ever read, he says in effect, can be summed up in a sentence— they all have as their theme "On An Unknown Country." Every book deals somehow with man's destiny, his yearnings, their frustrations, their partial fulfillments, in a word, with the happiness, the beatitude, for which Christian ethics teaches us man was made, and which daily living reinforces with its experience.

To some that "unknown country" is quite truly unknown; its mere existence comes to them as a rumor vague and distant, but clear enough to start the divine unrest working. To others of us, who have indeed been given a clear and beautiful picture and promise of that far country, it is known well and lovingly, for its Lord has not only told us of its mansions and invited us there as His brothers, but He has left us a map with every winding and turning of the road fair set forth, so that we may hurry on to enter its boundaries.

But for all, the ultimate country that beckons us is to some degree unknown, and literature is the seeking to catch a clearer glimpse of its outlines. In this sense, and it is not too wide a one, even a *Huckleberry Finn* is religious. It is a boy's search, in a boy's terms, and in an American boy's terms, for happiness. That his conceptions of it are dim and funny and often foolish only adds to the poignancy of our realization that as Huck doubtless in real life would have grown out of his adolescent dreams of happiness, so we have almost daily to grow out of incomplete concepts of it into an ever maturer realization of what happiness truly is.

This, then, is the human nature the novelist stands before as the matter to which his imagination will give form. But he does not, of course, except rarely, scrutinize that nature in these explicit terms. As will be pointed out in the study of Marquand, the normal atmosphere of the novel is not "theological." That its atmosphere is at least reductively "religious" is another matter. The novelist is not as a rule equipped to deal with the bare mystery and marvel of man. He will garb that concept, generally without recking that he is engaged in the act of vesting, in the myriad motley of society, of manners, of action. But underneath Hemingway's bullfighters, Fitzgerald's Jazz Age babies, Marquand's bank-clerks, is still man with his meaning, and the critic who knows that meaning will better judge the novel and the novelist.

It must be remembered, however, that the critic has no right to demand that the novelist write on the critic's terms. He cannot demand that the novelist realize the full extent or trace the final sources of the inquietude of the human heart. The novelist himself may indeed not know the truth and beauty of the Augustinian phrase. It would certainly seem, for example, that Fitzgerald had long forgotten, if he ever fully knew, the real reasons for his own rootlessness. Indeed, to be exigent that the novelist turn theologian would frequently be to demand that much of the poignance of modern fiction be jettisoned, for the significance not too seldom lies exactly in the fact that the novelist is writing of questing, unquiet souls who do not know that they are unquiet and searching. It can be shown at times, I conceive, that much of the poignancy lies as well in the antecedent fact that the novelist himself does not know.

What the critic must allow the author, then—and indeed demand of him—is that he write about men humanly. In his *A Companion to the Summa,* Fr. Walter Farrell, O.P., speaking of the place of the Incarnation in the proper view of human nature, has some observations that will illustrate this point. "Our human nature," he says, "can be seen from below; then it looms as gigantic, imposing. Seen from above it shrinks into humbling insignificance . . . Human nature can be seen from its own level; then it appears as an inspiring and humiliating union of the lowest and the highest in creation . . . [man] is capable of great love, of unstinting sacrifice, but he is also capable of great sin, of complete selfishness, of calamitous failure."

The novelist generally faces man on his own level, and that is all the critic can and will demand. It is only when the novelist approaches human nature on a subhuman level that the Christian critic will cry out against the distortion. It is only when utter naturalism fouls the picture that the critic will protest that the novel has become unhuman—and therefore, in a profound sense, irreligious.

But if the artist may not be castigated for not telling explicitly the source of man's unrest, the critic will be the more discerning and helpful if *he* knows that source. For the critic's function is mainly analytical, the novelist's function affective and imaginative. And it is only the reason that can discern the validity, the proper orientation of the imagination and the affections.

If this is to demand that the critic be more fully rounded in background, more steeped in the heritage of the past and more sensitive to the interrelations of past and present, then so be it. It is, of course, in a sense true. "The critic," Edwin Muir once remarked, "has three functions: to feel beauty when he sees it, and for that he must be an artist; to examine and find whether it is the true beauty, and for that he must be a psychologist; and to discover what significance it holds, and for that he must be twice a psychologist—in other words, a philosopher." Philip Toynbee has dwelt on the same thought, though with reference to the novelist rather than to the critic. In an essay, "The Future of Literature," contributed to a symposium, *The Prospect before Us,* he declared: "The task of creative writers will be to give expression to the complex spiritual problems of their time, and to do this they will have to abandon those minutiae of social and psychological realism in which the traditional novel has foundered." One may question the aptness of the adjective "traditional" (it is certainly the modern novel that has so foundered), and wonder if the "complex" spiritual problems of our time, as far as novelists can contribute to their solution, do not reduce simply to the most simple—a deeper awareness of the reason for man's sense of incompleteness. But certainly the awareness of those spiritual problems Mr. Toynbee would demand of the authors can with far more cogency be demanded of critics.

It seems to me, in this regard, that even such an excellent critic as Lionel Trilling unduly limits the scope of his own criticism in his chapter "Manners, Morals and the Novel," in *The Liberal Imagination*. The main function of this art-form, he claims, is to give "free play to the moral imagination." This is best stimulated by "moral realism," by which he means a portrayal "of the dangers of the moral life itself." These dangers come to a head in a refusal to examine our motives and to ask what lies behind even our good impulses. As an agent in this moral activity, says Mr. Trilling, the novel, though an imperfect form, displays

> its greatness and its practical usefulness . . . in its unremitting work of involving the reader himself in the moral life, inviting him to put his own motives under examination, suggesting that reality is not as his conventional education has led him to see it. It taught us, as no other genre ever did, the extent of human variety and the value of this variety. It was the literary form to which the emotions of understanding and forgiveness were indigenous, as if by the definition of the form itself.

This is true, and a noble statement which betokens that criticism in this country may be rising above the sociological comment which until lately consisted in noting that an author was a good photographer or reporter. But even this deeper appreciation of the function of the novel seems to me to miss *what* the novel deals with. It deals, to be sure, with morals and motives (and suggests the reader's examination of both), but morals and motives rest, in turn, on something else—the ultimates, destiny, the nature of man. The novel itself cannot be *disinterested* in these ultimates, though it may not advert to them with anything approaching explicitness. And the critic can even less afford a disinterest, though he is not to indulge in "theologizing" in his criticism. His interest will unobtrusively sharpen his sensibilities so that his criticism is, in a full sense, human.

That a critic so steadied, so guided by his preconceptions, will be enriched with keener insights is shown, I believe, in the studies that follow. It is precisely this appreciation of the true nature of man that enables Francis X. Connolly to see that the fundamental shortcoming that prevented Willa Cather from being among the very greatest of novelists was that "she never properly understood the Christian spirituality which is the informing principle of *Death Comes for the Archbishop* and *Shadows on the Rock*." And, to take another sample of this richness of critical insight springing from a Christian preconception, Michael F. Moloney seizes on the key fact that, though Hemingway had written that "a fourth and fifth dimension are possible in prose," his own prose lacks, "for the most part, a third" dimension because of "his refusal or inability to give evidence to that potential in man which either raises him above or sinks him below the rest of the animal world."

One aspect of the novel wherein the Christian critic is particularly attuned to deeper critical insights because of his basic preconception is, I believe, the meaning and depth of tragedy. Though it be probable that "tragedy is . . . impossible in a culture completely dominated by the Christian view" because "the Christian vision is of man's ultimate and certain triumph," it is even more probable, from another point of view, that it is the Christian who ought to be able most perceptively to sense the *hamartia,* the Aristotelian tragic flaw, that lurks beneath the potential (and the actual) majesty of the human personality, for man's greatness is the measure of his misery.

This sensitiveness to the tragic note will be discovered many times in the following studies. The essays on Hemingway, Faulkner and Marquand, for example, will demonstrate this perceptiveness springing from a rich preconception. Even when the tragic note sounds in our ears in the muted pitch of the "tentative inexorableness" of Marquand's titles—*So Little Time, Point of No Return*—the critic's insight, quickened and sharpened, will call forth the deep sympathy man's frail majesty does challenge and should evoke.

The tragic stature of man—or at least the tragic potentialities latent in man—viewed with appreciative sympathy: there is the deepest insight the Christian critic can bring to his work. It is, of course, the insight that the novelist must reveal, in greater or less degree, for his subject-matter *is* the frail majesty of humanity. He must not gloss over the frailty, else he attempts to deal with plaster saints. And if the critic is equipped to point out how the majesty and the frailty come through the work, he will be doing for the reader the greatest service at his command—he will be establishing a basis for a growth in the reader of the virtue of Christian charity.

For what are the characters of the novelist's creation? They are men and women endowed with a human nature that is actually here and now in history the marvelous and aweful complex we have been discussing. If the reader comes away from the reading of a book with a conviction that he has seen for a space that human nature in action, he will inevitably have been in contact with objective reasons, portrayed in the concrete imagining of a definite time and society, why human nature has within it the power to win consideration, esteem, sympathy, tolerance, understanding—in a word, charity.

This means that the critic will point out, if the novel give him grounds, the points of possible identification between reader and characters, the common ground that can be shared. Thus in books as in life, as Fr. Farrell puts it, "a door is thrown open and we are admitted to regions that are proper to God alone, for by friendship we stroll into the soul of another. It offers us completion for our incomplete, lonely human hearts, a fulfillment that is sought by every man from the beginning of his existence." So, though the author may not know or fully realize the fact of man's unquiet heart, or knowing it, may not divine its primary source, the critic, if *he* knows, will help in his little measure to bring the reader to a sense of completion.

There the critic's work stops, but the reader may still go on. He may carry over into life the motives for charity he has glimpsed through the author's creation and the critic's guidance. Let me quote Fr. Farrell's observations, which, aptly enough, fall in the section of *A Companion to the Summa* (vol. III, p. 245) where he is treating of "The Fullness of Religion." He remarks:

> The peculiar advantage of good books is that they are severe masters in whose company a man can grow, can perfect himself; they are towering mountains into which we can fly from the deadly flat landscapes of discussions on the weather or rehashes of newspaper accounts. They are higher places; superior to the level of our minds and

consequently a means of perfection. When we have learned all the book can teach us, we have reached its level and must look to something higher if our perfection is to continue. The rule is universal; it is not by contact with inferiors but by subjection to superiors that men and things reach their perfection. The mongrel pet of the lowliest of men improves from even such a contact with such a reason.

Or, as will be remarked in this volume of John P. Marquand:

This dual power of reflecting objective reality without distortion and, at the same time, fulfilling the old Morality function of representing Everyman to himself . . . ought not to be taken lightly in an age which, instead of holding a mirror up to nature, prefers to reflect back from a monomaniac monocle its own myopic eye. With Marquand's courteously relentless assistance we look at our natural face in a glass; and then go about our various businesses. Only, instead of forgetting what kind of men we are, perhaps, for the first time, we realize what kind of men we are.

It is to be hoped, of course, that none of the novelists treated here will prove to be among the "lowliest of men." It is true, however, that some of them have been rather "myopic" in their view of human nature and its frail majesty. That does not rule them out of all consideration. In their half-truths, their gropings, they may still manage to some extent to show us to ourselves, and in so doing to expand the boundaries of our charity—perhaps, indeed, all unconsciously—for men like ourselves. I believe that in every one of the critiques that follow the critic performs his function of collaborating in that expansion.

Edith Wharton:
Values and Vulgarity
ANNE FREMANTLE

OPULENTLY BORN into the New York bourgeoisie in 1862, Edith Newbold Jones married Edward Wharton of Boston in 1885, and died on August 11, 1937. Her first poems were published, through Longfellow's recommendation, in the *Atlantic Monthly* in 1880, her last novel, *The Buccaneers,* posthumously published, was unfinished at her death. In those more than fifty productive years, she wrote forty-five books.

Was she, as N. Elizabeth Monroe has claimed, "the greatest novelist America has known"? Was she the American equivalent of Jane Austen or George Eliot? Edmund Wilson has called her "a passionate social prophet," and Q. D. Leavis "an extraordinarily acute and far-sighted social critic." For Carl Van Doren, she was "first of all a novelist of civilization." Robert Lovett, on the other hand, complains of her "absorption in the somewhat mechanical operations of culture, her preoccupation with the upper class."

Some critics place her autobiography, *A Backward Glance,* between Henry Adams' *Education* and Malcolm Cowley's

Exile's Return, as the most significant American documentary of its period; yet others feel she was the bridge between Henry James, her acknowledged master, and F. Scott Fitzgerald, who dedicated his first book to her, and whose young genius she admired and encouraged. Eighty-nine years after her birth, what should be a mid-century evaluation?

She was a self-made writer if ever there was one. Her mother was considered the best-dressed woman of her day, and little Edith almost automatically assumed she would inherit this *toga feminea* when her time came. Handsome, distinguished, intelligent and well-educated, there was no reason to suppose that once she had left the schoolroom, she would ever open a book again, except for social or conversational purposes. Yet she wrote her first story at the age of nine and, except for some adolescent excursions into verse, she kept right on writing prose until her last days.

She found little encouragement among the members of her immediate family. Her first story opened with a hostess explaining to a matutinal visitor: "If I had known you were coming, I would have tidied up the drawing room." Upon this her mother's comment was: "Drawing rooms are *always* tidy." It was her only known reference to her daughter's literary output. In the rest of her family, Edith Wharton's literary success "created a kind of constraint which increased with the years. None of my relations ever spoke to me of my books, either to praise or blame—they simply ignored them; and among the immense tribe of my New York cousins . . . the subject was avoided as though it were a kind of family disgrace, which might be condoned but could not be forgotten."

Her husband also was completely uninterested although immensely proud of *her*. Thirteen years older than Edith, a sportsman and an outdoor type, after several happy years in which they shared travels in Europe, yachting in the Mediterranean, country life in Newport, and later in Lenox, Massachusetts, he fell into a melancholy and thence into a madness. His father had done so before him and, unfortunately, Edith Wharton, who was an heiress, had, as was usual at the time, made over her fortune to him when they married. His madness took the form of certain irresponsibilities with money, and Mrs. Wharton, after devotedly nursing him for many years, was reluctantly obliged to divorce him, in order to save her considerable fortune.

The Whartons had no children; indeed, Edith Wharton always showed a marked distaste for them. When sight-seeing, for example, if she saw a crowd of youngsters outside a church, she would carefully go around by a side door to avoid them, and it was not only underprivileged children to whom she so reacted—the children of her friends caused her the same, almost physical, distaste. Perhaps they were an interruption of the well-ordered life Edith Wharton believed in and lived. Her life, like her mother's drawing room, was *always* tidy.

Walter Berry, a young lawyer of good family, had fallen in love with Edith when she first came out. He had proposed, she had refused; gossip said because he was not a dazzling enough match for the young heiress. In any case, he remained one of her most devoted friends, upon whose judgment, both worldly and literary, she came heavily to rely. Too heavily, some of her friends thought, who feared that constant criticism by what to them seemed a second-rate mind might halt the full development of Edith Wharton's genius.

After her divorce, most of Edith Wharton's friends thought that she and Walter Berry would now marry, but they did not, and he died many years before the novelist. She left instructions that she was to be buried beside him, and on her grave, according to her own instructions, a cross was placed, upon which the words *O crux, ave, spes unica* were carved.

As a vastly popular author, a best-seller translated into every European language, as a member of the smartest international set, socially and intellectually, Edith Wharton lived her whole life very much in the public eye. Yet, almost uniquely, she never occasioned the least breath of scandal. Her private life was never public property and, at whatever cost, she always behaved with dignity and discretion. What that cost may have been is perhaps hinted in this sentence, from her *The Writing of Fiction:* "One good heartbreak will furnish the poet with many songs, the novelist with a considerable number of novels. But they must have hearts that can break."

And how nearly hers did is proved by the fact that she began to write fiction in earnest at the suggestion of Dr. S. Weir Mitchell, a specialist in female neuroses, during a period of nervous breakdown. "At her strongest and most characteristic," Edmund Wilson wrote of her, "she is a brilliant example of the writer who relieves an emotional strain by denouncing his generation." In other words, she is a triumphant example of sublimation: whatever she suffered from the tragedy of her own marriage was translated by her genius into an antennal awareness of the sufferings of others. But because her own suffering was genuine, she had also an acute perception of pretense.

Her compassion is immense, and encompasses all except the hypocrite. She can, and does, include the drug-taking clockmaker who destroys the Bunner sisters, in her story of that name; she includes the spiteful spinster who prevents her brother's mistress from bidding him goodbye; she includes Ethan Frome's bitter wife, and the Countess Olenska's triumphantly juvenile rival (in *The Age of Innocence*). She can write with sympathy of the near-moronic, in *Summer,* and yet "can take the view that there may be something inside when one spends one's summers at Newport" (Alice Gorren in *The Critic*).

Yet her sense of justice is never corroded by pity, that rust on good and evil, that most terribly presumptuous of all virtues, which should be reserved to the Author of virtue alone. For pity implies pride, and pride's *sequitur,* patronage: "poor Blank, how sad for him, how glad I am it's not me." Not the slightest smear of such pity blurs Edith Wharton's compassion. Her chief concern always was with truth: moral truth, artistic truth, social truth. And of moral truths, one of the first she knew was that "there, but for the grace of God, for a sheltered life, a good education, an assured income, a sense of security and a good digestion," went Edith Wharton.

To her, all reality was relationship, and as God is personal when He creates, so also is the writer. You get nothing for nothing, not an ounce of affection, not even from an animal; not a moment of triumph, even over the other woman, or the man who did you wrong. As Wystan Auden puts it:

> Every farthing of the cost
> All the bitter stars foretell
> Shall be paid.

Edmund Wilson has described her as "haunted by the myth of the Eumenides and filled with a sense of inexorable doom." Less dramatically, it is perhaps truer to say that to her very logical mind there was an inevitable connection between effect and cause, and she never forgot the nursery adage, "as you make your bed, so you lie on it," and that other about "he who takes what isn't his'n, when he's cotched, he's sent to pris'n."

Authors can be divided into those who write from inside-out, and those who write from outside-in; those for whom character is destiny, and those for whom circumstances alter cases. For Edith Wharton, character was implacably destiny; nothing simply happened, the teacup never just came to pieces in the housemaid's hand, always it was by her fault, by her fault, by her very grievous fault. The doom that awaits each one of her characters is their own, inescapably, but it is also collective: she condemned the whole society she portrayed, with her axiom, "a frivolous society can acquire dramatic significance only through what its frivolity destroys." So she saw clearly how power, as conferred by wealth, without the concomitant responsibility implied by nobility and its obligations, was the nemesis of American society, and of the individuals making up that society.

But she also saw how the European evasions of responsibility, by hypocrisy, subterfuge and all the devious forms of lying and cheating, were no less horrible in their destructive effects. In *Madame de Treymes* as in *The Custom of the Country*, the conscious American, aware of fundamentals, although only roughly and rather naïvely aware, is preferred to the Pharisaical aristocrat, who uses his position as excuse and escape from normal human obligations. In her last book, *The Buccaneers,* she almost overreaches her literary patriotism: the half-Italian governess, Laura Testvalley, is a sort of female St. George, defending her innocent American charges against the engulfing mire of a marriage with a selfish British Duke, who poisons a supremely selfish society at its source.

Hardly less important to her than moral truth was artistic. In *The Writing of Fiction,* "there seem to be but two primary questions to ask," she wrote, "in estimating any work of art: what has the author tried to represent? and, how far has he succeeded? And a third, which is dependent on them: was the subject chosen worth representing, has it the quality of being what Balzac calls, *Vrai dans l'art"?*

Edith Wharton's life until her marriage had included an annual visit to Europe, and for some years after, she and her husband traveled together each year. Settled at first at Newport, in a big rambling inconvenient family house, they later bought The Mount, in Lenox, Massachusetts, although they kept a small house in New York. Mrs. Wharton was very much a *femme d'interieur,* and her books on interior decorating and on gardening are professional in their knowledge and in the wisdom of their experience. She was good at her job, whether it was being a debutante daughter, a wife, a hostess, a gardener, or a writer. And she had no inferiority complexes about her sex. Being a woman never phased her, as it phased George Eliot, for example, or George Sand. She did simply and without fuss and supremely well, whatever had to be done, and would have thought to do otherwise were conduct unbecoming a gentlewoman.

It was to Edith Wharton's house in Lenox that Henry James came in 1905 on a first visit. Edith's stories had been sent to him in 1902, and he had written: "Her stories have made me want to get hold of the little lady and pump the pure essence of my wisdom and experience into her." Percy Lubbock has described how the enduring friendship with James, which began with Edith as the devoted pupil, ended with something almost like envy on James' part, for in his

20

total acceptance of European standards he had come to deny to his Americans a moral mainspring. For him, the pragmatic responsibilities of Europe were infinitely more valuable than America's sliding scales, based on money and success. But Edith Wharton saw deeper, and in several of her best stories —for example, in *Souls Belated, Glimpses of the Moon* and *The Reef*—she has shown she believed in categorical imperatives, in values *an und für sich,* which are natural and native to man, whatever his country. In all of these tales the high personal standards of some Americans are favorably contrasted with the unintegrated and superficial conventions of the Europeans.

No social novelist, not Jane Austen nor Henry James himself, believed more strongly than did Edith in the value of conventions when they represented, and were securely based upon, a social or collective conscience. But when that conscience had ebbed, leaving only an empty shell of custom, she was as eager to clean house as Swift or Dickens.

Edith Wharton's sonnets in the *Atlantic Monthly* had been on appropriate subjects: happiness, Botticelli, Ilaria's Tomb. But her first story, published in *Scribners Magazine* for July, 1891, was far removed from such suitably patrician themes. *Mrs. Manstey's View* showed that the "little rich girl" was a social historian, and that her literary inheritance was rather Russian and British than French: her somber, serious views of her responsibility recall George Eliot and Turgenev rather than Flaubert or Balzac.

Mrs. Manstey's View is frankly a sentimental-melodramatic tale of an invalid widow whose only joy is the view of a neighbor's yard from her own window. When this view is threatened by a new building, the widow unsuccessfully tries to commit arson, and dies of exposure. *The Fullness of Life,* her next story, shows Edith Wharton's ethical intransigeance, and, as well, her enchanting sense of humor. A woman, bored by her husband all her life, yet now on the threshold of Paradise, refuses to enter without him, preferring to wait outside than go in unaccompanied. This theme, which occurs in the life of various Bodhisattvas, who will not enter Nirvana so long as a single person suffers on earth, might have been handled in a mystico-moral vein: Edith Wharton, lighter in hand, is yet no less emphatic in making her point. She is always very subtle in her appreciation of the infinite varieties of love, which, as Aldous Huxley has pointed out, is the function both of the blessed and the bull, and is the motive power of Creator and created alike, from the Almighty to the amoeba. For Edith Wharton, love is unique because the condition and ,circumstances which surround it can never be identical in any two cases. But the laws which regulate it are always the same, they are the laws by which we exist, and love's uniqueness is no excuse for broadmindedness, nor for letting up on behavior, for evading the laws or our responsibilities.)

Morality, she insists, is a function also of biology and anthropology and a man's duty to his neighbor conditions all of his existence. As another member of the Jones family (Enid Bagnold) has put it: "unpleasant people are unhappy, and there is nothing you can do about it." I must live to love or I don't live. I must love to live or I don't love. Thus all Edith Wharton's characters, from Mrs. Manstey in her first published story to Laura Testvalley in her last novel, are primarily involved in the moral situation: their fate depends wholly upon their character. And all her characters are set in history, at a particular time, in a specific place. Otherwise, they would have behaved differently. The crimes of Clapham *are* chaste in Timbuctoo, she insists, and she is nourished, as a novelist, by the "manners, customs, usages, habits, forms, matured and established," upon which, Henry James insists, every novelist must live.

It was Edith Wharton's peculiar genius to be able to describe, from the inside, four cultures: Italian, French, English and American. The Italy of her first novel, *The Valley of Decision*, the England of her last, *The Buccaneers*, the America of *The Age of Innocence*, and the France of *Madame de Treymes* are equally authentic. Her triumph, Carl van Doren has said, is to describe rites, surfaces and burdens as familiarly as if she loved them, and as lucidly as if she hated them. Being first of all a novelist of civilization, she would agree with

Oscar Wilde, that nature learns from art, the sunset seeks to imitate J. W. Turner, and landscape is always infinitely preferable to scenery.

Yet three of her greatest stories, *Ethan Frome, The Bunner Sisters* and *Summer,* deal with what in England would be called the lower classes. For she did not necessarily equate culture and civilization with education or evolution. Ann Eliza, giving up her savings so her sister can marry a drug addict she loves, who later deserts her; Chatty Lovell, giving up a safe marriage to Joe Ralston to save Clem Spender's child, whom she loses to her cousin Delia; are equal and parallel in their Judeo-Christian context, but also their values are equally and parallelly bowdlerized, etiolated and generally watered down by the all-too-human natures funneling so great a tradition.

Edith Wharton was always a master of form. "The fundamental difference," she herself pointed out, "between the amateur and the artist, is the possession of the sense of technique, that is, in its broadest meaning, the necessity of form." And perhaps her most successful form was the *nouvelle,* that essentially American medium. For, though it derives from Madame de la Fayette's *La Princesse de Cleves* and Samuel Johnson's *Rasselas,* it has been perfected here, by Edith Wharton in *Ethan Frome, Sanctuary* and *Summer;* by Willa Cather in *Death Comes to the Archbishop;* by Thornton Wilder in *The Bridge of San Luis Rey;* by John Steinbeck in *Of Mice and Men* and *The Red Pony;* by William Faulkner in *Spotted Horses.*

When *Ethan Frome* came out in 1911, *The Nation,* reviewing it on October 26, commented:

> The wonder is that the spectacle of so much pain can be made to yield so much beauty. It is only possible because the gamut of human experience, the exaltation of anguish which makes a solitude for itself, reveal beneath the writhing torment the lineaments of a wronged and distorted loveliness. It is the piteous and intolerable conception of the Medusa head, but the face is the face of our own people.

23

Mr. Arthur Miller, writing in 1950 in the New York *Herald Tribune,* made the distinction between pathos and tragedy: a dog is run over, there is pathos; a child, here is tragedy. And Edith Wharton always writes tragedy; her characters are human beings, totally engaged. The pity is that she had this tragic gift at perhaps the "only moment in the world's history when the tragic view was impossible." And perhaps it was even more tragic, both artistically and personally, that her recognition of the supernatural bases of life was so uncertain, so hesitant and halting. For the only reason a child's death is more tragic than a dog's, is that the human is more than the brute. And for Edith Wharton, the supernatural seems to have been the spooky: her ethic comprises no duty towards God, and her recognition of nemesis does not seem to have included a glimpse, however faint or broken, of that "super-impending design" of which Cardinal Newman so magnificently writes.

And to see only tragedy is slightly suburban, to say the least. For example, in the stark ending of *Ethan Frome,* when young Mattie, whom Ethan loved, and Ethan himself are left dependent upon Zeena, his ailing virago of a wife, some suggestion that human misery and suffering are not part of God's original plan, but rather are the inevitable results of our own disgusting disobedience, might have strengthened the story. And the conclusion, that Mattie's death were better, is an admission only of the failure of life, and is weak. Because life cannot fail, only the living, and they only if they refuse Him through whom they can be "more than conquerors."

Edith Wharton has spoken in her autobiography of her own doubts, even after "I had groped my way through to my vocation," of whether she would "be able to cross the chasm which separated the *nouvelle* from the novel." But the publication of her first novel made her feel "story-telling was my job" and her joy in this discovery made her "like a homeless waif who, after trying for years to take out naturalization papers, . . . has finally acquired a nationality." Henceforth "the Land of Letters was to be my country, and I gloried in my new citizenship."

24

She was continually studying her craft. When she came to know other writers well, she confesses she was truly shocked at how few "were greatly interested in the deep processes . . . their conscious investigations seldom go deeper than syntax." They seemed, she found, constantly in quest of attractive and rewarding subjects, whereas she, "crushed by the multitude of subjects calling for presentation," was in quest of exactly the right mode of presenting a subject. She was never satisfied: towards the end of her life she confided to a great friend, Mrs. Winthrop Chanler: "O, to write like Proust and Lytton Strachey! I would like to throw away everything, and to start learning to write like those two."

The world, for her as for many, was divided into "the Gothically and the classically minded," and she agreed with Henry James that "no good novel will ever proceed from a superficial mind" and with Flaubert that "the greater the thought, the more sonorous the phrase." She was insistent that "Order the beauty even of beauty is," as Thomas Traherne put it, and that "Virtue is the order of love," as St. Augustine so finally concluded. One of the chief obligations of the short story, she wrote, "is to give the reader an immediate sense of security. Every phrase must be a signpost. Every subject must contain within itself its own dimensions." No subject can keep a novel alive, she adds, only the characters can. And the art of rendering life in fiction "can never be anything nor need be anything but the disengaging of the crucial moments from the welter of existence."

In this sentence she puts her finger on the whole duty of the writer: to make what he writes significant. The *how* and *why* of that making and that significance are what differentiates one writer from another. When that significance is universal, the writer is immortal: the soldiers' curses stopped in their mouths by the beauty of Helen walking on the walls of Troy, Prince Andrei, dying flat on his back after the battle and looking up at the pale sky, the Bishop running after Jean Valjean with the second candlestick—these are as significant for us as for the Greeks, Russians or French, for whom they were written, and are as valid today as then.

Edith Wharton, in her short stories, is always careful to be sure she has a story to tell, for, as she points out, in the short story it is the dramatic rendering of the situation, the episode, the anecdote, that matters, and action is the chief affair. The novel, on the other hand, depends wholly on character. So the novelist graduates from the short story, thickening and deepening his characters, until they become three- and even sometimes four-dimensional. Some writers are novelists born, who write an occasional short story; Tolstoi is an obvious example. Others yet are short-story writers who stretch into a novel, as a steeplechaser will sometimes stretch out into a long gallop—of such, it may be suggested, is Somerset Maugham.

Edith Wharton was a writer, *tout court,* who learned first to write short stories, then *nouvelles* and, lastly, novels. Being a woman, she liked learning for its own sake, and writing, perhaps because of the infinite variety of the things to learn. She had no message; she had nothing, even, that she very desperately wanted to say, but she quite desperately wanted to tell, and that only by writing her tales. Such a dedication is rarely possible to a woman: husbands, kitchens, children, clothes, all the four k's that, worse than in any Kakfa story, haunt each poor female, usually crowd and clutter out any singlemindedness from the public thoroughfares of her heart. But Edith Wharton had the rarest of good luck: money enough to buy time and an unobstructed heart.

The short stories gathered in *The Greater Inclination* (1899) are all about Americans. This was her first book of fiction: her first actual published book was the (to us) slightly Helen-Hokinson *Decoration of Houses* (1898). *The Touchstone,* a long tale, its author called it, with "a quiet title carefully chosen for one of the quietest of my stories," published in 1900, had little success in America. John Lane, "naturally taking care not to consult me," wrote Mrs. Wharton, "renamed it *A Gift from the Grave,* and "the book sold rapidly in England, to my mingled wrath and amusement." *Crucial Instances,* another collection of short stories, followed in 1901, and then, in 1902, her first novel, *The Valley of Decision.* This instantly placed her absolutely in the front rank: it is one of the best historical novels ever written, and won the acclaim of such cranky, meticulously accurate authorities on Italian eighteenth-century history as Vernon Lee. Theodore Roosevelt gently rebuked Edith Wharton because the hero, the Duke of Palinura, does not make an honest woman of the humble bookseller's daughter who loved him, but this seems to have been the only serious peeve made against this triumphantly successful first novel.

When asked if she studied hard to achieve such a mastery of detail, the author always denied it, and explained that although she did not travel and look and read with the writing of the book in mind, yet "years of intimacy with the Italian eighteenth century gradually and imperceptibly fashioned the tale and compelled me to write it." Thus it is the very opposite of *Romola*, George Eliot's equally erudite novel, of which Herbert Spencer said that it "smelt of the lamp" by whose light it had been written, and which has more than served its time as the most boring of all holiday-task-reading assignments.

Sanctuary, which appeared in 1903, is one of Edith Wharton's subtlest stories. Kate, engaged to Denis Peyton, "who has the gift of carrying one over the chasms of life through the closed tunnel of an incurious cheerfulness," discovers that his elder brother, a wastrel luckily dead, has left a widow. The money Denis thought safely his belongs rightfully, therefore, to this woman and the child. Denis' mother knows the truth and cheats quite horribly, and Kate, aware of the treachery, wants to break her engagement. She is nauseated: "she felt herself petrifying under the warm drip of Mrs. Peyton's platitudes. . . . Kate had begun to perceive that the fair surface of life was honeycombed by a vast system of moral sewage. Every respectable household had its special arrangements for the private disposal of the family scandals; it was only among the reckless and improvident that such hygienic precautions were neglected." But Kate, who is curiously like Celia, in T. S. Eliot's *The Cocktail Party*, recognizes "the moral need for expiation." The "sacrificial instinct of her sex" makes her do the right thing, and "in her anguish, she is conscious of that lift of the heart which made one of the saints declare that joy was the inmost core of sorrow, the old *credo quia absurdum* which is the secret cry of all supreme endeavor."

Denis dies, and Kate, having reared his son in the noblest pattern she knows, is faced with another crisis. Her son is tempted to cheat in an exam: his fiancée, like Mrs. Peyton senior, wishes him to yield. She will marry him only if he wins the contest; he can win only if he sends in as his own the wonderful drawings of his dead friend. The son triumphs where the father fell; his mother in him wins without a word, and Miss Verney, the callous fiancée, is wonderfully epitomized: "her lips seemed to listen as well as speak . . . all her features betokened a nature through which the obvious energies blew free, a bare open stretch of consciousness, without shade for a tenderer growth."

After some more distinctively tailored short stories, and two more "art books," one on *Italian Villas* (1904), the other on *Italian Backgrounds* (1905), Edith Wharton published in 1905 the first of her really major novels and confirmed her place as a superb American novelist. The love story in *The House of Mirth* lifts it above social satire, and makes it eternally true and always readable. Lily Bart is destroyed by the system which produced her, and ends up making hats in the shop where she used to buy them, but in the course of her life something has happened: by her behavior she has killed Lawrence Selden's love for her, but it has kindled in her "an imperishable flame . . . the passion of her soul for his."

The Fruit of the Tree (1907), rather an unsuccessful labor-management story, was followed by *Madame de Treymes* in the same year, and this study of two fundamentally noble human beings recognizing each other amid the jungles of aristocratic family behavior, with a sort of "Dr. Livingstone, I presume" poignancy, is one of Edith Wharton's masterpieces. To read it is like watching a fast fencing match, or figure skating, and then at the end, to see over the shattered possibilities of human happiness, thoroughly and mercilessly destroyed, the eternal verities come thundering by.

The publication of her only book of verse, *Artemis to Actaeon,* added nothing to her reputation, but one at least of the longer poems, "Margaret of Cortona," is still worth reading. All her life Edith Wharton showed a dilettante's interest in the Church: she was student of Catholic liturgy, and would often go to Mass, to Lenten sermons, or would discuss aspects of theology with her Catholic friends. But she entirely lacked humility as a person. As an artist, and a great one, she was extremely humble; as a person, she remained the imperious, assured young Protestant, never feeling in her life that absolute necessity for the truth of which she was so conscious as a writer.

In 1911 she published *Ethan Frome,* in 1912 *The Reef,* and in 1913 *The Custom of the Country.* These three are all of her very best, and she was now at the height of her powers. *The Reef,* a study, profound, analytic, passionate, of the effect of a casual sin on the relationship between a man and a woman who truly love each other, is the most interior of all her books. Anna, "who hadn't a drop of poetry in her, but had some of the qualities that create it in others," is in her late husband's French castle, expecting that George Darrow, a man she had always loved and who always loved her, will come, now she is free, and propose. She is quite certain all will be well: only her daughter must be properly prepared for the new relationship. He is on his way; she telegraphs him to come a week later, an unexplained contingency has occurred. He picks up a chance acquaintance, Sophie Vines, has a casual affair with her, joins Anna, and nothing is well. Anna, at first, does everything to blot out the spot; she even becomes George Darrow's mistress. But the flaw was not in his behavior, it is in his nature.

Anna recalled having read somewhere that in ancient Rome the slaves were not allowed to wear distinctive dress lest they should recognize each other, and learn their numbers and power. So, in herself, she discerned for the first time instincts and desires which, mute and masked, had gone to and fro in the dim passages of her mind, and now hailed each other with a cry of mutiny.

Through her suffering, she learns to know herself, and also to know her lover. Watching him, "he won't grow any older, she thought, because he doesn't feel things. And, because he doesn't, I shall." He, of course, poor man, hasn't the foggiest idea why Anna is making all the fuss; but something has so definitely died in their love that the story ends with their final farewell.

The Custom of the Country, with its cold heroine, so suitably named Undine, who lets men kiss her and can't understand why it means anything to them, and after three husbands still has not learned, is a *tour de force.* The old New York, the Middle West and the European aristocratic backgrounds are each in turn marvelously "done" and the men are much more alive than most of Mrs. Wharton's men, who are apt to be a trifle colorless: rich, handsome, leisured, well-educated, but rather bland food.

During World War I Edith Wharton remained in France and threw herself heroically into war-work and into writing about the war. She was decorated by a grateful French Government, and indeed, was taken to their hearts by the French people. Thereafter France was not only her second physical home, but the home of her heart, as Italy had never been— it had been but the home of her head.

Summer, published in 1917, is the strongest of her "proletarian" studies. This and *Ethan Frome* "were the result of explorations among villages still bedrowsed in a decaying rural existence, and sad slow-speaking people" as she wrote of them. It is curiously monochrome, in spite of the suggestions of violence. The poor heroine, Charity Royall, marries an old man who, having raised her, had tried to seduce her. After a hopeless affair with a poor, handsome boy her own age, she is punished with almost sadistic intensity for her brief fling.

In 1920 Edith Wharton published the last of her really great books, *The Age of Innocence,* a novel set wholly in the New York of her girlhood. Countess Ellen Olenska, fleeing from a disastrous marriage, is welcomed home with various degrees of cordiality by her vast clan. Among them is her dewy twenty-two-year-old cousin, May Welland, just engaged to Newland

Archer, a most suitable young man. Newland and Ellen fall
in love, but May keeps him, first by putting the date of their
marriage forward, and then by starting a baby. Only after
May's death, when his son is grown, does Archer completely
realize how deliberate her innocence has been. And then, twen-
ty-six years after, when he and Ellen can meet, he sends his
son, Dallas, up to her apartment in Paris, while he himself
remains outside on a bench in the gardens. Life is over, one
does not reheat its leavings, for they are indigestible, and it
would be indelicate.

Thereafter, Edith Wharton's novels were always competent
and distinguished, but never again great. She had, after all,
produced a remarkable *corpus* of sustainedly first-class writing and, in *The Writing of Fiction,* a first-rate primer of her
craft, which ranks with E. M. Forster's *Aspects of the Novel*
and Sir Arthur Quiller Couch's *On the Art of Writing.* She is
undoubtedly the greatest American woman novelist to date,
with only Willa Cather and Eudora Welty within even chal-
lenging distance.

Perhaps what she lacked was a sense of glory. Certainly
not form, nor art, nor morality, nor a sense of beauty—she
had an almost painful awareness of it—nor even a sense of
eschatology, for all her novels state, if only implicitly, a belief
in the four last things. Or, at any rate, in three of them—
death, judgment and hell. She misses heaven and glory—good
old knock-down glory, as Humpty Dumpty called it. But not
completely—it was rather that she sensed her loss and re-
gretted it. She describes the process of pursuit so well, in her
story, *After Holbein,* that it is more convincing to quote than
to comment:

Anson Warley had his moments of being a rather remarkable man. But they were only intermittent. They re-
curred at ever-lengthening intervals and between times,
he was a small poor creature, chattering with cold inside
in spite of his agreeable, and even distinguished, exterior
. . . except on the increasingly rare occasions when . . .
he mounted to the lofty water-shed which fed the sources

of his scorn. The view there was vast and glorious, the air was icy but exhilarating. But he soon began to find the place too lonely and too difficult to get to.

And so, by degrees, he not only refuses to go, but begins to sneer at himself for ever having wanted to go. Until one day at lunch, he talks "with a feverish loquacity, the only thing he could do, for he could not tell all these people . . . that he had that very morning arrived at the turn in the path where the mountains look as transient as flowers, and that one after another they would all arrive there too." All except those whose strength is from the everlasting hills. And, alas, Edith Wharton's own strength seems, in the last analysis, to have come instead from a stiff upper lip. But at least she knew the difference, as her tombstone indicates.

Sinclair Lewis, who dedicated *Main Street* to her, and who, with his then new wife Dorothy Thompson, paid Edith Wharton a pilgrimage, told her that what he admired most about her was that she was so vulgar. Whatever he meant—he never explained—perhaps had something to do with the "vulgar error" of failing "to be still and know that I am God"?

Theodore Dreiser:

Shifting Naturalism

EDWARD J. DRUMMOND, S. J.

BOTH THE man Theodore Dreiser and his work seem to offer quite proper material for simple, straightforward analysis, yet there are some complexities to resolve and some paradoxes to explain. Although he was a professed agnostic, there was in most of his work an implied frame of reference and a norm of values. He was a determinist, but one who worked hard to find success and recognition and who urged reform through socialism and communism. He was a materialist who not only was sincerely sympathetic (as many materialists have been and are), but who had a streak of soft idealistic monism in his make-up that was eventually to lead him to a position which Emerson could have understood. He struggled with censorship for over two decades, yet it was censorship which focussed light upon his work and, indirectly at least, assisted much in having his real importance assayed and recognized.

A controversial figure then, his work now seems clearly, almost curiously, dated. He is rather generally regarded as one of our foremost writers; but when he died in 1945 critics were reserved in their words of praise for his literary efforts.

Perhaps some of these are only seeming complexities and exist chiefly in the minds of various critics. Others concern mainly Dreiser the man rather than his work, and my concern is with his novels. Since the paradox, however, of his search for standards should prove to be a point of vantage for the critic who wishes to be sure what this novelist was attempting to do, and since this has been partially overlooked in interpreting his fiction, some direct attention will be given to this aspect of Dreiser the writer.

He was the twelfth of thirteen children. His mother, a convert, and warm and sympathetic by nature, seemed to have understood her children better than the father who appears to have been very faithful in the practice of his Catholicism but rigid and perhaps formalistic in that practice. At one time the father had been manager of a large woolen mill, but a series of financial reverses had left him a defeated man. Poverty and domestic quarrels resulted, which left their mark upon young Dreiser and gave him a growing sense of insecurity.

Some of the older children on leaving home to make their own way showed their reaction by turning down the more questionable side-streets of life. Yet to one of Theodore's dreamy imaginative nature these brothers and sisters had a flash of color to their lives and ease and warmth. There was paternal criticism, but such judgment of their lives began to seem to Dreiser like mere negative fault-finding. From what he had experienced at home, poverty, religion and the forbidden appeared to follow one upon the other; success, pleasure, money belonged to an entirely different world. In those first years after leaving home he placed a quite uncritical evaluation upon them as objectives. His later public confessions in four autobiographical books—*A Traveler at Forty* (1913), *A Hoosier Holiday* (1916), *A Book about Myself* (1922), *Dawn* (1931)—relate how frankly and how timidly he sought them.

Inclined in that direction by his imaginative nature, bent

thereto by reaction which began even at home, he was strengthened in these tendencies by the world he came to know through
his newspaper work. Encouraged to read by his fellow re-
porters, he found in Huxley, Tyndale and Spencer arguments
which enabled him to rationalize his impressions. Through
these experiences, however, a serious inconsistency was to develop which Dreiser only gradually came to realize. If life was
without meaning, if men were merely chemical compounds,
some strong, some weak, some "trig," some unstable, why pretend to be free in seeking any goal? Yet he could not reconcile
himself to poverty, to failure. Struggle might be futile, but he
could not accept the prospect of going down. Dreiser had no
answer when he wrote *Sister Carrie* (1900).

Carrie Meeber left a rural community to find employment
in Chicago, but the drabness and drudgery of life she saw in
her sister's home and at the factory in which she worked left
her dissatisfied. As the mistress of Drouet and later of Hurstwood, she finds security and contentment, though only for a
while. By the time Hurstwood's disintegration is complete she
has found a successful career on the stage. She rises to stardom
but remains unsatisfied with life. On that note the book closes.

The tone of the book was quiet and apparently marked with
the objectivity of a first-rate journalist who lets the story tell
itself, for Dreiser was here less concerned with a thesis than
in his other novels. Here was a true set of facts (Dreiser could
have verified every one from a world in which he watched it
happen). What did the reader say about this? In spite of its
quiet air of objectivity, the author, whether he completely
realized it or not, was using only half a deck to tell the fortunes of his characters. Morals, whether regarded as ethical
principles or purely social norms, were not adverted to; religion was hardly noted; ideals of even the most general kind
were not taken into account. He was fairly sure as he wrote
Sister Carrie that human beings were motivated by money,
pleasure and success; other motives were so inoperative as to
need no real consideration by the mature and honest person.

At the level of external fact, however, *Sister Carrie* stands
up very well. As usual with Dreiser, the book is weighted

with an abundance of detail; the urban scenes and backgrounds are carefully assembled and accurately handled. The plot is carefully worked out and the events are accounted for. But the causality is extrinsic. There is no dramatic development growing out of the clash of will upon will or mind upon mind. The characters in the story remain figures rather than living persons. Even Carrie Meeber is a nebulous personality; we are told about her, this quality and that; but we do not see her clearly. Veracity of background cannot by itself make characters in the foreground live if of themselves they do not have life.

All of this was part of the dilemma of the determinist. However much his reading and experience might persuade him of the credibility of a mechanistic world, Dreiser's experience would likewise make him realize the penalties of going down in the struggle. This antinomy he saw, and events in the next few years forced him to look hard at it again and again. But at this time his resolution of the difficulty and his analysis were, like Sister Carrie's, those of a dreamer. She could hope that a "new socialism" would evolve, that the world might better understand the uses of money, that free will would replace mere instinct, that ideals of beauty could be realized—but it was all a half hope. Hawthorne, working in an earlier era but with the same human material, knew better than this. Actually, Dreiser was never to solve this difficulty at an intellectual level. Only in terms of voluntarism was he able to resolve it temporarily. And such resolution runs the danger of sentimentality which, whether it be hard or soft (Dreiser's could be both), was nothing to live by.

Dreiser the man was very conscious of this aspect of the dilemma of determinism and its consequences for life; Dreiser the artist was much less aware of its effects on his writing. It is the inner qualities of mind and will which distinguish a man, mark him out, personalize him. If everything was to be explained by "chemisms," treatises on colloids were possible but nothing that had fundamental human significance. In later years this same defect would flaw his greatest novel. His inability to develop characters would always remain Dreiser's most serious shortcoming as a writer. It was the more regrettable since he had a real comprehensive sympathy for mankind and was by nature sensitive; he possessed, moreover, the patience to work away at small details that the careful psychologist requires.

For all the difficulty he had in handling character, Dreiser had been workman enough in other ways to make this an important novel and one of his best. That did not, however, immediately gain him an audience. At the turn of the century such magazines as *Century, Harpers* and *Scribners,* each important in the field of fiction, were very careful not to offend the tastes of their readers.[1] This did not mean that only such writers as Gene Stratton Porter and Harold Bell Wright were being read; Crane, Wharton, Glasgow and Upton Sinclair would in one year or another be high on the book-lists. Moreover, various facets of naturalism were reflected in the "moral confusion of Twain," "the harsher forms of realism" in Garland, "the robustious action tales" of Norris and London, the "bold miniatures" of Bierce and Crane. Students were beginning to think of a new and deterministic social science as taught by Comte and Spencer. And on the European continent naturalism had already been recognized.

The whole force of this movement in the United States, however, "was dulled by a traditional optimism reinforced by prudery."[2] Various forces were to change the standards of

[1] Dreiser's remarks made a few years later (1909) when he was directing the Butterick Publications are worth setting down. He explained to a correspondent: "We like sentiment, we like humor, we like realism, but it must be tinged with sufficient idealism to make it all of a truly uplifting character. Our field in this respect is limited by the same limitations which govern the well regulated home. We cannot admit stories which deal with false or immoral relations, or which point a false moral, or which deal with things degrading, such as drunkness. I am personally opposed in this magazine to stories which have an element of horror in them, or which are disgusting in their realism and fidelity to life. The finer side of things—the idealistic—is the answer for us, and we find really splendid materials within these limitations." (Quoted from a letter by Dreiser in *Theodore Dreiser,* by R. H. Elias, Knopf, 1949, pp. 140-41.)

[2] Cf. *Literary History of the United States,* edit. Spiller et al., Macmillan, 1948, Vol. II, pp. 943-999 and 1016-17.

American readers, but they were not yet ready to accept a book like *Sister Carrie*. It was not so much the events described, for, as at least one critic has noted, Hawthorne and Thackeray had handled such material before. It was not any salacious quality in the writing; Dreiser drapes no silks to give a glamorous sheen to the story; in this he is bare almost to austerity. Rather it was the raw newness of his material. Actually it was only in their taste that the majority were offended; theirs had been a bland diet, and their eyes and palate rebelled when uncooked potatoes were offered with the skin and the earth still on them.

The point for Dreiser was that the book was not accepted. This failure brought discouragement and a breakdown in its wake. With the help of his brother Paul he recovered and carried on editorial work from 1904 till 1911; the last four years of this period he spent managing the three Butterick magazines. Encouraged by his editorial and financial success, he was ready once more to take up his work as a novelist. The next few years were to be his most productive.

Jennie Gerhardt (1911), like his first novel (probably its materials were gathered about the same time), was a story of persons whose lives were shaped completely by the events around them. On the whole it is a weaker book than *Sister Carrie* and less convincing. Jennie and Lester are not equipped for hard and ceaseless battle in a very materialistic world; one is an idealist, the other lacked single-minded ruthlessness. This book shows, however, that Dreiser was moving nearer to the strong-man theory of life which is found in the Cowperwood trilogy.

As a boy Cowperwood had watched a lobster devour a squid at the fish-market. "That's the way it has to be, I guess," was his comment. "Things live on each other." The quick and the strong win out; they win because nature had made them strong and because they put no restraints upon that strength. Cowperwood might not know the meaning and significance of life, but he was sure he understood how it was organized. Get what you could and hold it fast; ". . . he genially ignored or secretly pitied those who believed otherwise." "I satisfy myself," was his motto and only principle. He followed it successfully as a "merchant prince" and a "sexual freelance" in Philadelphia through the pages of *The Financier* (1912) and in Chicago through its sequel, *The Titan* (1914).

As documented studies of the world of finance these are probably the best by an American man of letters. With patient labor the novelist set down all the facts of that complicated world and outlined how the labor of the ditch-digger, the ambitions of the society matron, the machinery of ward politicians, the cool avarice of bankers, affected their different lives. The result was not the portrait of a rugged individualist so much as it was a mural of a period. As such, shortcomings of languages, plot construction, characterization, imperfectly organized detail, did not materially prevent the success of the novels.

There is no need to quote from his naive speculations in *Hey-Rub-A-Dub-Dub* nor from his autobiographical books to assure ourselves that Dreiser at this time believed in the creed of naturalistic *laissez-faire* and in the survival of the fit. The whole construction and weight of Cowperwood's story revealed the author's awe and wonder of, his agreement with and belief in, this gospel of the strong. Yet with a difference. If one part of Dreiser was certain that only power and sex were realities and that the strong could win them in the struggle called life, another part of Dreiser apparently remained unsatisfied with such an answer and noted its doubts, though only at the end of each book.

If he was sure of the way that life was organized, Cowperwood did not know or understand its ultimate significance. And whatever that meaning might prove to be, facts like that of the "black Grouper" raised questions about the righteousness or beneficence to be found at the bottom of life's significance. Not even the fated strong who could handle life successfully for a while (because they understood the laws of nature) were able to reach final success. The witches in *Macbeth* might have hailed Cowperwood and have cried to him, "You shall be famed hereafter." "But like the Weird Sisters, they would have lied," comments Dreiser in *The Financier,* "for in the glory was also the ashes of Dead Sea Fruit—an understanding that could neither be inflamed by desire nor satisfied with luxury; a heart that was long since wearied by experience; a soul that was bereft of illusion as a windless moon."

At the close of *The Titan* Dreiser attempted another answer. Life was an equation; in the end a balance is struck and the mass subdues the individual or the individual the mass, but only for a time. "For, behold, the sea is ever dancing or raging."

> In the meantime there have sprung up social words and phrases expressing a need of balance—of equation. These are right, justice, truth, morality, an honest mind, a pure heart—all words meaning: a balance must be struck. The strong must not be too strong; the weak not too weak. But without variation how could the balance be maintained?
>
> Nirvana! Nirvana! The ultimate, still, equation.
>
> What shall we say of life in its last analysis, "Peace, be still"? Or shall we battle sternly for that equation which we know will be maintained whether we battle or no . . . ?

The question had but returned. "To each according to his temperament," was, he knew, no answer; so he wrote as the concluding paragraph of *The Titan:* "In a mulch of darkness are bedded the roots of endless sorrows—and of endless joys. Canst thou fix thine eye on the morning? Be glad. And if in the ultimate it blind thee, be glad also! Thou hast lived." Such an answer gives life only the significance of ultimate unintelligibility and requires the acceptance of a stoic. Dreiser would once more approach this problem in *The Stoic* (1947) when shortly before his death he wrote the last pages to the third volume of Cowperwood.

All this irony and skepticism came only in the conclusions to these books. It was too little and too late to change notably the reader's first reaction and interpretation of the novels; in any case these were glosses by the author and really outside the framework of the stories. As comments they add nothing to our understanding of Cowperwood though they do lead to a fuller understanding of Dreiser.

Before he had taken up the study of Cowperwood and of life as a quest for power, Dreiser was well along with another book. Published a year after *The Titan,* the story of Eugene Witla, the artist, attempts to examine life as a quest for beauty. Not even friends like Mencken, who had been championing Dreiser since *Jennie Gerhardt,* found much to praise in *The "Genius"* (1915). It is easily Dreiser's weakest novel and can muster strong claims to be being nearly the worst novel written by any important American writer.

There are inconsistencies in factual statements about the characters. In one place philosophy is said to be an open door to Witla; thirty pages later he is learning about Kant, Hegel and Schopenhauer. The genius of Witla is not convincing; it calls for repeated acts on the part of the reader to keep his disbelief suspended. Witla's search for beauty turned out to be something very much like the pursuit of young women: "He was interested to see how full and complete mentally and physically so many girls appeared to be at eighteen." It is not surprising for a character so conceived to be described as— "Here he was dramatic, impassioned, fiery, hungry. There was a terrible light in his eyes and he was desperate. He must be in love." And the speeches which Dreiser constructed for this cross-gartered lover fit with the all too accurate consistency of parody. "Oh, Flower Face! Oh, Silver Feet! Oh, Myrtle Bloom! Divine Fire! How perfect you are!"

One probable cause of the general weakness of the book was that Dreiser was not merely drawing upon his own experiences for a good deal of the material of the book—he was to do that consistently and often quite successfully—but he was unable to objectify this material as adequately as he was usually able to do. Some of Witla's tensions and problems were at this time Dreiser's own. This subjectivity of correlation helps us to understand the conclusion of the book. "Religious abstrusities" had given Eugene "a refuge from himself, from his doubt, and despairs, as religious thought always does."

Religion [Dreiser went on to say] gives life a habitation and a name apparently—though it is an illusion. So we are brought back to time and space and illimitable mind—as what? And we shall always stand before them attributing to them all those things which we cannot know.

Yet the need for religion is impermanent, like all else in life. As the soul regains its health, it becomes prone to the old illusions.

Dreiser himself at this time was again being troubled by the dark angel of skepticism. And like Witla he made some endeavors (wondering in the interim whether they were only temporary indications of a failure of nerve) through spiritism, Christian Science and his own speculations about mind and spirit to find a meaning which might explain the very pressing and disquieting forces of the material world.

It is not difficult to understand, in view of the weakness of the book, that Mencken was at first not very eager to take up any cudgels in behalf of the author when *The "Genius"* was cited by the New York Society for the Suppression of Vice. On Dreiser's urging, however, he did what he could to rally the clans and for a time the issue was hotly discussed. But the publisher wanted to risk no law-suits; so most of the copies of this book remained in store-rooms until it was re-issued in 1923.

The suppression of the book and the whole public argument which followed, however, had several effects so far as Dreiser himself was concerned. It brought his name and his work before the public and did much to prepare the way for a recognition that might otherwise not have come as early as it did and within his lifetime. Secondly, it caused him to lose something of that detachment of the observer (which he had or thought he had) and to take instead a more active part in changing the social scene. Finally, the lack of acceptance of a novel he had regarded highly was one of the reasons for his turning from the novel for nearly a decade.

During the next ten years Dreiser kept busy writing short stories, sketching the lives of men he had known, setting down his views and observations about life, and making his autobiographical confessions. In the meantime, especially during the years following World War I, a larger public had been prepared "to accept his frank, amoral attitude towards sex, his scientific materialism, and his disillusion."[3]

It was not, of course, merely the change in the audience which caused *An American Tragedy* to be acclaimed so widely when it appeared in 1925. Dreiser had produced an impressive novel and his best work. In essence the plot was an old story. Clyde Griffiths, a weak, impressionable young man, leaves his home and evangelical-minded parents to find work eventually in the factory of a rich relative. He falls in love with Roberta, a factory employee, but soon shifts his attention to Sondra, whose family is wealthy and socially prominent. Roberta demands marriage because she is pregnant. To solve his dilemma Clyde permits Roberta to drown. For this he is convicted of murder and dies in the electric chair.

But Dreiser had used such old material skillfully and to advantage. The earnestness and absorption of the author with his theme, the brooding and somber atmosphere, the dramatic tension which is maintained despite the length of the book, give this novel something certainly of the power of great tragic literature. Although the reader must make his way over some of the stumbling faults characteristic of Dreiser's prose and push through an accumulated mass of detail, he does feel the strong power of the work while it is immediately before him. That feeling, however, tends to dissipate as the book is set aside; its significance lessens as reflection and critical analysis have their way.

For many years Dreiser had regarded man only as a social-biological fact to be explained by the laws of nature. Within such a framework he shifted his point of view and his sympathies, now upholding the strong individualist, now the freedom of the artist, now the unintelligibility of the whole pattern of life. In spite of his agnosticism, therefore, which veered this way and that as he sought for some fundamental verity, Dreiser continued in his belief that man's problems were the

[3] Taylor, W. F., *A History of American Letters*, American Book Co., 1936, p. 372.

result of conflict between man's biologcial urges and the conventions of society.

In that struggle the strong win and the weak are crushed. Clyde Griffiths would, of course, have gone down in any social system, for he was a weakling; he could not counter the divergent pulls of his desires with any fixed norm of action. On no level from the religious to the economic was he agent; he was acted upon. His downfall, however, was an American tragedy because the potential weakness of his character was actuated by the goals contemporary society proposed to him; American society, as Dreiser saw it, furnished Clyde no standards save the huckster norms of wealth and ease and social position.

The main point is not whether Dreiser was pointing out the tragic implications in such a weak and passive character as Griffiths or whether he was indicting American society for its false conventions; from the intent of the author and the intent of the book, both were probably true. A more basic critical question is rather—what real significance at the level of tragedy was possible and consistent with such thoroughgoing naturalism?

Suffering and death, where human will has played a determining role, have the possibility of tragic meaning. But Dreiser's construction of *An American Tragedy* involved two intrinsic difficulties. The first was Clyde Griffiths himself; here was a weak keystone to uphold an arch of tragic action. That difficulty could have been and in part certainly was met by making Clyde a symbol for all the irresolute and confused who were destroyed by ambivalent desires and by the untrue and inconsistent standards of society. The other difficulty was the *hamartia* of the naturalist who works with tragic material. If human beings were ultimately only biochemical compounds modified by social environment, the resulting reactions could take on only that significance. The reader is indeed impressed with a sense of tragedy while he reads this story, because he brings to it, at least half-consciously, a truer understanding of man; but when the book is laid aside and the reader critically reflects on the premises of Dreiser's theme, its meaning as tragedy diminishes despite the power in its dark and bleak austerity.

Not long after the publication of *An American Tragedy*, Dreiser wrote that he saw man only as an "utterly infinitesimal individual" who weaves a "wholly meaningless course." But towards the end of the 'thirties he had begun to look on every phenomenon of life as being caused and operated by a universally pervasive creative energy. An experience with a snake,[4] which he encountered one day and told not to be frightened, and some botanical observations about the design in flowers were catalytic in his reaching the conclusion that this creative energy was intelligent and involved love in its plan.

Such a change in outlook would be reflected in *The Bulwark* when he determined in 1944 to complete it. As originally planned it was to follow the Cowperwood trilogy and "was to tell ironically of a puritan Quaker father whose devotion to the Decalogue does not bring success and does result in the disruption of his family."[5] Now as Elias notes, ". . . he remembered his father and his father's wayward children, and he thought that perhaps at last he knew and understood his father's real character. The Solon Barnes who might once have been a harsh portrayal of his father, or even a gently ironic one, now became his father lovingly transformed into the embodiment of Dreiser's own feeling of affection."[6] He even conceived of the book as a kind of atonement for his irreverent attacks on God and as a tribute to the creative force.[7]

The book itself is far less turgid and more clean of line than any of his previous work, save perhaps *Sister Carrie*. There is unity in its construction, at least a unity of purpose and design, and strong sincerity. Still the sympathy in it, for all its sincerity and reverence, has a certain invertebrate quality, which affects both the tone and the thesis of the novel. But of its message and the appeal which Dreiser meant it to

[4] This incident, which happened to Dreiser himself (cf. Elias, p. 288), is described near the close of *The Bulwark* as happening to Solon Barnes.

[5] Elias, p. 166.

[6] *Ibid.*, pp. 298-99.

[7] *Ibid.*, p. 304.

45

have, there can be no mistake. "Surely," he writes near the end of the book, "there must be a Creative Divinity, and so a purpose, behind all this variety and beauty and tragedy of life." And again:

> In this love and unity with all nature . . . there was nothing fitful or changing or disappointing—nothing that glowed one minute and was gone the next. This love was rather as constant as nature itself, everywhere the same, in sunshine or darkness, the filtered splendor of the dawn, the seeded beauty of the night. It was an intimate relation to the very heart of being.

Dreiser had not become a mystic nor turned to orthodox Christianity; in reality by the end of the book the "inner light" of the Quaker had been so interpreted that it would have been acceptable to a yogi; still this softened and somewhat Emersonian cast of thought (it had more of warmth and feeling and less of intellect than Emerson's) of Dreiser's last years was markedly different from what had gone before. Yet for all the difference, its possibility was always there. Witla had experimented with spiritism and Christian Science; even in *The Financier* and *The Titan* occasional hints were dropped. More than that—the possibility was there because Dreiser was always a man of the heart who could not have found more than temporary contentment in being a cool, detached and purely intellectual observer of life. This urge of will and feelings to see life as other than a meaningless flux of action and reaction did not make Dreiser's own vision true, but it did make it understandable.

After writing *The Bulwark* Dreiser set to work on *The Stoic,* for he wished to complete the story of Cowperwood within the time he still had before him. He had begun this novel in 1922 and gathered some background material for it when he visited Europe four years later. But now with his changed outlook on life, the difficulty of finishing the book and rounding out the trilogy becomes clear. He strove, especially in the conclusion, to give the book a different turn, an explanation in line with this deeply felt philosophy of life he now possessed. That it was only partially successful as an ending was not altogether due to his death and his editors; the material itself had become refractory because contradictory.

There are likewise contradictory aspects to be considered in any appraisal of Dreiser as novelist, for as writer his were the virtues of the will, not of the mind. Sincerity, laborious patience, deep sympathy, are quite apparent in his work; mental confusion, inability to discriminate and lack of craftsmanship are just as apparent. His choice of themes enabled Dreiser to exercise his power in the massing of details. And if he has not directly influenced later American novelists, his work has helped greatly in making it possible for them to examine life more fully in all its phases, to handle other than surface materials and themes. If he has not provided example and leadership under the aspect of mind, he has in terms of seriousness and determination of will. At that level his work in American fiction will endure.

Ellen Glasgow:

Ironist of Manners

N. ELIZABETH MONROE

THOUGH PASSED over in silence by many present-day critics, Ellen Glasgow will always enjoy a secure place in American letters. Her historical novels represent the fictional equivalents of major historical and social movements in Virginia from 1850 to 1912; her comedies of manner and her more serious works create a number of memorable characters, apply a delicate craftsmanship to the American scene as it was being drawn in Virginia during the early part of the twentieth century, and delineate manners with unerring rightness and vision. Her art is formal in the extreme, and her skill with descriptive prose that gives the effect of narrative and with incidents that reveal and define character might well be envied by greater novelists. All her stories bear re-reading because the characters establish themselves in the imagination long after the author has done with them.

Then why has she been neglected? Her death on November 21, 1945 was followed by no important critical evaluation and today there is no sign of a literary revival nor of the banding together of readers determined to read all of her works as the Trollopians have done with their idol. Michael Sadleir's introduction to Trollope's *Autobiography,* first published in 1883, explains why he was neglected in the years immediately following his death, and these same reasons may be applied to Miss Glasgow. Sadleir says that Trollope's name was on too many title-pages; that he chose to be known as a gentleman rather than a man of letters; and that his autobiography showed too much horse-sense to be relished by any literary cult.

Miss Glasgow follows the same pattern. *In a Certain Measure,* published in 1938, explains her technique and the inception of her stories. Though it is a book no one concerned with the technique of the novel can afford to miss, it is too simple and unmannered to catch the attention of critics who live by discovering something new and striking every day. She knew that no small voice can expect to be heard in America, certainly not for a long period of time, but continued to practice her exacting art for almost forty years in serene disregard of that knowledge. She thinks that to move freely in an imagined universe is success, whether it be recognized or not. She never went out deliberately to observe a scene or way of life and never invented one out of the whole cloth, but waited for her observation of life to sift itself down in her imagination before beginning to write. She never wrote the first line of a story without knowing what the last line was to be, and though her characters came to her complete with names and habitations supplied, they were allowed to grow and develop with their author before she sent them out to live in the world.

Dorinda Oakley, for instance, had been in her mind ten years before she began to write *Barren Ground,* and even then was given room to grow and change. Miss Glasgow worked hard over her stories, always preparing three drafts (except with her last novel), and never beginning until she had distinguished the point of view or points of view from which the narrative was to be told. As with Trollope, there is no literary patter in *In a Certain Measure,* but merely an honest appraisal of her art. Like Trollope, too, she has written too much to be sorted out by the run-of-the-mill reader and, as Cabell points out in his *Ellen Glasgow: An Inscribed Portrait,* there was always much of the *grande dame* about her, a fault not easy to live down.

The fact of the matter is that anyone who elects to write about the *haut monde* in America has a bad time of it from the start. There has been no social tradition inclusive enough with us to be accepted as a matter of course in literature or in life. We are in too much of a hurry to get things done to bother with manners, customs, codes of any sort, and though morals have not been completely abandoned, they have been so far removed from the scene of action that they are likely to appear merely quaint to the bright young people who write too many of our novels.

All this constitutes a great loss to the novel to which manners, customs, codes and traditions are the very stuff of life. It is true that Ellen Glasgow was born into a relatively stable social tradition, but she was given no encouragement from the general public, which knew little and cared less about the chivalric tradition. This kind of work is tolerated by the critics only when a novelist takes the big stick to his characters, and this Ellen Glasgow was unwilling to do. She sees to the core the vanities and pretensions of the world she describes, its apathy and disenchantment, its evasiveness and disorientation, and yet is unwilling to condemn it outright. The intention of such an art is to discover character not only to the reader but to the characters themselves, and here an urbane and ironical treatment is invaluable. As a result we have a whole assemblage of people who have lost their way in the world, but who are not without some of the dignity proper to man.

Miss Glasgow knows, for instance, that Judge Gamaliel Bland Honeywell (*The Romantic Comedians,* 1926) is something of a pious fraud, yet she allows him his hour of bliss, before dismissing him from the scene with the dignity a Virginia gentleman deserves. He is not taken directly from life; he is rather a stylized version of life, and placed in the perfect setting his illusions call for. Miss Glasgow says that from the time life pushed Judge Honeywell into her mind, his biography bubbled over with an effortless joy and that this novel is one of those happy marriages of form and idea which could not have been different.

Mr. Virginius Curle Littlepage (*They Stooped to Folly*, 1929) is still less a figure of fun, though he has amusing moments—had he not contemplated infidelity over the better part of a lifetime, only to become the victim of his own good habits? Every now and then his creator prods him, but never harshly and, though she laughs at his antics, she never lets him lose face with the reader. When he analyzes the causes of his disenchantment he speaks for a whole generation of men who, unable to find a center either within or without themselves, give themselves up to a futile daydream of what might have been. Why is it, he asks himself, that a man who has risen to the top of his profession and has always had the influence of a good woman—why, at fifty-seven, should he feel that he has never had anything he wanted? The war, perhaps? And he concludes: "The worst thing is this sense of having lost our way in the universe. The worst thing is that the war has made peace seem so futile." Only a limited self-knowledge is open to men like Mr. Littlepage, but there are moments when they see the cause of their malaise, if not its cure.

Into this long reverie Miss Glasgow has woven the theme of the book as illustrated by the three women who, in one way or another, have "forgotten themselves." How does the chivalric code operate toward the woman who has fallen not only from the pedestal on which man has placed her, but from virtue as well?—women like Millie Burden, who says she has the right to her own life, but who finds nothing worthy of love in the world about her; Amy Dalrymple, who, in spite of her heroic war record, has never been forgiven, because she has recovered and been happy; and Aunt Agatha, who has retired to the back bedroom, emerging now and then for a soda or the movies.

The Sheltered Life (1932) slips a sharp rapier into the cult of devotion to beauty. Miss Glasgow knew intuitively that in this novel the point of view must determine the form, and so the romantic legend is viewed by an old man whose futile life is behind him and by a young girl who, in throwing herself at her friend's husband, says in essence, "I didn't mean anything. I only wanted to be happy." The story that flows between these two points of view is too slight to be told in straight narrative; besides, the real subject is what happens in the minds of the two observers. Miss Glasgow says that the old man is the center of the book and that she has put into his reverie much of her own ultimate feeling about life, but even though his reveries are rich and varied, he himself is not representative enough to be civilized man still standing when the world breaks up around him. He is not compelling enough to occupy the center of the stage.

Miss Glasgow is at her best in the delineation of manners, a task for which she was prepared by birth, temperament and experience. She lived in a society that liked ideas, liked pleasure, and still, in spite of the inroads of modernism, practiced a becoming decorum in all things. Thus her medium was ready at hand. The comedy of manners requires precise observation of manners, a sense of form, a detached point of view, wit and charm, the ability to make little things interesting and, above all, a civilized society. It requires also the ability to see beneath and beyond details to what Miss Glasgow calls the eternal verities. Miss Glasgow, who had been observing the life about her from early childhood, never had to go in search of subjects or characters, but only to let her mind work on this rich store-house of memories before the outlines of her imagined universe became clear.

The comic spirit breathes through all her works. She is never heavy-handed or tedious, never didactic, never exaggerated. Concerned with a society in search of happiness, yet with no plan or chart to guide it, furnished only with a code of manners divorced from its religious and moral bases and almost without social meaning, she sees that she must treat her characters with ironical deference. Even though leading a tranced existence, they are so clear that they seem to be suspended in crystal. They never act except in conformity with other people's ideals or with the exactions of an inherited code. In fact, reverie has taken the place of action, yet every now and then, these reveries flower in beauty—for a moment the character seems about to discover the clue to his own identity. But only for a moment; then the lights are dimmed and twilight closes in on his universe again.

The young who rebel against this code are really no different from their elders; they never reason about life, never succeed in breaking through the tight shell of their ego, but are driven hither and yon by their own emotions. They go about shouting their right to rebellion, only to find nothing in the world about them worthy of love or rebellion. When they are radical, it is because they are projecting their own inner disorder upon the universe about them. In fact, the universe exists for them only as an extension of self. Their elders lived in a disenchanted, but not a lost world—not while courage, gallantry, integrity and laughter remain; they will live in a broken, disrupted world without meaning, without compassion, without love.

As an ironist of manners Miss Glasgow bears comparison with almost any of her contemporaries, especially with Edith Wharton and Henry James, both of whom are concerned with the technique by which manners are to be delineated or with the way significance is to be given to a society that has lost its sap. Ellen Glasgow keeps her eye on nature; Edith Wharton, who had an almost photographic memory and highly developed critical acumen, loses her way only when she tries to give moral significance to a confused and unworthy character; Henry James eschews observation in favor of invention and ingenuity.

Except for geographical differences, Miss Glasgow and Mrs. Wharton view the same scene—the *haut monde* in America during the last of the nineteenth and the early part of the twentieth centuries. Ellen Glasgow describes the decline of the agrarian aristocracy in the South; Mrs. Wharton gives the outer pattern of fashionable and aristocratic life in New York from the Civil War to World War I and, by implication at least, the reasons for its disintegration. The society in which Mrs. Wharton grew up was idle, rapacious and cruel; it had no important religious, social or political ideas and, though the rich Dutch families who ruled over its fixed pattern of decorum were pleasant and well-bred so long as they could pull the blinds down on everything disagreeable, they had less to fall back on than Ellen Glasgow's characters, for their society had never put its roots down in anything but money. That is sandy soil for the novelist, and yet Mrs. Wharton's work seems more significant than Miss Glasgow's, because through it she represents the tragedy of waste and because most of her novels are studies of moral consciousness which follow inexorably the logic of cause and effect.

There is bound to be a certain monotony in the descriptive and ironical method Miss Glasgow uses. There are too many frustrated people, too many despairing moods, too many gallant poses. Miss Glasgow is not responsible for the malaise that afflicts her characters, but she might have broadened her subject and given here and there a positive quality to her treatment. That is to say, her elegiac note could have been fuller, richer, more varied while still remaining true to itself. Miss Glasgow has other limitations that limit her characters. While it is not the novelist's duty to solve the problems he sets for his characters, there ought to be nothing in his point of view that gets in the way of their *being* solved. There is every reason to believe that Miss Glasgow saw no way to escape futility except through courage, gallantry and integrity. These are great qualities, but not great enough to redeem an age from futility.

Surely there must have been someone in the society she represents who saw that natural values will not remain at the human level without the support of supernatural values. Some of her characters besides Grandmother Fincastle and Aunt Meggie (*Vein of Iron,* 1935) must have tried to apply Christian principles to their lives, if not to the world about them. Instead, religion is always treated skeptically and ironically, as though the novelist herself saw religion only as part of an outworn code.

Ellen Glasgow's comedies of manners have been compared with Tchekov's *The Cherry Orchard,* but they are alike only in that they both celebrate the death of an age. Tchekov's characters are futile, too, but their reveries are rich and varied, outlined now with nostalgic longing for an age which is slipping away, again with love and tenderness and compassion, with vision and faith and a sense of the mystery that lies all about them. They can or will do nothing about their fate, but they *have* known love and happiness in the past, so that the young daughter can say: "The cherry orchard is sold, it is gone, that's true, that's true! But don't weep, mamma! Life is still before you, you have still your good, pure heart." That note of love, of affirmation, is never sounded in Ellen Glasgow. Edith Wharton's stories never strike the note of love either, but with her, situation and plot compensate somewhat for the lack of tenderness and warmth.

No one, of course, would compare Ellen Glasgow and Henry James as to style, scope and adequacy of conception, or imaginative consistency, but as an historian of manners, Miss Glasgow is certainly superior to James. It takes patience and a degree of humility to study manners, and by temperament and training James was prepared to devote his life to his impression of things, not to things themselves. Everything in his novels—situation, character, dialog, ethics—was pure Jamesian. He was prepared to defend the thesis that life was made for art, not art for life, and also the extension of this thesis that when life gets in the way of art, it can and should be sacrificed to art.

I think it is evident, too, that his whole elaborate craftsmanship was devised to hide the fact that he knew little about manners and customs at first hand. His powers of invention were prodigious, but they were set to work on his impression of life, subtle and involved as it was, and taken at two or three removes from life. Even the thinnest of Miss Glasgow's fictions are rich with the detail of day-by-day living; characters who come into the action only for a few minutes are clearly realized for us, and scenes and backgrounds are vividly described.

These three novelists are all interested in people who,

56

through rationalization, have lost the clue to their being, who think and act in two separate spheres, and who lose themselves in the meshes of their sensibility and spend their days and nights in idle dreams. In describing this kind of disorientation, Ellen Glasgow is much less obscure than Henry James. In fact, she is not obscure at all, though she limits her observation largely to the intellectual elements of life. The reader must know who is being deceived by the code of "beautiful behavior," the characters themselves or their author and, though the novelist need not part the curtain and declare himself, he must indicate what he is about in the maze of psychological subtleties in which his characters are imprisoned.

James takes his characters at their own evaluation. He considers them as examples of how noble intelligences will react in certain situations. When challenged as to the validity of his characters because they had no counterparts in life, he said that if such characters had never existed, they should have existed, and so there was nothing more to be said on that subject. Ellen Glasgow knows that her Virginia gentlemen never quite succeed in deceiving themselves and much less her and, if given a second chance, would do no better than the first time. She is saved from deception by the comic spirit itself. But James' characters teeter back and forth on literary occasions of sin, advance, retreat, advance again, explain their scruples to the point of exhaustion, then begin all over again with the delaying tactics their creator has worked out for them.

And what is their author doing in the meantime? Laughing at them? Indeed, no. He is preparing more and better defenses for them or waiting for other clouds of glory to descend upon them. His point of view is often ambiguous, too. What does he think, for instance, of the man who, deceiving his wife, says that he wants to do the noble thing? Or of the man who is sent abroad to spy on his friend with the reward in sight of marrying his friend's mother if he succeeds? Or of the woman who punishes her husband and his mistress by making them continue their sin after he, at least, is tired of it? James is not laughing at them—he thinks rather, that he has enriched their consciousness to the point where everything about them is of interest. After all, he invented them out of the whole cloth, did he not? And as superior beings they have the right to their own peculiarities.

A writer who tries to transfer his experience in the raw into fiction has by-passed the whole process of art, but the writer who, having little experience to depend on, invents his subject-matter as well as the technique by which it is interpreted, is bound, sooner or later, to arouse only the interest of curiosity. This is the stage toward which James is headed.

Ellen Glasgow did better than James in the delineation of manners because she was closer to the world around her, more sensitive to people, and much less concerned with self than James. Her mother's people belonged to the Tidewater aristocracy, her father's to the band of hardy Scotch Presbyterians who settled the upper reaches of the James. When she was born, April 22, 1874, in Richmond, Virginia, Federal troops still occupied parts of the South. It was an age of vivid contrasts that stretched out before her. When she began to write in 1897, the bitterness of the Reconstruction had worn off and a new and vigorous civilization was being built over the ruins of the old. When she died on November 21, 1945, she had lived long enough to witness the death of this new civilization.

All her life she must have been perceptive, quick to enjoy people and to get their stories, and intelligent enough to find the fictional counterparts of the people and movements about her. In her comedies of manners she celebrates the passing of an era whose exterior grace never quite covers up its internal decay. But she celebrates it not from a great distance, not by escaping into another milieu, but with wit and irony and a faithful representation of its manners and customs. She uses invention, too, not to take the place of observation, but to give form and permanence to her vision.

While all of Miss Glasgow's novels may be classified as historical, it seems useful to break them down into three groups. First come *The Battle-Ground, The Deliverance, The Voice of the People, The Romance of a Plain Man, Virginia, Life and Gabriella,* all of which have definite historical backgrounds, covering the period from 1850 to 1912, and which portray the bitter aftermath of the Civil War and the Reconstruction, the rise of railroads and industry, the development of democratic principles, and the gradual merging of the problems of the South with national and international problems. There follow the three comedies of manners which I have discussed, *The Romantic Comedians, They Stooped to Folly* and *The Sheltered Life,* in which manners are treated as the fruit of history. Finally, the third group consists of *Barren Ground* (1925), *Vein of Iron* (1936) and *In This Our Life* (1941), in which Miss Glasgow varies her descriptive method, creates character in the round instead of rolling it out flat, and broadens her theme. These are not novels of situation, though they are more dramatic than her earlier works and the separate incidents bear a causal relationshsip one to the other. Wherever a character does not seem to be filled out, it is not because Miss Glasgow has little to say about him, but because she is describing a community or the passing of an era. In her comedies of manners she succeeds in objectifying many of her own moods; in these works of the third group the organization of material makes that task unnecessary. The characters are further away from her background than are the main characters of the comedies, but they are brought close to her and the reader by the intensity of her observation and vision.

This is especially true of *Barren Ground,* where nothing is allowed to come into the story except what the heroine might have been expected to experience. Miss Glasgow says that this novel, which, by the way, she considers her greatest work, became for her almost a vessel of liberation and that everything she had written before, except *Virginia,* seemed by comparison thin. She is her own best critic here. She wrote so well and had so much to say that she might have gone on for a long time as a competent novelist with a distinguished style, had it not been for this new impulse of creativity. This was a great moment in her life. From here on she was free to ask searching questions about the life she had been observing since childhood on and to create characters who are not always passive before experience, but who sometimes take a hand in their own fate.

Barren Ground is the story of a woman who transcends all the bitter reversals of life through hard work and an enduring spirit. Belonging to the race of the undefeated, Dorinda Oakley would have been a great character wherever the author might have placed her, but in this story she is given the perfect setting for her courage and power to endure. The land is low and flat and endless with its field on field of broomsedge and scrub pine, the down-at-the-heel farms, its general air of poverty and near despair. The farmers go on year after year sowing the same crops, unwilling to change, because the people in these parts have always farmed in this way. These are good people rather than good families, as Miss Glasgow explains, sons and grandsons of Scotch-Irish pioneers, who settled this part of Virginia and made the land yield in spite of the hazards that beset them.

Only austere courage could fit into this scene, fill it out, redeem it from impoverishment and despair, and that is precisely what Dorinda Oakley brings to her task. Betrayed in her deepest affections on the threshold of life, she comes back to Pedlar's Corner determined to turn her father's land into a dairy farm. Though the community is skeptical, she sets to work, learns how to select and breed cattle, how to rotate crops, where to find markets for her produce. The land yields slowly —each failure is met with new energy until, after years of hard work, Dorinda can view her fields and livestock with pride. If, in this long, upward pull, she is ever discouraged, she says nothing about it. Not that she thinks of herself as heroic— she doesn't—she has an inexhaustible supply of energy and courage and wants only the chance to use it.

Yet all during her life the thought of Jason Greylock, who had loved her, then allowed himself to be tricked into marriage with another girl, has the power to bring anguish into her heart. Each time she closes the door quickly, turns the key on grief, knowing that he is not worthy of anguish, knowing also that love cannot be assessed in terms of worth. He calls her hard, but that is the revenge weakness takes on strength, on people who do not allow themselves to nurture the luxury of defeat.

At the last, she brings him to her home from the poorhouse, eases the burden of his passing, cares for him with a tenderness and objectivity she had not thought herself capable of. No word of the past ever comes between them. A lifetime has passed between their first meeting and this moment of death, nothing but drunken despair for him, but for her a lifetime of hard work, rewarding and, in its way, fruitful. A note of austere triumph sounds through this restrained and beautiful narrative; Dorinda has redeemed the land, has turned defeat into victory, has kept the door barred against futile grieving.

But this is not a love story, as is clearly indicated by the structure of the narrative. A bare third of it is given to Dorinda's love for Jason, the remainder to her triumph over the land. Miss Glasgow has portrayed this kind of heroine before, but always as the victim, not one who knows how to mold circumstances to her own needs. As I have said, the novel is remarkable for its close unity of theme, character, mood and place—every detail is set to work to tell the story of Dorinda. Time passes slowly in the changing seasons and as it affects Dorinda's character. As she wrings her victory from the reluctant hours, both she and the reader have a sense of fulfillment—self has been lost in the work of creation.

In *Vein of Iron* and *In This Our Life,* Miss Glasgow broadens her theme still further. What happens to man, she is asking, when all the props—home, family, religion and society—are taken away? Is it the "vein of iron" that keeps him standing upright, an inexhaustible instinct for survival, or individual integrity? What makes these questions all the more poignant is the fact that Miss Glasgow is seeking the answer for herself as for her characters. In her preface to *Life and Gabriella* (1916), she says that when she began to look around her she found most of the world sunk in despair, that it seemed wrong to be happy in the midst of all this suffering, and that in some obscure way, she was in part to blame for it. From then on she was casting about for means of alleviating the general suffering, not by articulating a moral in her stories, but by asking the questions humanity cannot ask for itself and by accepting the burden of creativity and by refining more and more the tools of her medium.

Of *Vein of Iron,* Miss Glasgow says: "I was striving in this book for a way of writing that was strong, terse, without extraneous adornment, and impeccably true to reality." There is no doubt but that she succeeded, though here and there she has not filled out a character because her canvas is too wide or because she is testing the "vein of iron" against too many pressures. In the opening chapters she distinguishes five different points of view through the prose cadences the characters employ and through the use of dissonant and harmonious sounds in their recollections, and though she succeeds in the experiment, she has a little trouble getting the story under way. However, after this initial difficulty, the story moves with certainty through the crowded years before and during World War I and the depression that followed.

Vein of Iron is the story of the Fincastle family, whose roots go back to the Scotch pioneers who settled the upper valley of the James, tamed the land and made it their own. On her paternal side, Miss Glasgow is descended from these same people, so that her understanding of them runs in the blood. In this story the problems of the frontier are replaced by social and political problems that indicate the passing of an era. Grandmother Fincastle's doughty heart can sustain any burden. Her son, John, is preoccupied with philosophy in an age which thinks in terms of science. Unable to find work, he is forced at the last to eat in soup kitchens, yet at no point in the story does he lose his quiet dignity. Standing in the breadline he thinks that the one thing society can never take away from him is fortitude; then he adds: "There is an understanding deeper than words, deeper than sound . . . below consciousness. He was a shell, or less than a shell, washed up and left by the tide. Yet the tide had ebbed and flowed over him, and he remained himself; he had endured; he was alone."

His daughter's marriage, as the author explains, represents the break with tradition and channels the story into the future. But Ada Fincastle has the vein of iron as surely as her fore-

bears. As far back as she can remember she had been in love
with Ralph, and when he is forced into marriage with another
girl, she takes their life into her own hands, rears his child
while he is at war, moves the family into town and holds them
together by getting a job in a department store. After Ralph
comes back she waits for his sign of love, which rarely comes,
as he is steeped in despair. He gets jobs and loses them, has a
cheap affair with a girl on the block and, though he is honest,
never sees that his chief trouble lies within himself. Ada carries on without complaint because she has schooled her will to
take hold of life; he will always be something of a failure
because he lacks the vein of iron.

In This Our Life is not a sequel to *Vein of Iron,* though
structured like it and similar in theme. Here again we have a
family as subject matter, a love story which is not the central
situation, and the passing of an age as the theme. Asa Timberlake, sacrificed in vain to the family, has always wanted a
little time of peace and quiet and is still hoping for it when the
story closes. His wife enjoys permanent ill health; the
younger daughter, Stanley, confesses that she cannot see happiness in other people without wanting to tear it apart; her
sister Roy is searching for something to hold on to that is not
an outworn tradition, a faith to live by which will not limit
the freedom of others but will give significance to her life;
Uncle William is the sensual man who, in his 'eighties, is still
pursuing women, but who is respected because of his money.
The skeptical, rather negative treatment only adds to the disillusionment; Miss Glasgow's theme here is greater than her
solution.

What is important here is the fact that Miss Glasgow puts
style, structure, even language to work in interpreting her
theme. All the characters in this story are searching for happiness, but whether they approach it obliquely or head-on,
they find it slipping through their fingers at the very moment
certitude seems to be theirs, and all this is symbolized for us
by recurring images which show the illusory nature of experience and the insubstantial nature of a universe that has slipped
its moorings. The images start up all about us: the flight of

pigeons, shimmering pools of water, invisible wings in the October sunlight, billowing waves of asters, golden-rod and life-everlasting, and blurring horizons, so that the reader experiences far more than is explicitly stated for him.

In conclusion, what has Miss Glasgow to say about the great moral and spiritual questions that have always exercised the mind of man? What has she to say to man himself? If, as Henry James asserts: "Works of art are capable of saying more things to man about himself than any other 'works' are capable of doing," then any novel, however concrete in its preoccupations, ought to have a general meaning. Miss Glasgow's general meaning appears to be that there are men in every generation who can sustain any loss and remain human. The lights have gone out in her world, but man holds on in the darkness, not pitting his strength against the universe, but merely holding on. It is a negative fate, but not an inglorious one.

Although Miss Glasgow's treatment of morals is skeptical and ironical, her stories never run counter to or against the grain of morality. In fact, the reverse of this is true. Suffering for her still has a purgative value. Dorinda Oakley goes through a lifetime of suffering and disappointment without becoming bitter; she has learned how to mold life to her own purposes instead of being molded by it. John Fincastle *(The Vein of Iron)* knows defeat, but not loss of identity—at the end he can still say he has lived, he has endured. Asa Timberlake *(In This Our Life)*, after a lifetime of servitude forced upon him by his ailing wife, is still hoping for a little time of peace and independence. Death scenes are often touched with nobility and, now and then, a character feels that something beyond time and space is trying to reach him. Even the hard, rapacious little heroines who get what they want find in the end that they do not want it. We are not asked to admire what is ugly or cruel, as so often happens in Henry James, but to contemplate life with the author's unwavering objectivity. Seen thus, the universe is still a moral universe, though man has lost his way and become almost a stranger to its laws.

The fact that her characters do not know the consolations of religion, the sweetness of God's love or the nearness of His presence, only deepens our pity for them. They do not experience suffering as part of the pattern of life—man's opportunity to ease the burden of Christ. They do not see that it has a redemptive value not only for the individual but for the whole human race. But they have not lost the divine image in its entirety, only its glory and radiance; their natural virtues rest on supernatural values which they cannot discern, and the fact that many of them retain their courage until the end is indeed remarkable.

The characters in the novels of manners are afflicted with a sense of futility. Having lost their center, they are driven round and round the periphery of consciousness, hardly aware of what moves them or of where they are going. Rationalization has become second nature with them. If they cannot cope with the outer world, they are helpless in the face of the interior world. They have moments when the pall lifts and they are on the verge of self-discovery, but these are only moments; then the darkness descends again, and they are lost.

There are two things to remember about this. The first is that Miss Glasgow is satirizing states of mind and emotion, and the second that self-deception and rationalization, superficiality and fear are the besetting sins of our day, that they can and do co-exist with religion, and that helping man find himself by losing self can be implemented through irony as well as through the usual direct means. At least, Ellen Glasgow never confuses scrupulosity with subtlety of mind, as James so often does; she is describing moods which at various points might be penetrated by light. Disassociation has always provided an opportunity to God—when a man loses his pride of place and the compactness of a world he has always depended on, he begins to question, to search for clues, to ask what it all means. It is precisely here that God may find an open door.

It must also be said of Ellen Glasgow that she does not shy away from dogma as so many modern humanists do. Henry James thought (and many of his critics think) that his great triumph lies in the fact that his mind was violated by no dogma whatsoever, political, social, moral or religious. If such a theory were acted upon, it might argue a kind of insanity, a living alone in a world of one's own making. At its best it argues a barren pride, a too-cautious caution, a determination to fix not only the conditions of one's own life, but that of one's characters as well. This accounts for the fact that so much of James' work seems contrived; it is a demonstration of how the creation should have taken place—a large order, but not too large for Henry James. One of his critics (a sensible and amusing one) shows how James worked up his knowledge of life by sitting on the edge of the abyss and sending his characters down in the pit, then questioning them sharply as they came up. This is his way of determining character and action and the rationale by which they are to be judged. But Ellen Glasgow did not invent the chivalric code (she lived in it over the better part of a lifetime) nor did she invent her characters, their actions or their morality. She did not feel the need of a particular milieu in which to write but, except for a short period in New York and Europe, lived quietly in Richmond. Remembering that Gide had to go all the way to Africa to preserve the purity of his vision, we must admit that Miss Glasgow's methods were simple indeed.

What this comes to is that the novel is a social art, which cannot be cut off from life and expect to thrive. As individuals, we are being admonished on all sides that we cannot save our souls merely by retiring into ourselves, but must achieve our destiny in the market-place, working with and for other men. How much more must this be true of the novel, which has been molded by humanity to express its fears and longings, its improbable dreams, its sins and suffering, its high dedication and shameful denials, its courage and hope and love.

While Ellen Glasgow had no taste for the supernatural, she never works at cross-purposes with it, and her treatment of social and moral questions is guided unconsciously by eternal values. She is deeply aware of the failure of the old South, of the harsh realities of the Reconstruction, of the re-emergence of the old life in the form of legend. She knows, too, of the eternally recurring problems of man, how to endure in the face of a hostile universe, how to achieve freedom without destroying others or being destroyed by others, how to narrow the gap between thought and action, between feeling and thought. These are not literary questions argued in the studio, not the contrivance of humanists, who think that nothing is settled yet, but questions taken out of the heart of life.

Many times her characters choose the right action in spite of themselves. Under the pretense of weeding out her husband's lower nature, Victoria Littlepage has completely frustrated him. But at the end there are for her, too, echoes of another, deeper consciousness than the one she has been aware of through life, and we are surprised but not unbelieving when we learn that she, too, has not been happy in their relationship, that the myth of woman as a good influence—man's invention, by the way—has not satisfied her, either. The myth has not pervaded the whole of her life, as her exquisite friendship with Louisa shows, and her actions in general are guided by good sense and prudence. Miss Glasgow says that she had intended to keep Victoria Littlepage in the background of her story as a "tiresome good woman," but that she came alive and played her own role before the story got under way.

Amanda Lightfoot *(The Romantic Comedians)* lived out her life under the same myth, in a sense was destroyed by it, but her charm and grace and delicacy of perception helped her to fill out the space allotted her and to play her part in the social life of Queenborough. The fact that she was identified time and again as one of Miss Glasgow's circle shows how much vitality she really had. By rights the Judge should have married her in the beginning; then, after being released from bondage to the memory of a perfect marriage, he had his second chance but, wanting to feel like a bird on the wing, he chooses to pursue youth instead of a perfectly preserved woman of his own generation.

General Archbald *(The Sheltered Life)* still continues to articulate a civilized point of view in the midst of disintegration and decay. Virginia Pendleton *(Virginia)* lives by the highest principles of religion and culture without ever having thought in her life—in fact, she has been taught that the best preparation for life is to know nothing about it. She is an exquisite creature, full of grace and charm and selfless in her devotion to her husband and children; when, in the end, she is cast aside, she accepts her fate with patience and forbearance. In short, these characters, without the visible support of religion, live in unconscious harmony with it, an achievement which shows how pervasive and enduring the influence of religion really is.

One final point about Miss Glasgow's treatment of morals. She never becomes didactic, never tells us what we are to think about her characters, never explains them, but lets them speak for themselves. Even the most brittle of them seem to have been created from within. In other words, she has reduced everything—morals, political and social ideas, manners and customs, beliefs, the whole of experience—to character and action.

This is not an easy thing to do, especially with characters who, living in a transitional era, are certain of nothing except their own futility. Miss Glasgow is careful to keep out of their reveries everything but what they might be expected to feel; they can explain themselves only up to a certain point. Beyond that their author is never tempted to go, even in the interest of enlightening the reader. Their reveries, taken together, articulate a multiplicity of attitudes, sentiments and ideas which do much to explain the consciousness of the South. The remarkable thing about this is that she never goes outside her medium to reflect the qualities of an age; the characters themselves and their actions carry the burden of social history.

Willa Cather:

Memory as Muse

FRANCIS X. CONNOLLY

OF THE two opposing impressions of Willa Cather [1] the favorable one is, at present, predominant. Like all popular admirations, its source is not altogether clear. The springs of devotion are deep in instinct, disguised in latent assumptions, and they often bubble up in generous but imprecise enthusiasms at very great distances from the true source of the pleasure they inspire.

Miss Cather is admired, one gathers from a large body of comment, for her profound sense of the larger motives, for

[1] Willa (Sibert) Cather was born of Irish, English and Alsatian forebears near Winchester, Virginia, on December 7, 1873, according to one account, early in 1874, according to Dr. James R. Shively, in 1876, according to the epitaph on her tomb-stone in East Jaffrey, Vermont. In 1882 she moved to a farm near Red Cloud, Nebraska. Her early education came from her parents, relations and neighbors from whom she acquired a sound taste for the classics, and from the frontier environment of the wild prairie and pioneering French, Bohemian, Scandinavian and German immigrants. She was one of three graduates from Red Cloud High School in 1890. From 1891 to 1895 she attended the University of Nebraska where she wrote for the college literary magazine and a local newspaper. Upon graduation Miss Cather entered journalism, then turned

her serene artistry, her purity of language, her moral poise, her ardent but controlled desire for perfection of art, of mind and of spirit. Her principal characters, chiefly artists, pioneers and saints, are valiant spirits who live and die for ideals. Their immense, epic vitality, conveyed by mood rather than through action, derives from intrinsic virtues of mind and heart. But their vitality, far from being abstract, operates in a special region and a special moment of history, so that we are as often aware of the landscape, and the movement of time across it, as we are of the symbolic figures which dominate it.

In a literary age characterized by negative capability—the accommodation by an author of logical contradictions and conflicting sensibilities—Willa Cather has been taken to stand for positive values. Her attitudes are clear and precise; unequivocally and unambiguously for the artist and against the boor, for the pioneer and against the commercial exploiter, for the saint and against self-centered mediocrity. She gave her readers fictitious men and women they could admire and ideas which they could absorb into the business of life. Occasionally, as in O*ne of Ours* or in *Sapphira and the Slave Girl,* she tended to describe states of mind rather than persons, and once or twice, due to her imperfect assimilation of the Jamesian technique, she seems to have assaulted rather than to have wooed her subject. But these infrequent lapses—indeed it is right to say with René Rapin that she never published a really *bad* book—merely called attention to the greatness of her other achievements.

to teaching English at the Alleghany High School near Pittsburgh. She became a magazine editor, traveled in Europe, vigorously practiced and studied the art of fiction. In 1911 she began to devote her time wholly to writing. Although she had published a volume of poetry as early as 1903, a book of short stories *The Troll Garden* in 1905 and a novel, *Alexander's Bridge,* in 1912, it was not until the appearance of *O Pioneers* in 1913 that her splendid talents were clearly recognized. From that date she advanced steadily towards the highest honors in American letters. When she died in 1947 she had become *la plus grande dame* of our artistic life, a title which earned her the privilege to dissent sharply with the spirit of her times and to display with impunity some of her most forgivable eccentricities.

70

Speaking by precept, in *Not Under Forty* and in *On Writing,* as well as by example, she opposed the raw and capering naturalism which colored the literary generation of which she was perhaps an involuntary member. Essentially a biographer of the spirit of man, she could not respond to the literature of sociology, of journalism, of mere documentation. Having striven, from her earliest stories, to cultivate a silver style capable of conveying the quiet, melancholy underground tones of memory and mood, she was not unexpectedly oppressed by the violence and crudity, the insufficiently humanized passions of contemporary fiction. Like many of her own heroines she seems too magnanimous to be understood rightly by a generation from which true greatness had passed away. She rejected with deliberate anger the contemporary surrender to disorder and anxiety, and turned to those moments of the past when tradition, decency, a classic sense of life could permit her imagination to soar without strain, to hover without danger of collapse.

Those who shared this mood—this irritation with the taint of feverish being—followed her into retirement. They found that her increasing austerity added to her charm, and that visits to the high places of her spirit, symbolized by her choice of settings in the incredibly blue mesas of the southwest or on the rock of Quebec, braced them to resist the warm and liquefying dissipations of life in the cities on the plain. She was, in the best sense of the word, a natural contemplative, holding in her mind and caressing chastely the disciplined endeavors, the dignified manners, the hard-won hearts-ease of men who conquered themselves and their environment.

That her rejection of her own generation should be taken for escapism or, as Maxwell Geismar characterizes it, as infantile malice (the most recent contemporary phrase is "failure of nerve") may readily be understood. Her early great reputation was secured by *O Pioneers, The Song of the Lark* and *My Antonia,* books which were immersed in the real memory of her childhood. Her characters had been remembered, rather than created, her plots had the force as well as the assymetrical form of a memoir, and her writing or composing had come

71

to count for less than the reality they pointed out. "I'd like the writing to be so lost in the object that it doesn't exist for the reader," she had said. She had, all the critics agreed, found herself and her subject at the same time, and the subject was native, realistic American experience.

To turn from this rich vein to the elegiac middle-aged disillusion of *The Professor's House,* and then to the Spanish southwest in the nostalgic *Death Comes for the Archbishop,* and immediately afterward to the French northeast in her reticent and frosty *Shadows on the Rock* certainly could appear to be "evasion of social environment, broken creative framework, dissipation of true energies." Some color is given to this last judgment of Mr. Geismar by Willa Cather's reconversion to her American material in *Lucy Gayheart* and *Sapphira and the Slave Girl.* Her reliance in these two novels on personal childhood memory rather than on the historical memory of tradition, could be interpreted as an unconscious confession that, in *The Professor's House* and *Death Comes for the Archbishop,* she had committed the great artistic sin of avoiding contact with her own direct and immediate experience.

Now the fact that there are at least two opposite impressions of Willa Cather should suggest that she is far more complex than her admirers at least have supposed. If she is not actually ambiguous, she is at least a fascinating blend of opposites. She is as romantic as Walt Whitman in *O Pioneers,* as classic as Henry James in her short stories; democratic in her love of simplicities, aristocratic in her artistic reticences. Fond of the traditional, as her loving descriptions of emigré European manners testify, she rebels against the formalism of the little bourgeoisie. She is earthy but fastidious; simple and subtle; full of passionate desire but desirous of prudent restraint. She admired enormously the great personal styles of her literary masters while she was theoretically committed to an impersonal kind of writing in which language merged completely into the reality it expressed.

Literary form was her constant preoccupation and yet she allowed her books to carve out their channels, to follow a will of their own, to shift in time and point-of-view, to run up-hill at times, as in *The Professor's House,* where one digression continues for a quarter of the novel. She had the robust mentality of a man, but remained ineluctably feminine in her spontaneous and detached insights. Preeminently a chronicler of affairs of the spirit, her eyes wandered after the lustier life of her Lena Lingards. She was so devoted to the individual "existential" person that, excepting *Alexander's Bridge,* she refused to plot a course which might interfere with their independence. Nevertheless she is an "essential" novelist, for the central idea—the theme—is nowhere more controlling than in Willa Cather.

These themes, moreover, are often curiously ambivalent, and thus frequently defy her professedly single intention. They concern both the frontier *and* the drawing room, self-realization *and* frustration, constant change *and* eternal truths, Martha *and* Mary. The symbols which she selects to convey these controlling ideas, while less equivocal, are not less rich in contrast. Professor St. Peter, an artistic temperament sprung from pioneer French and Yankee stock, has two houses; one enshrines a silver memory of a golden past, the other the prosperous, brassy and pressurized present. In *My Antonia,* the great grassy sea of plains is characterized by the plow, the coming age of meanness by the town. In *Death Comes for the Archbishop,* the majesty of the desert, the Cathedral and the Virgin, the civilized amenities of gardens, cookery, music and French language are figurative contradictions of the drunken, desecrating cowboys, the vile avarice of the mining towns, the malicious vulgarity of the Anglo-Saxon Smiths.

There are tensions in Willa Cather, but they are rarely revealed in the same character, never wholly revealed in the same book; and, more often than not, they rarely rise above the tight smooth surface of story. Neither are they resolved explicitly; even when, in an attempt to do so, Miss Cather breaks almost all the conventions of prose fiction.

For the direction of Willa Cather's art, as it may be determined from her crucial books—beginning with *My Antonia* and ending with *Shadows on the Rock*—moved steadily away from dramatic form and "solidity of specification" towards the literature of statement, of legend, of mood, towards the fusion of fiction and reality.[2] The normal preoccupations of novelists with contemporary manners and morals, with the cycle of stimulus and sensation, thought and motive, motive and act, act and memory, memory and stimulus, with the dialectic of subject and style, the concern with the growth of a character through successive incidents to a full personality—in short, their attempt to give a complete sense of life—these are not Miss Cather's chief preoccupations. There is memory of growth and change in her novels, but it rarely takes place before our eyes. There is report of stress, even of horror, but the event is quickly succeeded by the shadows which it casts. For the truth is that, for all the realistic tone and texture of her stories, Willa Cather is at heart a symbolic writer. She is far more concerned with the foreshortened essential meaning than the lengthy existent fact, and at one stage of her career more concerned with residual moral value than with elaborate intellectual meaning.

Indeed the crucial books mentioned above, particularly *My Antonia, The Professor's House* and *Death Comes for the Archbishop*, record progress from one level of meaning and value to another; from the level of nature to the level of mind, and from the level of mind to the level of spirit. In harmony with this progress, one may detect a gradually shifting point of view, in which the ultimate values of life are seen successively in the memory of youth, of middle age and old age.[3]

---

[2] How closely Willa Cather's novels depend upon her own life, especially her intimate childhood memories, may be inferred from her literary essays and from the many allusions to the function of art scattered throughout her fiction. *The World of Willa Cather*, by Mildred R. Bennett (Dodd, Mead, 1951), a recent study published after this essay was completed, contains a wealth of oral and documentary evidence supporting the idea that Willa Cather's stories were fictionalized biographies of the people she had known in Nebraska and elsewhere. Mrs. Bennett's book is an indispensable aid to the understanding of Willa Cather's literary life.

[3] For a convenient paraphrase of the plots of Miss Cather's novels, also published subsequently to the writing of this essay, see David Daiches' *Willa Cather, a Critical Study* (Cornell University, 1951).

II

"Optima dies . . . prima fugit" is the Vergilian motto of her effort in *My Antonia* to recapture "the precious, the incommunicable past." And the past is, as it was so often for Conrad, for James, for Evelyn Waugh in the *"Et in Arcadia ego"* section of *Brideshead Revisited*—youth.

Jim Burden, middle-aged, successful, romantically in love with the wide western country, has never ceased to treasure the primitive truths of his boyhood. He is, his sometimes tired tones suggest, burdened with his "handsome, energetic, executive" wife who is incapable of sharing his quiet enthusiasms. Stimulated by a visit to his home in Nebraska, he began to think of Antonia Shimerda, "this girl who seemed to us the country, the conditions, the whole adventure of our childhood."

Of the five books comprising this relatively short novel, only the shortest, Book IV, deals wholly with Antonia. Books II and III are more concerned with Antonia's friends than they are with her, and Books I and V really depict the family life of the Burdens, the Shimerdas and the Cuzaks rather than Antonia's personal life. Yet Antonia is the organic center of the story. Because of her Jim Burden's memory grows warm with recollections of the sod house on the prairie, of that first glorious autumn when Jim anticipated true happiness in being "dissolved into something complete and great." It is Antonia who witnessed with him the snake fight and who shared his thrill of horror at the story of the Russians, Peter and Paul, it was she who introduced him to the music-loving Harlings, who stimulated his scholastic ambitions, who rebuked his adolescent impurities. When he thought of the good life— laughter, generosity, enthusiasm, whole-hearted labor—he thought of Antonia. Tragedy, too, clustered around her. Her father's suicide, Wick Cutler's foulness, her seduction by Larry Donovan—these were almost as much a part of his life as they were of hers.

It is by knowing her deeply and wisely that he knows everything else. "Do you know, Antonia," Jim says to her, since I've been away, I think of you more often than of anyone else in this part of the world. I'd have liked to have you for a sweetheart, or a wife, or my mother or my sister—anything that a woman can be to a man. The idea of you is part of my mind; you influence my likes and dislikes, all my tastes, hundreds of times when I don't realize it. You really are part of me.

The idea of Antonia—she incarnated kindness—the idea thoroughly realized through brief perceptions, is summarized in the concluding book when Antonia, the fulfilled wife and happy mother, entertains Burden on her husband's farm.

I lay awake for a long while, until the slow-moving moon passed my window on its way up the heavens. I was thinking about Antonia and her children; about Anna's solicitude for her, Ambrosch's grave affection, Leo's jealous, animal little love. That moment, when they all came tumbling out of the cave into the light, was a sight any man might have come far to see. Antonia had always been one to leave images in the mind that did not fade— that grew stronger with time. In my memory there was a succession of such pictures, fixed there like the old woodcuts of one's first primer: Antonia kicking her bare legs against the sides of my pony when we came home in triumph with our snake; Antonia in her black shawl and fur cap, as she stood by her father's grave in the snowstorm; Antonia coming in with her work-team along the evening sky-line. She lent herself to immemorial human attitudes which we recognize by instinct as universal and true. I had not been mistaken. She was a battered woman now, not a lovely girl; but she still had that something which fires the imagination, could still stop one's breath for a moment by a look or gesture that somehow revealed the meaning in common things. She had only to stand in the orchard, to put her hand on a little crab tree and look up at the apples, to make you feel the goodness of planting and tending and harvesting at last. All the strong things of her heart came out in her body, that had been so tireless in serving generous emotions.

It was no wonder that her sons stood tall and straight.

76

She was a rich mine of life, like the founders of early races.

It was this "idea of Antonia" that enriched Jim Burden's life. It made him aware of the moral and artistic resources of despised foreigners—Bohemians, Swedes and Germans. It disgusted him with the "respectable" Black Hawk society, with the refined daughters of shopkeepers whose "muscles seemed to ask but one thing—not to be disturbed"; with the Black Hawk boys who looked forward to marrying Black Hawk girls, not because they loved them, but because "the respect for respectability was stronger than any desire in Black Hawk youth." Because Antonia had taught him to ignore prejudices, he could fall into love with Lena Lingard and part from her with a mature understanding of her kindness of heart. When Lena sends him away, "with her soft, slow, renunciating kiss," she says, "I guess I've always been a little foolish about you. I don't know what first put it into my head, unless it was Antonia, always telling me I mustn't be up to my nonsense with you." It was Antonia who then blessed his escape to the east, gave him all her affection but demanded nothing in return, except that he become the man he should be. Antonia sustained him, would sustain him, we are left to understand, all the days of his life.

Between the publication of *My Antonia* in 1918 and *The Professor's House* in 1925—the period of shattering disillusionment following World War I—Miss Cather seems to have remembered her heroic pioneers less vividly than she did the materialistic exploiters who succeeded them. The Middle West of *One of Ours* (1922) and *A Lost Lady* (1923) is no longer a theatre of valiant, energetic struggle, but a drab, commercial side-show. Claude Wheeler, the hero of *One of Ours,* finds no Antonia to fortify him in his desperate battle with his hard-headed money-minded father and brothers. He finds instead Enid Royce, sterile, frail, withering. An atmosphere of "poisonous reticence" contaminates family gatherings, makes it almost obscene to utter his inmost conviction that "there was something splendid about life."

When he is deserted by his wife on the frigid pretext that she was "called" to nurse her sister, a foreign missionary of a puritanical sect, Claude feels that he is choking in the thin platitudinous air of his native environment. He rages, almost hysterically for a Cather character, for freedom. Eventually he finds escape by joining the Army and dying on the fields of France, happy in the sense that he could contribute his life to the noble purpose of defending Western civilization. "Men could still die for an idea," Claude thinks before his death, for "ideals were not archaic things, beautiful and impotent; they were the real sources of power among men."

In *A Lost Lady,* the immediate predecessor to *The Professor's House,* the same vein of disenchantment persists. Here Neil Herbert, a more reticent Jim Burden, recalls his own youth in a western town at its moment of transition between its spring splendor of achievement and its early autumn of decay. Marian Forrester, the symbolic lost lady, is first remembered as a figure of brightness—so long as she is loyal to her eldering, dignified, pioneering husband. She withers in the face of hardship, gives herself to Ivy Peters, the shrewd, self-seeking young man "who had never dared anything, never risked anything," eventually is heard of in the Argentine as the parasitic wife of a rich rancher. The Forrester home, once an outpost of pioneering chivalry and hospitality, becomes the property of Ivy Peters.

The narrow sterility of Enid Royce and the fitful selfishness of Marian Forrester are in ugly opposition to Antonia and to Thea Kronborg of *The Song of the Lark* (1915) and to the artist heroines in *Youth and the Bright Medusa* (1920). Miss Cather's preoccupation with them did not signify, however, either reversal of her values or a permanent change of emphasis. They illustrate what happens to people who have no ideas and no ideals themselves, and no incarnation of an idea and an ideal like Antonia to fortify them. They are, as the title of a later book (1926) in the same vein suggests, their own mortal enemies.

Thus, by the time Miss Cather addressed herself to the writing of *The Professor's House,* she had a far more complex sense of ideas and ideals, of memory and of personality, than she had displayed in *My Antonia*. One feels that Jim Burden's problem was perhaps a little too easily solved by his recovery of the past he shared with Antonia. Were all his frustrations really shaken off because he had been accepted by the Cuzak family and could look forward to playing with Antonia's children and, after the boys grew up, to tramping the streets of Black Hawk "with Cuzak himself!"? Does this second-hand hope constitute "the sense of coming home to myself, and of having found out what a little circle man's experience is"? Jim Burden's destiny is hardly complete, for, if he possessed with Antonia "the precious, the incommunicable past," he has not faced the present or the future. There is no solution here of his own unhappy marriage, no accounting for his career as a lawyer, no hint that he has actually retrieved an essential independence of spirit. Jim Burden's problem is, in short, romantically simplified by his recovering the memory of his youth.

III

Professor Godfrey St. Peter, on the other hand, Janus-like faces the past and the future while living in the acutely sensitive middle-aged present. Looking backward, to his intense, idealistic scholarly life, he accuses himself of "never having learned to live without delight." Looking forward, from his terrifying apathy, he realizes that he must "face with fortitude" a life that promised neither "joy nor passionate grief." In the past he found his Antonia partly in Tom Outland and partly in Augusta, the seamstress. But the memory of Tom Outland is tinged with irony. It was Tom's posthumous fortune that corrupted one daughter, embittered another, drew his wife away from the spartan disciplines which had hitherto preserved her integrity. But Augusta, the pious, practical, middle-aged German Catholic spinster who had mysteriously shared his inner life and saved him from asphyxiation—he would rather have her around him "than anyone he could think of. Seasoned and sound and on the solid earth she surely was, and, for all her matter-of-factness and hard-handedness, kind and loyal. He even felt a sense of obligation toward her, instinctive, escaping definition, but real. And when you admitted that a thing was real, that was enough—now . . . There was still Augusta . . . a world full of Augustas, with whom one was outward bound."

Willa Cather's increasing maturity, and disillusion, may be seen in comparing the respective reliance of her two heroes on Bohemian Antonia and on German Augusta. Antonia was, despite her Christian piety, a child of nature, warm and intuitive; Augusta is a strict Catholic, a practicing and practical devotee. Antonia trusted her sensibilities (indeed her right-heartedness was the only donnée she could cultivate), while Augusta abides serenely in the habits formed by reason and custom as well as by her good heart. But if the one symbolized a youthful memory of woman, the other does not stand merely for woman's companionship in middle age. One feels that the young Augusta must have been very different from the young Antonia. Her reality is not merely a temperamental trait, her uncultivated poise no accident. It is a quality of spirit which St. Peter yearns to possess for himself, a grace which he quite clearly recognizes in his wife's seamstress.

There is a difference, too, in Burden's and St. Peter's sense of the past. Professor St. Peter like Jim Burden is haunted by history, but Burden's sense of history extended only through his lifetime. St. Peter, on the other hand, has absorbed European history and the timeless American southwest into his immediate present. From his French-Canadian ancestors (in symbiotic tolerance with a Yankee Methodist strain) he inherited ardor, a love of beauty, delicacy of taste, a sense of order which is expressed both by his penchant for gardens and fine wines and a sympathy for the great European past that inspired his great work on the Spanish adventurers. From them, too, came a reverent sense that art is a form of belief "in the mystery and importance of . . . little individual lives" and that "art and religion (they are the same thing in the end, of course) have given man the only happiness he has ever had."

The professor's search for form in life, in art and religion, in his own scholarship, is a search for the meaning of experience, and a willingness to submit to that meaning. Unlike Jim Burden who sometimes brought ideals to things as a measure of their value, the professor finds the truth in things. Even the success of his scholarship could be traced to a characteristic intuition of the objective movement and pace of events, which he caught and stressed, rather than to any deliberate making of his own. Here is how his book—and very probably Willa Cather's too—took shape:

> . . . All day long they were skirting the south coast of Spain; from the rose of dawn to the gold of sunset the ranges of the Sierra Nevadas towered on their right, snow peak after snow peak, high beyond the flight of fancy, gleaming like crystal and topaz. St. Peter lay looking up at them from a little boat riding low in the purple water, and the design of his book unfolded in the air above him, just as definitely as the mountain ranges themselves. And the design was sound. He had accepted it as inevitable, had never meddled with it, and it had seen him through.

St. Peter, unlike Burden, actually faced the incoherencies of contemporary life; the growing estrangement of his wife, the politics of a university campus, the irrepressible vulgarity of one son-in-law and the frustration of the other. He endured the dinner table banalities of the slowly sophisticating Mid-Western town, the commercial emphasis of an entire civilization. Through his connection with Tom Outland (whose memoir, it will be recalled, constitutes a quarter of the book) St. Peter reflects the pioneer's contempt for the bourgeois life. A scholar and artist himself, he is repelled by the patronizing babbits with their glossy substitutes for the abundant, precious realities.

As a result he is too complex to be satisfied with the honest but relatively simple natural perfections which supported Jim Burden. He is too aware of too much to return to primitive, preadolescent boyhood desire, "the truth under all truths . . . a first nature . . . untouched even by the tastes and intellectual activities which have been strong enough to have given him distinction among his fellows . . ." He can revert, at times, to a sense of that natural goodness of which Antonia Shimerda is the perfect embodiment, but he cannot stay there. He cannot escape reflection. The silver style of the book is the healthy pallor of this reflection. St. Peter's idea of life is at once more realistic than Jim Burden's, more commonplace, more mysterious. This idea, in which resignation plays so large a part, becomes St. Peter's ultimate humanistic ideal.

The symbols in *The Professor's House*—the shabby old place which is a home of the spirit as opposed to the new house which is a mere convenience, the unclouded joy of Tom Outland's blue mesa as opposed to the contaminated pleasures of life in the university town of Hamilton, Augusta's rough-textured trustworthiness as opposed to the humid sensibilities of his own family—contain the seeds of Willa Cather's future growth.

It is already half evident that the momentum of the reality she perceived so clearly in her succession of novels must carry her at an increasingly rapid pace beyond the heroism of heart and of mind to the heroism of spirit. The prominence she gives to Augusta, who is superficially static and undeniably drab, can hardly be explained save by regarding her as an unconscious precursor of Willa Cather's next novel, *Death Comes for the Archbishop* (1927).

IV

Long before writing *Death Comes for the Archbishop* Willa Cather had found the country of her soul in the desert places of the American southwest. The poetic paragraphs in *The Song of the Lark* sing of her heroine's response to the brilliant earth colors, the blue sky with its belled fire of stars and the meditative mood-making power of that mysterious, wonderful country. Tom Outland's story, which breaks into the main narrative of *The Professor's House* and serves to sharpen the contrast between the enthusiasm of the pioneer artists and the neurotic spasms of the money-makers, contains descriptive passages unrivalled in American prose. The land was lean, its contours

82

sharp, its winds stirred the soul with "something soft and wild and free, something that whispered to the ear on the pillow, lightened the heart, softly, softly picked the lock, slid the bolts, and released the prisoned spirit of man into the wind, into the blue and gold, into the morning, into the morning!" It was the exact, the right environment for her Archbishop, her hero who was pioneer, artist and saint, a kind of glorified fusion of all the things she had been admiring and striving to express during her life.

One perceives immediately the crepuscular tone of this book from the prolog set in Rome—that of the "unaccented legend" in which reality, not so much altered as distilled, is truly the remembered past, the impression of history and biography, the sum rather than the content of experience. There is no plot, but a life lived among lives, distinguishable from those other lives only as the highest peak is distinguished from the other peaks of a range. Father Latour is highly intelligent, handsome and severe. "Everything showed him to be a man of gentle birth—brave, sensitive, courteous. His manners, even when he was alone in the desert, were distinguished. He had a kind of courtesy towards himself, towards his beasts, towards the juniper tree before which he knelt, and the God whom he was addressing."

There follows a series of gently moving pictures describing the Bishop's arrival at Santa Fe, his own and Father Vaillant's missionary journeys to remote ranches and Indian villages, his encounters with an undisciplined clergy. But each unrepeated visit of the Bishop and Vaillant, however short, has an epiphanic quality. To have met the sheep-herder Benito at Agua Secreta, seventy-year-old Padre Herrera "still full of the sweetness" of his pilgrimage to Guadalupe, Don Manuel Lujon at his ranch near Bernalillo sadly parting with his prize mules, the horrifying murderer Scales and his victimized wife Magdalena, is to encounter in each case another immemorial human attitude. The Navajo chief Eusabio, Kit Carson, Fray Baltazar, still alive in legend, imperious Padre Martinez, "his full lips thrust out and taut, like the flesh of animals distended by fear or desire"—each highly individualized figure reveals the infinite capacity of the human spirit for the service of love and hate.

No literal reporter of social facts (indeed Miss Cather is careless of many details, including the spelling of proper and place names), she is nevertheless as attentive to the variety of the social background as she is to the difference between individuals and the quirkiness of nature. Life in a pueblo differs from that in a Navajo hogan, the cultivated society of Don Antonio Olivares and his wife Dona Isabella from that of hearty Don Manuel. The story of Sada, the Mexican slave of the low-caste Protestant Smiths, permits a brief horrified stare at the vicious camp-followers of the American conquerors. In contrast, a slightly romanticized Kit Carson, the dignified but still active patriarch of Taos, carries in his person the heroic attitudes of the Anglo-Saxon. For a glance at the larger world of Europe and the manners of France and Rome, there are many mirrors—among others the letters of Father Vaillant's devoted sister, the domestic refinements of the two priests, the tranquil and triumphant recollections of the aging Archbishop.

Indeed, so rich is the texture of this memoir of the southwest that one may become pleasantly lost in the details of the individual characters and of their contrasting social manners. It is only when one consciously searches for the meaning of the book as a whole that one realizes how all the "pictures" do more than develop a mood. *Death Comes for the Archbishop* is not merely a slightly fictitious history of a region. It is that, and many things more, but it is primarily a tribute to the transforming power of the disciplined intelligence of a Latour illuminated by his faith, assisted by the driving energy of that friend of his soul, Joseph Vaillant. The Archbishop and Vaillant are in effect one complete personality, since each exists completely in the other by virtue of their common inspiration and culture. Their temperamental differences serve to render credible the co-existence in that one complete personality of the healthy coarse grain of the pioneer and the tender sensibility of the artist. Take either man out of the book, or separate their life stories, and the whole idea of the book falls apart. Taken together, Latour and Vaillant stand for that fusion of action and contemplation, of doing and being, of enterprise and art which was latent in *My Antonia* and emergent in *The Professor's House*.

To say this is to suggest that in *Death Comes for the Archbishop* Willa Cather reached the end of her search for self-expression. But the pattern of her progress towards the spiritual poise of *Death Comes for the Archbishop,* from the lower levels of *My Antonia* and of *The Professor's House,* together with the analogous rhythmical pattern of youth, middle age and old age, is not wholly satisfactory. And it is not satisfactory because the pattern of progress does come to an end. Her next book, *Shadows on the Rock* (1931), maintains an exquisite poise of spirit. It repeats and reinforces the theme discovered in *Death Comes for the Archbishop,* even extends the note of contemplation. But *Shadows on the Rock,* for all its splendid episodic action, reveals a fundamentally closed world, too great a sense of contemplation, with an ending which does not contain a new beginning. Four years later, with the appearance of *Lucy Gayheart,* Miss Cather seems to sense this exhaustion of theme and to have returned once more to her familiar conflict between the immature artist and small-town Philistia. In *Sapphira and the Slave Girl* (1940), *Obscure Destinies* (1942) and *The Old Beauty* (1948) one finds little awareness of the ideas which had directed the movement of her art from *My Antonia* through *Shadows on the Rock*.

If this brief recapitulation of Miss Cather's last phase is even partly correct, one may account for her lack of continuous growth by two possibilities. One view, already stated, sees her spiritual impulse as a mistake which she recognized and attempted to correct by a return to the realistic path from which she had allowed herself to be diverted. This may well turn out to be the biographical fact.

The other possibility is that Miss Cather had never properly understood the Christian spirituality which is the informing principle of *Death Comes for the Archbishop* and *Shadows on the Rock*. Her "idea" of Christianity was perhaps too esthetic, too historical, too French, an admiration of Christian art and manners, its order and decency, its culture and its codes. She tried to remember what she had not experienced and perhaps found that her response, that of the culturally starved Protestant, to the greatness of the past, her noble desire to participate in an aristocracy of spirit, did not suffice to capture the reality she aimed at. She had fused art and life. When her vision of reality failed, her art failed with it. She was too honest to feign what she could not represent.

One senses this predicament even in the most affecting scenes of *Death Comes for the Archbishop*. In setting forth the qualifications of the new vicar of Santa Fe, the missionary Bishop Ferrand says: "The new vicar must be a young man, of strong constitution, full of zeal, and, above all, intelligent. He will have to deal with savagery and ignorance, with dissolute priests and political intrigue. He must be a man to whom order is necessary—as dear as life." The Spanish Cardinal comments that these are the marks of a Frenchman, adding wryly that "our Spanish Fathers made good martyrs but the French accomplish more." The French arrange, they "have a sense of proportion and rational adjustment. They are always trying to discover the logical relation of things. It is a passion with them." And all throughout the book it is this wholly admirable virtue of proportion and rational adjustment and courtesy that is stressed. Even in the case of the more fiery Father Vaillant, Miss Cather admires his civilized common sense rather than the communicated power and wisdom and love of his calling.

Now the passion for order has its term in order, in a real or illusionary tranquillity of spirit. But unless this passion tolerates a kind of divine impatience, an anguish of dissatisfaction with oneself and one's world, it can convey, even during a display of surface agitation and admirable energy, a feeling of passivity. For some types of the orderly mind everything is over before it is begun, the idea suffices for the experience. Once the idea has been clearly expressed there is no longer a need for the sweaty, arduous wrestle with the brutality of flesh and the obduracy of matter. Such a mind is perilously satisfied with its own knowledge of past solutions.

That this attitude is dangerous for the artist is readily apparent. It tends to focus his concern on previsioned salients or it restricts the memory to select and tested recollection. Too rarely, perhaps, does it permit the actual forging of peace in the hot furnace of the immediate moment. Too often does it suggest that order is as much a matter of temperament as it is the painful submission of the wayward mind to the reality of being. It encourages the belief that peace and order do not require daily, and possibly, an increasingly difficult struggle. Finally, it shuts off our blind participation in a thousand mysteries simply by classifying them as mysteries beyond the scope of idea.

Willa Cather did not of course succumb to all the difficulties inherent in such an immoderate passion for order. But she did have an imperfect sense of what the struggle for spiritual perfection actually meant. For this reason she made no progress beyond the position developed in *Shadows on the Rock,* or for that matter in *Death Comes for the Archbishop.* She failed to keep pace with the movement of her own vision, and losing the pace, she lost momentum, too. She had gone as far as she could go.

To say this is simply to say that her immense and imperishable contribution to American literature is not the most perfect one can imagine. Had she been able to understand that *Death Comes for the Archbishop* and *Shadows on the Rock,* while far superior in their vision of reality to their predecessors, were themselves incomplete, that there were still higher levels of spiritual values and greater depths of spiritual suffering; had she been less content with her ideas of things and with the esthetic gratification of those ideas; had she, in other words, felt fire as well as seen it, she might have been the greatest novelist of her time.

Sinclair Lewis:

Reviver of Character

C. CARROLL HOLLIS

A FEW years ago the editors of the *American Mercury Reader* went through the twenty volumes of that magazine to collect representative material. In the published result, top place was given to Sinclair Lewis's 1928 contribution, "The Man Who Knew Coolidge," because, to quote the editors, "Sinclair Lewis, during the 'twenties and 'thirties, said in lusty fiction what the *American Mercury* was saying in many of its articles and sketches," and because "this long and hilarious story, which eventually became a book with the same title, displays Mr. Lewis in all his glory."

Now one may validly object to the inclusion of the 1930's in this reference, but to say that Lewis and the *Mercury* were up to the same thing in the 'twenties is an enlightening and useful observation. And if "The Man Who Knew Coolidge" shows us what they were up to, so much the better.

But what does it show us? In Lowell T. Schmaltz's long monolog, the greatest bore in American fiction is self-revealed. He epitomizes much that Lewis, the *Mercury* and the 'twenties delighted in caricaturing, parodying, ridiculing. He is the stereotype formed from all the smug, sniggering, materialistic and egotistic mock-virtues of the decade, but whereas there were stock-characters before this time, for Schmaltz the stereotype is complete. He has not one redeeming virtue, not even a vice that relates him to the reader. That he moves and talks means not that he is a character, but that he is a caricature, parody—ridicule personified. We listen to Schmaltz's self-revelation with the same fascination that we watch monkeys at the zoo—he and they satisfy a morbid curiosity because they seem so much like men.

But monkeys and parrots and Schmaltzes are not men. And yet a novel, whatever else it may be, treats of the actions of men. It presents the actions of men for our contemplation in such a way that our curiosity about life is in some way satisfied. It is an axiom of art that there must be some relationship between the imitation and the thing imitated. In novels that relationship is found in the characters; they are and must be human. Notice that even in an animal story we make the animal characters human; they reason, they make choices, they have virtues and vices, they react to life as men do. So, because we read Lewis's work as a novel, we are forced to accept Schmaltz as human, but in violence to our knowledge of what man actually is. No man could be as unlovable as Schmaltz: his very existence as a man makes Creation a fairy story, the Incarnation an impossibility and the Redemption a joke. A novelist may portray the most wretched of sinners, but a sinner is at least a man with whom in imagination we can feel a basic human identity. Schmaltz is not even a sinner; he is a phonograph record, cleverly constructed to mouth assorted inanities. Indeed, Lewis's major deficiency as novelist is that he fails to individualize his characters, to give them that humanity without which the novel as an artistic imitation of life is impossible.

This is not to say that *The Man Who Knew Coolidge* (1928) is not important, but only that it is not a novel. The technique used in the sketch has been called "merciless" by any number of critics. They speak better than they know, for it is *merciless* in a fashion that goes far beyond technique. It is *merciless* literally. It refuses the speaker humanity, yet permits him every other attribute of men. It gives us a speaker in whom there is not a single redeeming feature, for whom there can be no involuntary flow of charity—for there is no object of charity. If one may say so without being blasphemous, not even God could love Lowell T. Schmaltz.

Presumably one can't go farther than this in condemning a novel, yet note that it is *as novel* that it is condemned. One may grant all the assorted tributes that have been variously made as to Lewis's verve, his capturing of middle-class phrasing, attitudes and institutions, yet still assert that a novel is something more. Whether one calls *The Man Who Knew Coolidge* satire or caricature or ridicule, the attitude and the technique it clearly reveals have a limited place in the novel. Lewis's singular merit in American fiction is that, consciously or not, he has extended the range of fiction by encompassing this danger zone. That he went beyond it in *The Man Who Knew Coolidge* is evident and, even so, important as marking by its failure one of the boundaries of the novel.

That this work will continue to be classed as a novel is inevitable, for critical terminology is always far behind literary experiment. What it ought to be called, if we can borrow a seventeenth-century term, is a Character, with an admixture of a Victorian poetic device, Browning's dramatic monolog. To say that Lewis's work is not a novel but a Theophrastian Character is not as far-fetched as it may seem at first glance. Everything about *The Man Who Knew Coolidge* from its title on is so completely in the Theophrastian tradition that it is surprising that no one has made the comparison earlier. There is, of course, no direct indebtedness; one may doubt, in fact, that Lewis would have felt any professional interest in Hall and Overbury and Earle, let alone Theophrastus. It is, indeed, somewhat ironical that Lewis with his scorn of tradition should be so clearly a part of a tradition that stems back to Aristotle.

The question here is not, then, Lewis's indebtedness to the Character writers. Rather, the point to be made is that the Character and the novel are two separate, almost contradictory things, for although they are related, they are yet distinct arts, each with its own end, its own discipline, its own pleasure. The whole notion of Character writing as a specific genre has been lost for centuries, yet it was once a remarkably adroit and skillful accomplishment for doing a special thing that no other art could do as well.

What it does, consciously and artistically, is to create *types*. The Character writer, when he contrives the Character of the Flatterer, the Petty Proud, the Braggart, the Pinch-penny, the Pretender to Learning, etc., intentionally ignores anything that is individual, that explains the particular psychological motives in different men, resulting in this common outward manifestation. He selects from tradition and from his experience the expressions, mannerisms, attitudes of any number of individual men in the light of some character-trait he wishes to exemplify, removes from this data anything that relates to individuals, and creates with what is left the type or the man who never did or could exist.

Now this Lewis does also. But the Character writer worked in an obvious, although narrow and difficult, convention, and accordingly the reader knew always and from the patterned opening sentence just what he was getting. The common human need that the Character or the creation of types satisfies is simply stated but profound in implication: the need of men to organize and to evaluate their experience. That we can abstract traits from many men and unite those traits into one imaginary man in such a way that we can make an intellectual judgment or appraisal of a certain aspect of life is a valuable and satisfying accomplishment. When a skillful writer does this for us, and by his handling of his subject aids us (without our being consciously aware of it) to make the judgment, we honor him.

The Character is much more intellectual in its appeal than the novel. To say this the other way around, the novel necessitates and demands far less participation (either instinctive or acquired) in an ordered society with its standards, classifications and hierarchy of values. In the eighteenth century, with the changes in philosophy, in religion, in economics, in science, and with the growth of a new middle-class audience cut off from the older traditional Aristotelian and Christian view of life, the Character gave way to the less demanding, more emotional and more immediately satisfying art form that we now call the novel. Specifically, the novel, through its representation of real characters, through its imitation of life, permits the satisfactions of vicarious experience which are directly and consciously abjured in the Characters.

The Character-idea did not die out completely. It is seen in various forms in both the eighteenth and nineteenth century. Generally, however, the remnants of it are found as adjuncts of other art-forms, notably the drama, the novel and, later, the movie, and always in the extremely low-brow or extremely high-brow levels of those popular arts. On the low level, types are seen in the stock characters of melodrama, in the formula fiction of our pulps, in nine out of every ten movies. That this should be so is a continual witness to the healthy, instinctive, but ever commercially thwarted need of people to organize their experience; that this need is so naively and simply satisfied does not justify the condescending "writing down" of our exploiting technicians, as Shakespeare forever testifies. On the upper level, the survival of types is less evident, but is seen chiefly in one kind of humorous writing, in Thomas Love Peacock, in Thackeray's snobs, in Meredith, in Max Beerbohm, in many essay writers. The relation of the Character to humor is close, for humor itself (in its intellectual form) implies recognition of order and the absurdity of any departure from it.

With the artistic novel itself, as we normally think of it today, the Character influence has practically vanished. Now, indeed, it is a term of opprobrium to say of a novel that its characters are only types. And this is right and proper. A novel cannot do what it is supposed to do if it works through types. Yet the need for what the Character used to do is still present. Sinclair Lewis—to get back to him—merits our serious critical attention because in a few novels he attempts and partially succeeds in extending the artistic range of the novel to include some of the forgotten values of the Character.

Until we are told otherwise, we may assume that Lewis was

unaware of the Character writers and was wholly unconscious that he was reviving, if in an oblique form, an ancient tradition. What, then, can we say of how he came to write the famous novels of the 'twenties? First, we must put him in his age.

Scholars and historians have done much to dissect and explain the 'twenties. It was a post-war decade, with its lost generation, its luxury of despair, its expatriates, its scorn of prohibition, its sneering rejection of Puritanism and Victorianism with all that those ubiquitous terms could possibly signify. All of this is true, but what is sometimes forgotten is that all of this posturing, this scorn, this rejection provides a vantage point from which one views the contemporaries one dislikes, the past one rejects, the institutions one laughs at. That vantage point, that precarious position from which the writers of the 'twenties confidently asserted their view of life, may seem, in the light of the depression-'thirties and the war-'forties, somewhat adolescent and cock-sure to us today, but it was definitely present.

The vantage point from which Lewis and the *American Mercury* viewed the rest of America was that of an intellectual and cultural superiority drawn from the quite tenuous inferences of the new science, the new psychology, the new sociology. There was little serious intellectual defense and justification for their attitude, but such books as Lippmann's *Preface to Morals* and Krutch's *Modern Temper* indicate, even in their titles, the nature of the defense. As far as the *American Mercury* was concerned, the easiest way to assert one's superiority was to ridicule whatever had no place in the bright new order, and thus the "American Credo" and the successive volumes of *Prejudices*. The clearest expression of this attitude is the magazine's own proclamation of its *modus operandi* that appeared in the first issue:

> The Editors have heard no Voice from the burning bush. They will not cry up and offer for sale any sovereign balm, whether political, economic, or esthetic, for all the sorrows of the world. The fact is, indeed, that they doubt that any such sovereign balm exists, or that it ever

will exist hereafter. The world, as they see it, is down with at least a score of painful diseases, all of them chronic and incurable; nevertheless, they cling to the notion that human existence remains predominantly charming. Especially it is charming in this unparalleled Republic of the West, where men are earnest and women are intelligent, and all the historic virtues of Christendom are now concentrated. The Editors propose, before jurisprudence develops to the point of prohibiting skepticism altogether, to give a realistic consideration to certain of these virtues, and to try to save what is exhilarating in them, even when all that is divine must be abandoned. They engage to undertake the business in a polished and aseptic manner, without indignation on the one hand and without much regard for tender feelings on the other. They have no set program, either destructive or constructive. Sufficient unto each day will be the performance thereof.

The quotation speaks better than volumes of what the magazine and Lewis wanted to do and in some measure did in the 'twenties. And for this gay work, a revived Character *genre,* the personification of the virtues and vices of the day, was an almost ideal form.

The tradition of the Character was, as far as we can tell, not even recalled. But, as is always the case, traditional artforms continue or are revived because they are needed, not because one writer submissively follows another. The major value of a live tradition for the artist is that he is freed of the trial-and-error system in attaining a mastery of his artform. When the occasion arrived for the revival of the Character, the form itself was known only by a few scholars, and Lewis was not likely to take pedantic advice even if it were offered.

In an age or, better, a decade, when the Character would serve the needs of the time, Lewis's novels came nearest to satisfying that need. That he used the novel form to do something that is outside the sphere of the novel is unfortunate, because he was at best a second-rate novelist, who subordinated a valuable if unrealized gift for Character-writing to a contrary art-form.

In spite of this, perhaps because of this, his novels of the decade are important and significant. Had he not used the novel form in *Main Street,* the Character approach might not have caught on at all, and *Babbitt, Arrowsmith, Elmer Gantry, The Man Who Knew Coolidge* and even *Dodsworth* could not have appeared. On the other hand, had he been a better novelist, the very discipline of that form would have prevented the inclusion of the alien Character element.

To trace Lewis's career in the light of this Character-*versus*-novel construction of his major works is difficult but rewarding. The difficulty arises chiefly from both his and his readers' almost continual unawareness of the merits of this Character insertion. All through the 'twenties and later, one finds critics and commentators reading these works as novels: they are forced to admit the importance and are yet baffled by the exaggeration, the caricature, the types that are inherent in these works. Yet, when Lewis's major work is seen as a combination of Character and novel, the puzzling stages in his career fall into place.

The need for the special kind of Character presentation that Lewis alone could do with great effectiveness was inevitably temporary and short-lived. For a brief decade only it was possible to make a Character of Gopher Prairie and its Main Street and its inhabitants, of Babbitt and American bourgeois business, of Gantry and the revival preacher, of the man who knew Coolidge. But in the 'thirties, the never fully thought-out standards, upon which these Characters had merit, vanished completely. When Gopher Prairie had its farms foreclosed, when Babbitts jumped out of office windows, when Gantry's success was seen as depending not on his charlatanry but on the eager groping of countless spiritually blinded Americans, when Lowell T. Schmaltz became only a bitter joke—then the Character disappeared. And with its disappearance, the novel that carried it was now only a novel, and as the novels before *Main Street* were without distinction, so are all of Lewis's works as novels, as everyone has recognized from *Prodigal Parents* on.

The dichotomy of the major works of the 'twenties is best seen in *Babbitt,* but begins in *Main Street* (1920). We are told that this novel was formed in Lewis's mind in 1905 in a work to be called *The Village Virus*. It corroborates the present analysis that Lewis waited another fifteen years to write this work, for in that interval much had to happen so that *Main Street* could be written and received as it was. As a novel, it tells the story of Carol Kennicott's eager desire to transform Gopher Prairie into an Arcadian village with Parisian overtones. She fails, is hurt by her doctor-husband's lack of sympathy, encounters a succession of misadventures, runs away, but ultimately comes back to Main Street with no real change in either her character or that of Gopher Prairie.

When we examine both the book and the tremendous effect it produced, a number of things are evident. Foremost is that it is not and was not accepted as a novel. When we look at the book as a novel, Carol Kennicott is the nominal heroine— the notable passages should concern her and should portray her with depth and insight. Actually, Carol is a ninny, a perpetual adolescent whose charitable endeavors are selfishly motivated and who, in justice, deserves all that she gets and more. Here is material for a Character, but instead she is one of the few persons in the book who is individualized (Miles Bjornstam is another). Though we may object to Lewis's apparent approval of her, no one mistakes Carol for a *type*. Yet, actually, no critic or reader seemed very much concerned with Carol as a *person*. The same applies to Will Kennicott and Guy Pollock, who are something more than the country doctor and small town lawyer. Rather, what created the furor was the Characterization, as seen in the Dyers, the Clarks, the Haydocks, Raymie Wutherspoon, Mrs. Bogart and others, who collectively make the composite Character that gives the book its title.

In a period when "realism" was a battle-cry which demanded that one take sides, critics and readers made comical blunders in trying to come to grips with the book. The Character is at the opposite pole from realism, and the solemn affirmation, supported by statistics and references, that the small town was or was not what Lewis claimed must have amused Lewis and the *Smart-Set* critics, even though they themselves seem hardly to have realized what *Main Street* did signify artistically. The efficacy of the Character itself cannot be tested by statistics and historical facts, for its merit does not lie in its factual basis in Sauk Center, Minnesota.

It is likewise critically inept to question the historical authenticity of *Babbitt* (1922). Someone once said that the book became an over-night best-seller because all the Babbitts read it, and each of them said to himself, "How true—of my neighbor." Such a comment has the merit of neat simplification, but misses the point of the book completely. If anything may be derived from the remark, it is that George F. is quickly accepted for what he is—a type—and that one characteristic of the type is its automatic self-blindness. The book is a major development, if not complete, in the use of Character. In *Main Street* the Character and the novel are inevitably at odds, and the thing characterized is itself diffuse. In *Babbitt,* the two art-forms become as nearly fused as they can be.

Babbitt is a resident of Floral Heights, a suburb of Zenith, in the state of Winnemac—the whole series of non-existent persons and places establishes that this is an abstraction; but an abstraction created from a rigidly-bounded area of American life. In the book as novel there is little plot in the conventional sense. Babbitt is, to be sure, in conflict with that part of middle-class society represented by the Zenith Boosters' Club, but it is not a valid conflict for any sort of dramatic and meaningful presentation. This is not to say that a spiritual conflict between an American businessman and his social environment is not possible, but only that Babbitt (as Lewis presents him to us) cannot become significantly engaged in such a conflict. The various episodes which make up the action of the story are not Babbitt's attacks on the sterility, stupidity or grossness of bourgeois society. They are, rather, his attempts to avoid his bourgeois responsibilities. Such efforts as the vacation with the "bohemian" Paul Riesling, the liaison with the widow, Tanis Judique, and the active sympathy with the ideas of the socialist lawyer, Seneca Doane, are only temporarily successful, and in the end he accepts his role, having got safely through his "foolish forties."

As for the Character itself, it is too well-known to need analysis. We have, in fact, so long accepted Babbitt as the personification of the American businessman, that we forget the book. Actually, the Babbitt of a novel had to be more than a personification. And so he is. The best scene in the book, when we consider it as a novel, is the human, moving and compassionate episode of Babbitt at Myra's sick-bed. But the Character cannot be human, and yet the novel must be. What the 'twenties did, and what we still do (for Babbitt is now part of our national consciousness) is to forget George Folansbee Babbitt the man and to remember Babbitt the Character.

The history of Character writing reveals what Lewis and the 'twenties also found: that it is easier to personify vices than virtues. From the writer's position, it *is* easier, because virtue by its modesty almost necessitates recognition of personal achievement. In addition, although the 'twenties might scorn many things, there were few virtues ready made for Character treatment. Lewis did try it, however, in *Arrowsmith* (1925).

The difficulties inherent in combining a Character of a Virtue (in this case, science) and a novel were insurmountable in this work. Of Lewis's so-called novels of the 'twenties, *Arrowsmith* is most nearly pure novel and least Character (after it comes *Dodsworth,* 1929). In the story of Martin Arrowsmith, Lewis had both his own memories as the son and brother of a country doctor and the assistance of Paul de Kruif, the popularizer of medical science. With these, he could speak with persuasive authority of small-town doctors' offices, of laboratories, of medical institutes. The conviction carries over into the story itself, so that only on second reading do we note the inadequacies as fiction. Granted that Lewis's original intention was to satirize the callous exploitation of medical science by the vested interests, and granted, too, that we will one day be informed of the real people behind the fictional characters, we still expect the story to have its own logic and unity.

Yet, examined as a story, there are obvious artistic blunders: Martin's adolescent veneration for Gottlieb is understandable when he is a student but not when he is a colleague; his minor set-back when he fails to reform the public health system is not enough to warrant the consequent scorn for all forms of public service; the melodramatics of his professed credo as scientist, ending with "God give me the strength not to trust in God," are external rather than integral to the story; the self-imposed exile which terminates the story is not the logical or psychological consequence of anything that precedes it. Arrowsmith and Leora are not as carefully conceived and as consistent as one might wish; they are individuals, not types. Gottlieb seems much nearer a type—in this case the sardonic Old World scientist devoted to truth (or the only truth that the 'twenties could still venerate)—but the most obvious Character is Dr. Almus Pickerbaugh. Presumably Lewis intended us to contrast the virtue and the vice as represented by Gottlieb and Pickerbaugh (a device of the earlier Character writers), but the story gets in the way. In this book it happens to be a good story; in fact any defense of Lewis as a major novelist must inevitably rest on the evidence supplied by *Arrowsmith* and *Dodsworth*. Whatever one's total view of Lewis may be, it seems increasingly impossible to talk about *Babbitt* and *Arrowsmith* in the same terms. Lewis had a flair for Character writing, but in *Arrowsmith* the attitude of veneration and humility before science vitiates even those Character-insertions that are present.

Mantrap (1926) is unimportant as novel or as Character, and it signifies only that Lewis's forte was the Character-novel combination. When he had the assistance of family experience, Paul de Kruif's advice and a dramatic plot, he could write a good novel. But without such a happy circumstance and without the opportunity for Character creation, he could—and did —write third-rate novels for the market.

Elmer Gantry (1927) is something else again. This work happens to be a failure, but not at all because it magnifies any of the weaknesses previously seen. As a novel, the book fails chiefly because it is contrived to carry a thesis. Gantry, in terms of Lewis's indictment, must become increasingly successful as a revival preacher as he becomes increasingly venal, hypocritical, cynical—and so he does but at the sacrifice of artistic credibility. Throughout the book the attitude toward the material is that of amused condescension, of sophisticated superiority, both for Gantry and his kind and for those who are taken in by Gantry's tricks.

As in *Babbitt,* the titular character is a type, but here the type or Character of a Revival Preacher is hastily and inartistically done, in fact, over-done. Babbitt as a Character is skillfully created (excepting the novel-writer's insertions previously mentioned), and he admirably suited the need of the day to categorize and evaluate the ubiquitous businessman. But the success of Babbitt as Character ultimately rested in the general conviction that as a universal character he represented countless numbers of particulars. Gantry is similarly contrived, but we all know that it doesn't come off. Why? Not because of any novelist's error, but because Gantry is no universal character created by abstraction from particular men. Lewis's melodramatic sense vitiates the Character by creating a figure who cannot be a type for he is typical of no recognized group. We acknowledge that some revival preachers are hypocritical, others venal, others drunkards, others lechers, and others grossly stupid, but the traits are self-contradictory. Apparently Lewis studied the various evidence with a statistician's enthusiasm, but Characters are as much beyond composite photographs as universals are beyond the nominalist's composite. The book had notable trade success, but as with all successes *de scandal* its notoriety has little critical import.

The Man Who Knew Coolidge is, of all of Lewis's work, the only Character in the true and complete sense. Here, and here only, we have the Character, the universal, the personification of an abstraction by itself with no story interference. As such we have epitomized Lewis's greatest artistic accomplishment, seen in its tentative stage in *Main Street,* in its widest scope in *Babbitt,* misdirected in *Arrowsmith,* mishandled in *Elmer Gantry,* and brought to its narrow perfection in Lowell T. Schmaltz.

Yet, if this analysis is true, why was and is the work not widely read and loudly praised? The answer has three parts. First, Lewis or his publishers made a serious critical and commercial blunder by enlarging the sketch to make a novel out of it. Nothing is added in the book edition, and the Character, which depends on brevity for its impact, becomes burdensome as it is thinned out. Second, it was the age of the novel and our critical perspective has been limited by too many novels; the intellectual acuity demanded by the Character *per se* was present, but not in sufficient degree to make the writing of Characters commercially successful. Third, even as a Character the work is not completely successful. The use of the monolog device is eye-catching and permits Lewis to display his subordinate gift of creating what seems to be phonographic recording of lower middle-class speech, although Ring Lardner could do this far more effectively. But the monolog trick necessitates too many extra words to get over some necessary point and eliminates the details of dress, mannerisms, facial expression that objective description might have supplied. Indeed, Lewis might have learned much from the seventeenth-century Character writers, but even so *The Man Who Knew Coolidge* is the nearest thing to pure Character that we have.

With *Dodsworth,* the last of the novels of the 'twenties, the peak had passed. By 1929, the previous standards, which Lewis shared with the *American Mercury* and in terms of which he created his Characters, were beginning to seem empty, shallow and not sufficiently serious for the impending collapse that everyone sensed. If any outward event marked the change in attitude, it would be the excitement attendant upon the Sacco-Vanzetti trials and, perhaps, in literature the appearance of Wolfe's *Look Homeward Angel* in the same year as *Dodsworth,* and Dos Passos's *42nd Parallel* in 1930.

The whole story of the trip of Sam and Fran Dodsworth to Europe, and the results that follow, is well told and easily read. Sam retires as Zenith's automobile magnate to pursue the European culture his wife has been talking about for years.

He finds on the boat to Europe that Fran's idea of culture is to liberate herself from the petty conventions of American society, including her marriage vows. Ultimately Dodsworth rejects her, but throughout her various affairs he himself goes through a painful course of self-education. In the end he sufficiently realizes himself to know what he wants of life and, with the help of Edith Cortright, settles in Italy to enjoy it. The story has been eminently successful in both stage and movie versions, and to the extent that the time-element prevents a close scrutiny of motivation this success implies a criticism of the work as novel. Indeed, it is hard to see how Dodsworth, the shrewd industrialist blind for twenty odd years to his wife's shallow, selfish nature could suddenly about-face to see right through her and assume a cosmopolitan outlook besides.

Sam Dodsworth is not the *type* of the industrialist, but at the same time Lewis uses so many of the tricks of his previous Character portrayals in presenting him that he is not thoroughly convincing as a person. Fran is more nearly the Character of the Spoiled and Pampered Wife, but her use in the story is to offset and show by contrast Sam's growing self-awareness. The early part of the book is enough like *Babbitt* in tone and attitude to arouse anticipation of a similar work on a higher social and economic level, but inevitably or not the story of Sam's struggle toward self-knowledge becomes the dominant concern of both the novelist and the reader. As such, the novel is generally accepted as Lewis's chief claim to the role of major novelist. *Arrowsmith* makes the more exciting reading, it is said, but *Dodsworth* shows the greater insight. This seems reasonable enough, if one could only get around two facts: that Lewis might have shown greater insight by revealing potentialities for Sam's development before Fran's affair with Arnold Israel, and that a major novelist cannot default so completely and so continuously thereafter.

For default Lewis did in the 'thirties and 'forties. The projected work on the American labor movement was a grandiose idea (perhaps he felt an imposing theme incumbent upon him as a Nobel Prize recipient) but the novel never appeared. Instead appeared the minor novels. *Ann Vickers* (1933) sketched the social reformer whose interest in the Suffragette movement and prison reforms is a part of a total rejection of middle-class morality, which also includes a succession of lovers and an illegitimate child. *Work of Art* (1934) told the story of Myron Teagle and his devotion to the bourgeois ideal of building and managing the Perfect Hotel. *It Can't Happen Here* (1935) was tremendously newsworthy as the nation first realized the menace of fascism, but thin reading now that that war is passed and a new and quite different conflict approaches. As Professor Warren Beck says, in the only close and unflattering criticism of Lewis as novelist that we have ("How Good is Sinclair Lewis," *College English*, IX, 4, Jan., 1948, 173-180), "The brave antifascist editor worships liberty, not only as political principle, but in pursuit of another woman for whom he leaves his wife." For some years after *It Can't Happen Here,* Lewis worked at plays, but in 1938 he published *The Prodigal Parents,* which is totally inexplicable except in terms of *Babbitt* written for a widely different period and with the Character element omitted or perverted to make the disastrous Fred Cornplow.

From 1940, beginning with *Bethel Merriday,* the actress, and through the succession of novels written for the market and for one season's market, there is little of significance. *Gideon Planish* (1943) attempts to arouse our sympathy for a man who knowingly corrupts himself or, better perhaps, permits his wife Peony to vitiate his ambition and falsify his character. *Cass Timberlane* (1945) officially championed the Main Street-Babbitt society he had once scathingly attacked. Actually it is a feeble, unconvincing, tortured resolution of a triangle between an old Judge, his young wife and her lover. *Kingsblood Royal* (1947) was written for an audience "softened up" for its thesis by a number of nationally known incidents. As a melodramatic treatment of the race question, it was certainly financially helpful for Lewis, may possibly have been socially helpful to American Negroes, but can never be artistically useful to anyone. *The God-Seeker* (1949) was not meant to have been an ironical title, but the mixture of historical romance, history, underground railway, Indian fight, love story and material success have made the title something less than indicative. The last novel, *World So Wide* (1951), attempts a revaluation of American life through Hayden Chart's initial acceptance and later rejection of European culture in its Florentine manifestations. The theme is carried by a love story in which Hayden, after being tempted otherwise, finally marries the hometown American girl reporter. The Dodsworthian theme is not resurrected, as the blurb tells us, it is exhumed; it has no life, no art. Even the slang is that of twenty years ago.

It hardly seems necessary to apologize for Lewis's decline as a significant writer. Rather, what needs to be done is to rescue the important work of the 'twenties from the regressive effect of his later production. The defects of the 'twenties are palpable enough, but for better or worse that decade could and did assert its conviction of its cultural superiority. That most of its spokesmen reneged in one fashion or another was inevitable and inescapable. No sensitive person in his right mind could possibly maintain tenaciously the same viewpoint in the 'thirties and later as he did in the 'twenties.

The question is not whether they were right in their sometimes arrogant display of their cultural superiority; they thought they were right, and we must accept their sense of conviction if not their creed. What we may justly ask of them, however, is what artistic use they made of it. For Lewis, we may answer that he revived the Character form of writing (whether consciously or not) and extended the boundaries of the novel to include it. The challenge of art is to war against the intractability of the medium, and in *Babbitt* Lewis came nearest to doing what is ultimately impossible. Yet the effort and the result are significant, for we have in *Babbitt* the only work of its kind.

Habituated by the almost excessive reading of novels, we ignore the artistic merit of types or Characters. We have long scorned the use of types, or what we call stock-characters, because they always indicate the artistically ineffective shortcuts of writers who shirk the creative task. There is, however, a difference not of degree but of kind between the exploitation of stock-characters and the creation of Character-types. The latter is artistic literature in a high if limited sense, and it was recognized as such until a few centuries ago. The changes that occasioned the rise and growth of the novel also meant the cessation of Character writing as a highly developed, rigorous and traditional art.

There was, however, a brief period when the need for Character creation was again present, and Sinclair Lewis was the only artist capable of satisfying that cultural want. Before and after the 'twenties Lewis wrote books that can be judged only as novels, and as such they have been already judged by that pre-eminent critic of all literature, the reading public. Most of his *novels* are forgotten; those within recent memory, as *World So Wide*, *The God-Seeker* and *Kingsblood Royal*, are notable for their news-import, not for their literary significance. In a few years they, too, will be forgotten, and Lewis's role as Character writer will alone be remembered.

John Phillips Marquand:

Martini-Age Victorian

CHARLES A. BRADY

The operation was called "Operation Vanity" . . .
B. F.'s Daughter

Ah! *Vanitas Vanitatum!* Which of us is happy in this world? Which of us has his desire? or, having it, is satisfied?
Vanity Fair

Vanissas Vanistatum . . . O the vanity of Vanissy! All ends vanishing! Personally, Grog help me, I am in no violent hurry.
Finnegans Wake

The best of a bad job is all any of us make of it—
Except, of course, the saints . . .
. . . contented with the morning that separates
And with the evening that brings together
For casual talk before the fire
Two people who know they do not understand each other,

Breed children whom they do not understand
And who will never understand them.

The Cocktail Party

He shall never find out fit mate, but such
As some misfortune brings him or mistake;
Or whom he wishes most shall seldom gain,
Through her perverseness, but shall see her gained
By a far worse, or, if she love, withheld
By parents; or his happiest choice too late
Shall meet, already linked and wedlocked-bound
To a fell adversary, his hate or shame:
Which infinite calamity shall cause
To human life, and household peace confound.

Paradise Lost

Her dress, on that day, was of a most noble color, a
subdued and goodly crimson, girdled and adorned in such
sort as best suited with her very tender age. At that moment, I say most truly that the spirit of life, which hath
its dwelling in the secretest chamber of the heart, began
to tremble so violently that the least pulses of my body
shook therewith; and in trembling it said these words:
"Here is a deity stronger than I; who, coming, shall rule
over me."

La Vita Nuova

IT IS quite old-fashioned nowadays to begin with epigraphs,
especially the epigraphs of Puritan worthies; but then, except
for the uncanny expertness of his techniques, John Phillips
Marquand is a very old-fashioned novelist. What is more, he is
old-fashioned in a curiously Puritan fashion. He was, in fact,
halfway through his present publishing career before he abandoned the early seventeenth-century Puritan manner of Hawthorne for the late nineteenth-century Puritan manner of Howells. But he has never either denied or compromised his New
England Puritan heritage. Steeple-hatted, beruffed dignitaries
yet stir in his blood. For all their modern décor the glossy
portrait galleries of his novels darken disquietingly now and
then like the prophetic pictures of Hawthorne's allegory.

This innate, fastidious Puritanism is, very possibly the most significant critical fact that can be adduced in Marquand's regard; and, of all his critics, only Stephen Vincent Benét, who was an old hand, anyway, at telling a Puritan hawk from a Cavalier handsaw, had the acumen to note it. *Wickford Point,* Marquand's sole comedy, is also the House of Atreus which, in New England, bears seven gables and a brass-rod drugget in place of Agamemnon's crimson carpet of doom.

Like Milton, Marquand is preoccupied with the effects of original sin; original sin, untheologized, without benefit of Freud, is the burden of his stoically joyless epithalamia. His cocktail parties are full of Apleys *agonistes.* He is a martini-age Victorian. His whole novelistic output might be described as *Operation Vanity* in the Thackerayan sense of the word. " 'If you got what you wanted, did you always want something else?' " muses Polly Fulton, Burton Fulton's daughter. Marquand likes to orchestrate Solomon's old refrain of *mataiotes mataioteton.* " 'Have you got everything you want?' " Harry Pulham asks Bill King, and Bill replies: " 'That's a damned silly question, and you know it, boy. Nobody ever has everything he wants.' " One of the things you never really got was the girl you wanted; or, if you did, she didn't want you—at least, not with all her heart. Vanessa also spells Vanity. For Marquand the human condition always implies a Vanessa, whether he calls her Jessica, Marvin, Marianna, Polly or Mary Monahan. Jim Calder knows the rules of the games. " 'The boy has got to get the girl and he's got to get the money, and he must have a happy future.' " But that's for the slicks. In neither literature—not even in the Trollope Mr. Marquand so strangely resembles—nor in life does it work out that way. There boy never gets girl; or, rather, boy gets wrong girl— or else, as in *B. F.'s Daughter,* girl gets wrong boy.

But meanwhile, as Dante recorded in his blinding May Day epiphany of love, before the *trauma* comes the glory; and after the *trauma* stays the memory, bittersweet, autumnal clear, Malorian-sad in its slow record of the death of the heart. Marquand, too, has read deep in the book of Galleot. All his protagonists are foredoomed Balin-Balans. They have heard in their hearts "an horn blow as it had been the death of a beast. That blast, said Balin, is blown for me, for I am the prize and yet am I not dead. . . . And so all the ladies and gentlewomen wept for pity."

On the whole, Marquand's critics, both secular and Catholic, have been reluctant to accept him as a serious chronicler of Augustine's "unquiet heart." This is partly due to the organic nature of his novelistic communication. His art is too finely disciplined to allow either of Thackeray's overt puppet-mastership or of Steinbeck's no less overt sociological commentary. The sociological critics note with irritation that he has no ax to grind about the organization of society; they complain that in the realm of economics his *cor* is not *inquietum* enough. The Catholics argue that nowhere in Marquand is there the explicit acknowledgment of the source of human restlessness: *et inquietum est cor nostrum, donec requiescat in Te.*

It is an ungenerous and narrow parochialism on both their parts. A novel need be neither Augustinian nor sociological; it need only be human. John Henry Newman, who, esthetically speaking, did not object to the contraction of Augustine into Austen, never made that mistake about Thackeray or Trollope. The great Cardinal described their books as "ethical," as opposed to the category of "sensational." Even if he might have felt—and there is no assurance he would—that, like Galsworthy, Marquand was more *anima naturaliter Confuciana* than *Christiana,* he would still have admired his Roman qualities, which were Newman's qualities as well, of *pietas, urbanitas, humanitas* and *gravitas.*

Another undoubted reason why Catholic critics are slow to admit Marquand's essential *gravitas*—Harold C. Gardiner is a notable exception here—is that they have become conditioned in the past few decades to a theological dimension in the novel. Actually, the novel, unlike the drama, is not normally theological. Marquand is conspicuous among his contemporaries in writing the normal novel of the central tradition: the novel of Henry Fielding, Jane Austen and Anthony Trollope, as set over against the novel of Laurence Sterne, Emily Brontë and Graham Greene. Where the drama moved from the altar to the market place, the novel tends to move, in a circle, from bourgeois counting house and sitting-room back to bourgeois counting house and sitting-room. At its most average it deals in marriage and giving in marriage; and at this late date it ought not be necessary to have to justify anew the significance and value of this novel of the central tradition. The trans-human plane is all very well; we would be the poorer for its lack. But it is not quite so natural to the novel. As *Pride and Prejudice*'s Charles replied to Caroline's remarks on the merits of conversation over dancing at a ball: " 'Much more rational, my dear Caroline, I dare say, but it would not be near so much like a ball.' "

Considered sheerly as a novelist of marriage, Marquand's authority impresses itself upon the reader very forcibly. His vignettes of modern marriage are much more normal than the acid plates of Sinclair Lewis. Almost a decade before Sir Henry Harcourt-Reilly in Eliot's *The Cocktail Party*, Harry Pulham reaches the conclusion that perhaps love really was "not passion or wish, but days and years." *H. M. Pulham, Esquire*'s study of the estrangement of the personality in marriage is a basically religious theme. So is *Point of No Return*'s clear and compassionate perception of a certain quality of well-bred strangeness toward one another in marriage. All this is one of *The Cocktail Party*'s two dimensions. It is true that Marquand does not possess or make any pretense of possessing the other. Why should he? It is enough that each of his heroes has a Beatrice somewhere in his past; and that each of them, in his own Puritan way, manages to escape the romantic hell of Paolo and Francesca. Like the Roman in Dante, the Roman in Marquand knows that, in some circumstances, romance is a pander and so are writers of romance.

In addition to being a novelist of love and marriage—or perhaps it would be more precise to say love *in* marriage— Marquand is also a novelist of time. Of time past seen as time to come; of time past, both his and ours, reeled off a bewilderingly subtle shuttle. He is a University-bred Teiresias who specializes in foretelling the past instead of the future. "And the past," as Eliot intones, "is about to happen, and the future was long since settled . . . And all is always now." Even in the *Mr. Moto* melodramas one can hear, between the revolver snicks, time chiming like the bell on some ornate French clock in a Sardou drama. It is our own wrist watch that ticks away the seconds as we listen to this poignant chamber-music of memory. The effect is almost intolerably nostalgic. *Je me souviens des jours anciens, et je pleure.*

Somewhere, back in time, Jessica and Charles have never ceased being lovers. Somewhere back in time the Marquand young men, who are no more and no less heroes than Pendennis, choose again, as they did before, "the road less travelled by," while Harry Pulham's father, who is as much John Marquand as Harry Pulham is, lights his cigar and snorts disapproval of all this *Dear Brutus* business: " 'No one ought to have a second chance,' said Father. 'That's damned rot.' " But it doesn't help Harry much. He has stood in the garden of love's beginnings, *Burnt Norton*'s "arbour where the rain beat." And he cannot forget.

This element of tentative inexorableness extends into Mr. Marquand's titles: *The Late George Apley; So Little Time; Repent in Haste; Point of No Return.* It is a consciousness of temporal passage expressed emotionally rather than metaphysically. It neither steps out of time nor achieves a conquest of time. Except for an instant at the end of *So Little Time,* Marquand remains time's prisoner and time's fool. He cannot even think of God without remembering time. When, in the bar of the Harvard Club, Malcolm Bryant asked Charles Grey if he believed in God, Charles remembered that the Bank was waiting. "It must have been the mention of God that made Charles think of time. He looked at his watch and it was a quarter after two." It was a quarter after two and Charles knew he had to get back to the Bank. But he also thought, upon reflection, that he really did believe in God. As for Mr. Marquand and Mr. Marquand's readers, God can be felt in His absence as well as in His presence. This consciousness, keen to the point almost of being a sense of deprivation, constitutes a real spiritual dimension. God is by no means absent from the sad temporality of Marquand's novels.

Dante, who should have known, called art God's grandchild; and that is a relationship at two removes. Not every writer need be God's spy, as Lear called it. To be God's mirror is not by any means a dishonorable function; and there is no reason whatsoever why God's mirror cannot also be Stendhal's "mirror walking down a street." In Marquand's case this Stendhalian mirror happens to be a Thackerayan pier glass in which the reader constantly finds himself. This dual power of reflecting objective reality without distortion and, at the same time, fulfilling the old Morality function of representing Everyman to himself—and once again it should be repeated that Everyman has every right to speak with a Cambridge accent—ought not be taken lightly in an age which, instead of holding a mirror up to nature, prefers to reflect back from a monomaniac monocle its own myopic eye. With Marquand's courteously relentless assistance we look at our natural face in a mirror; and then go about our various businesses. Only, instead of forgetting what kind of men we are, perhaps, for the first time, we realize what kind of men we are.

In his autobiographical essay, *The Lost Childhood,* Graham Greene has recorded how early—it was at fourteen—he became aware of "the sense of doom that lies over success." Religion, he adds in retrospect, "might later explain it to me in other terms, but the pattern was already there." Unlike Greene, apparently religion has not explained it to him in other terms, but that same pattern is everywhere apparent in Marquand. It sounds through Jeff Wilson's memory of Ecclesiastes in *So Little Time.* It becomes explicit in Charles Grey's realization of the sadness of victory in the last chapter of *Point of No Return:*

It was like the time at Dartmouth when he had won the half mile at freshman track. He felt dull and very tired. . . . Tom's voice seemed to come from a long way off. There was a weight on Charles again, the same old weight, and it was heavier after that brief moment of freedom. In spite of all those years, in spite of all his striving, it was remarkable how little pleasure he took in final fulfillment. He was a vice-president of the Stuyvesant

Bank. It was what he had dreamed of long ago and yet it was not the true texture of early dreams. The whole thing was contrived, as he had said to Nancy, an inevitable result, a strangely hollow climax. It had obviously been written in the stars, bound to happen, and he could not have changed a line of it, being what he was, and Nancy would be pleased, but it was not what he had dreamed.

Literary criticism of contemporaries by contemporaries is necessarily inconclusive. The pendulum swings from over-praise to under-praise. So far Mr. Marquand has not been over-afflicted with over-praise. The sour grapes of his tremendous commercial success have undoubtedly set on edge the teeth of several of his critics. But, to do most of them justice, they appear to be in a very real sort of Marquandary. They find themselves there because of two fundamental misconceptions: the first a misunderstanding of the relationship between the novelist as social historian and the society which is the subject-matter of his social history; the second a misunderstanding of the nature of the Horatian-Thackerayan satirist.

Mr. Marquand does not pretend to be a sociologist, though his greater novels are, among many other things, good sociology, more especially *Point of No Return*. In this latter novel, by means of the favorite Marquand stereopticon device of a bifurcated point of view, we get, through the lens of Malcolm Bryant, sociologist, Clyde sociological, and through the lens of Charles Grey, onetime resident, Clyde pastoral, the whole adding up to a satisfactorily total town of Clyde. Insofar as he is concerned with society, he is a historian of society, and an admirable one. Class lines in America are fluid and subtle, but no less unmistakable for all their fluid subtlety. Marquand catches every nuance of the class to which he belongs.

But he has no ax to grind, political, economic, or otherwise. On this plane his fiction is neither philosophy nor journalism, but an imaginative and sympathetic series of insights into social man in our contemporary age of anxiety. From the standpoint of both capitalist and communist dialectic, he inevitably appears a pessimist even as, to the conventional bour-

114

geois judgment of his day, Thackeray appeared a cynic. (Both
Thackeray and Marquand are, as it happens, tender-minded
sentimentalists; it is their greatest weakness, but a relatively
amiable one.) Marquand neither indicts capitalist man nor
celebrates communist man. He merely judges acquisitive man
and, if he indicts at all, indicts human nature.

Once again Marquand's point of view is "straight"; un-
attended by any surrealistic distorting factor. Proust saw society through a glass darkly, as strange sea monsters in an
aquarium. Edith Wharton's world of the *beau monde* bloomed
like a cunningly made-up corsage under a glass bell; or, even
more expressionistically in *The House of Mirth*, Lily Bart
suddenly saw her hosts as great stalking carnivores behind the
bars of a cage. Even Thackeray looked out meditatively
through the heavy plate-glass window of a London club. But
Marquand, insofar as his perceptions are refracted through
any shielding medium at all, watches, without comment,
through apartment-house glass or some picture-window opening on the Boston Fellsway.

All through *H. M. Pulham*, Harry Pulham and Bill King
carry on a subtly argued non-Marxian dialectic that is, in a
sense, a dialog-soliloquy; for Harry Pulham and Bill King
are really two halves of one person. In every Marquand book
the hero is dichotomized—it is a biographical reflex; Marquand was simultaneously a poor relation and a boy whose
great-great-grandmother Searle had been painted by Gilbert
Stuart and whose aunt, Mrs. Hale, had been painted by James
Whistler. So his heroes find themselves dichotomized into a
Confucian and an *arriviste*. Sometimes, as in *Wickford Point*
(his most directly biographical if not most directly autobiographical novel), the Confucian is simultaneously an *arriviste;*
sometimes, as in *Point of No Return* and *Warning Hill*, he
is almost more a Hamlet-revenger than an *arriviste*. Always
there is this element of ambivalence. Both Charles Grey and
Jeffrey Wilson are as much provincials in the capital as either
Dickens' Philip Pirrip or Balzac's Rastignac. They have, despite their rueful retrospectiveness, great expectations. The
representative novel of the eighteenth century had concerned

itself with the foundling who found he was an heir; that of the nineteenth with the young man from the provinces who found his way to fortune. The typical novel of the twentieth century has dealt, rather, with life's shattering the youth of sensibility; taken all in all, it might be described as a portrait of the artist *manqué*. Its theme, in a word, is "lost," not "found." Marquand's sophisticated ringing of the changes, in however minor a key, on the centuries'-old, fairytale chord of "found" has hardly endeared himself to the *avant garde* critic.

Marquand is almost excessively conscious of society's displacement in time as well as space. He has employed a dowser to locate water on his Newburyport estate. His own forked dowser's rod has the witch in it when it comes to the far queasier task of tracing the unwritten conventions of a social milieu which no longer wells out of easily identifiable bed-rock springs. The profession of diviner grows even more difficult when those unwritten conventions, which are as immutable for their small leash of years as the laws of the Medes and Persians, shift their boundaries from year to year almost, to say nothing of from decade to decade.

Both in *Point of No Return* and in *B. F.'s Daughter*, Marquand thinks—and in an entirely un-Proustian way—of society as existing in an aquarium, but an aquarium that is constantly changing. The glass walls may look the same to the fish; but they are new walls all the same. " 'It's gone,' " says Milton Ouerbach to Bob Tasmin, " 'and I don't know when it went, and what's more, I can't entirely remember what it was, although we all lived in it. We're like fish being moved from one aquarium to another.' " *Point of No Return* links this same theme of social relativity in time with the graver moral music of the vanity of human wishes in this reflection of Charles Grey's:

> They were all caught in a current that jostled them and interfered with normal existence. All anyone could do was to try to adjust his life within the limits of a constantly changing frame. That was the difficulty. Even the limits were constantly changing.

The limits of happiness itself, Charles was thinking, were continually changing. You got somewhere and then you wanted to move somewhere else, to another, larger bar, to better, brighter company.

. It has become a critical commonplace to indict Marquand as a Tory. Actually, he is more of a Whig. But, if by Toryism one means a liking for tradition, then it does not hurt a novelist to be a Tory. Like Willa Cather, Marquand is fascinated by the older American capitalist. One meets him in *Pulham* and the *Moto* stories before his full-dress portrait as Burton Fulton in *B. F.'s Daughter*. George Apley is a more angular gentleman than Colonel Newcome. Minot Roberts of *So Little Time* is the fullest-blooded Stuart in his gallery; Roberts' flesh-tints have a positive port wine hue among the sparer Marquand characters. When Jeff Wilson reflects it "was disturbing to think that the world might no longer have time for what Minot Roberts represented, and it was not because Minot was old. It was because he looked so young," the reader nods approvingly.

Here is social portraiture at its best; neither approving, nor disapproving, simply capturing the multidimensional reality the great painter also knows how to catch. Bob Tasmin is a gentleman of at once an older and a newer vintage. His father had gone "to great pains, too, to teach him tennis and trap-shooting, bridge and poker, and an appreciation for a few Victorian novels." The reader has every right to wonder if this is sufficient equipment for the complexities of twentieth-century life. Since it is hard to repulse Potiphar's wife without looking like a prig, the reader may also question if Bob Tasmin is anything more than a grownup boy Percival out of an Episcopal Easter pageant in the kind of church where the organist gets paid more than the minister. Nevertheless, stuffed shirts have immortal souls; and one of Marquand's most sensitive achievements has been to capture the spiritual values of stuffiness.

His most confused protagonists possess a kind of certitude that Edith Wharton's more passionate personages are always struggling to attain. He assumes what she sets out so assiduously to prove, that "a slowly-accumulated past lives in the blood—whether in the concrete image of the old house stored with visual memories, or in the conception of the house not built with hands, but made up of inherited passions and loyalties." It is a mark of his spiritual sensitivity that he never really disparages this almost racial certitude, but that, instead, he finds it is not enough.

Nor is every representative Marquand figure by any means a respectable Confucian. Many of his people are residents of Tilbury Town, and John Grey's name leads all the rest. He never manages to beat the System, nor, in the last analysis, does his son Charles, even though Charles gets to be vice-president of Tony Burton's bank. Not one of Mr. Marquand's critics, incidentally, seems to have noticed that the System is the world and that the resigned Puritan in Marquand is consistently against the world which is, however, for ambivalent good measure, unfailing grist for his novelistic mill. But it is fatally easy to make a mistake here. That mellowest and most tolerant of worldlings, Justice Holmes, complained to Pollock that "mundane motives and interests seem to be Thackeray's own ultimates."

One can easily exaggerate Marquand's rigidity of social outlook. It is true that his Confucian mind prefers the caste-molds of smalltown Clyde to the plasticity of semi-fashionable Sycamore Park, to the "impermanence of a New York suburb with its shifting population of unrooted communities with order that existed only on the surface." But this preference is as much esthetic as sociological. Moreover, it is not nearly so constant as it seems. Society is a great chessboard to John Marquand. In one book red wins; in another white. Tom Brett, for example, is treated unsympathetically in *B. F.'s Daughter;* but the Tom Brett type had received very sympathetic treatment indeed in *Apley*. It isn't so much that Marquand changes his mind, either. He never really makes up his mind. Like a cool croupier in dinner jacket he registers the winning combinations; and the winning combinations change from game to game. If this is social bias, it is social bias with

118

a Pirandello twist. For example, Burton Fulton, in *B. F.'s Daughter* and *Point of No Return*'s Tony Burton—notice the persistence of *Burton* in the shifting identities—and the father of Marianne in *Warning Hill* are really one and the same person viewed from a different vantage point.

This kaleidoscope-shift appears especially apparent in Marquand's marriage combinations. It is very evident from certain bits of dialog in *B. F.'s Daughter* that Marquand intends his Polly Fulton-Bob Tasmin-Tom Brett-Burton Fulton quadrangle to counterpoint Philip Barry's design for marriage in *Holiday*. What is not so evident about his obsessive ponderings of marriage patterns is that, basically, *there is no marriage pattern for Marquand*. This has been missed in the facile assumption that, because Mr. Marquand is a patrician by temperament, patricians must therefore always marry patricians in his books. They do in *Apley* and *H. M. Pulham*. They don't in *Warning Hill*, *Wickford Point*, *So Little Time*, and *Point of No Return*. In *B. F.'s Daughter* they both do and don't. But this latter somewhat unsuccessful *tour de force* is exceptional, anyway, in that, for the first and only time, Marquand balances a feminine protagonist against a bifurcated deuteragonist instead of merely splitting his usual male protagonist into the customary halves: conformist and rebel; traditionalistic and *arriviste*.

As a matter of fact, Marquand's main interest in this particular aspect of the marriage coil is in the old Montague-Capulet opposition which has always teased the artist's imagination—in folklore, medieval romance and Elizabethan drama as well as in its nineteenth- and twentieth-century novelistic masquerade. It is, moreover, a theme which, despite critical superciliousness at its expense, is as significant as any other, and one which admits both of archetypal simplicity and sociological complexity. Mr. Marquand has even permitted himself the sly luxury of romantically resolving the star-crossed tangle in *Haven's End*'s happy-ending wedding of the Scarlets and the Swales. Add to this aboriginal Verona motif Marquand's favorite psychological sub-theme of time's attrition of the personality, and one has the basic formula for his marriage situations. This latter pattern is beautifully summed up in the nuances of Charles Grey's conversation with Dorothy Whitaker:

"You see," she said, "I'd find out what you used to be and how you got the way you are."

"It wouldn't be worth it," Charles said. "I've always been about the same."

"Oh, no," she said, "nobody ever is. We can't help working on ourselves."

He had a momentary picture of her working on herself, sitting before her mirror with her lipstick and her powder base, and brushing back her hair.

"Not on ourselves," he said. "Everyone works on us. Everyone wears us down."

"If you're tough enough," she said, "you don't have to be worn down."

Charles found himself laughing again.

"All right," he said, "what did you use to be?"

She shook her head slowly and her smile had gone.

"Nicer," she said, "quite a good deal nicer."

Marquand's range as a social historian is extraordinarily wide; it is also intimate and meticulous. It stretches in time from the Civil War to the Russian-Allied condominium over Berlin. It stretches in space from north of Boston to California —the Hollywood sequences in *So Little Time* are as competent as Fitzgerald's or Lardner's; more penetrating than Schulberg's. It stretches also from the South Pacific to the Rhine. It comprises both a folklore and an anatomy of the Brahmin caste and their stiffly wistful descendants. It catches New York and New York's suburban littoral. New York may not be in his bones like Clyde and Boston, but his New York scapes are more lyrically, impressionistically lovely in a Japanese sort of way—like Samurai *Hokku* on rice paper—than his darker-toned Boston still-lifes. In every case his interiors are modernistic Vermeers, selective, precise, complete, perfect, without seeming in any sense of the word like a catalog.

His range in time and space covers Harvard and two world wars. (Marquand is a capital war novelist; on the evidence of the early magazine installments of *Melville Goodwin, U. S. A.*, one can almost risk the generalization that, where Hemingway's Col. Cantwell had the Roman truth of a battered gladiator, Marquand's General Goodwin has the Roman truth of a pro-consul in the field.) It spans New Deal Washington; newspaper and magazine offices; radio; advertising; play carpentry; the businessman's Orient; and the world of finance. Especially the world of finance. Marquand is as good as Trollope or even Balzac on the place of money in human affairs. *Warning Hill* defines money not only as a power factor but as a kind of religious symbol, "like the rune on a pagan sword." In *Point of No Return* Charles Grey understands that "all human behavior was mixed in some way with money"; that the banker must be an ascetic of finance, not coveting money, but respecting it "in an impersonal way, as an astronomer might think of light-years in interstellar space." No such breath of mundane reality ever clouds the bland family silver of the Jamesian simile; but, when he wishes, Mr. Marquand is capable of that Jamesian specialty, the round-globed image that is also an organic symbol.

Like the themes of most social novelists, Marquand's themes grow naturally out of his own autobiographical experience; out of the deep waters of his personal well of the past as well as out of the shallower reaches of everyday journalistic immediacy. He was born both to the purple and to the sackcloth within the taciturn limits of a cultural complex where poorer relatives find themselves dowered with a very special status. From this dual accident of birth proceed the twin *traumata* that provide him with his psychic wound and compensatory bow of art; he was snubbed at Harvard; and either he was jilted by a girl or—both combinations appear on the Marquand chessboard—else he did the jilting. (Thackeray's twin *traumata* were grimmer: he lost his patrimony at the gambling table, and he married a mad wife.)

John Phillips Marquand was born November 10, 1893, the son of a civil engineer who later turns up, Micawber-wise, as John Grey in *Point of No Return* and earlier, as Alfred

Michael in *Warning Hill.* He was the grandnephew of Margaret Fuller and a cousin by marriage of the Hales of Curzon Mill. This makes him related through the Hales to Edward Everett Hale—old John Brill of *Wickford Point,*[1] the tribal fetish Marquand exasperatedly repudiates but which he cannot escape. Old Brill is not only a convenient symbol for the essential Marquand ambivalence. In his actual biographical capacity as Edward Everett Hale he once wrote a short story, "My Double and How He Undid Me," whose title is a perfect description of Hale's twentieth-century descendant's stereopticon formula for dichotomizing his protagonists; and a no less perfect description of Mr. Marquand's own psychological plight.

Somewhere, some place, lost in time—in Newburyport, Curzon, Boston, Cambridge, along the winding Meuse with the great guns booming out their somber obbligato—a young Marquand still ponders the roads that diverge in a yellow wood, while an older Marquand, all too poignantly conscious of the road he took, yet cannot forget the road not taken. Like that other Yankee of fable, Peter Rugg, he beats his way, book after book, back over the roads of a personal past; back beyond Edward Everett Hale and Margaret Fuller, beyond that ancestor who was painted by Gilbert Stuart, to the Cotton Mather whose *Marginalia* has provided Mr. Marquand with some of his favorite reading. We readers are the richer for the pleasant pangs produced by this witchery with time.

Mr. Marquand missed Exeter, but not Harvard. At Harvard he made the *Lampoon,* but no Clubs. Instead he lived in the same boarding house as President Conant, known in the days of Bo-jo Brown as "two-drink dash Conant." He did a stint on the Boston *Transcript;* got a brief glimpse of the Mexican War; attained the rank of Captain in Artillery at Saint Mihiel and along the Meuse-Argonne; worked on the *Tribune;* wrote advertising for a short time; and struck his stride, commercially speaking, as a "slick" fictioneer for the *Ladies' Home*

---

[1] This is the usual critical presumption, at least. But Mr. Marquand informs me that, if he had any actual person in mind when creating old Brill, it was John Greenleaf Whittier.

Journal and the *Saturday Evening Post*. He has been married twice; the first time to Christina Sedgwick of the *Atlantic Monthly* Sedgwicks; the second time to Adelaide Hooker. There are two children of the first marriage; and three—all young—of the second.

Since, by virtue of genetic circumstance, every writer is, of necessity, the prisoner of the material he works in, it is hardly necessary to apologize for that same material. The only valid question a critic may ask in this connection is: has a writer managed to enslave his readers? From Marquand's biography come also the characteristic ambivalences which stamp his satire with its humane and civilized complexity. Marquand is a born satirist; and, when he chooses, can be as urbanely lethal as Pope himself. The full-length portrait of Allen Southby, *Wickford Point*'s Middle Western Harvard don who drinks beer out of a pewter mug and keeps a "maid in a mob-cap," is a masterpiece of wickedly perfect malice.

But Marquand is by no means primarily a satirist. He tends to concentrate his satiric effects in Thackerayan set-pieces which can readily be detached from context and which already begin to appear as old-fashioned as the satiric set-pieces of *Vanity Fair* and *The Newcomes*. In so far as he is a satirist, he is, in the main, a satirist of compunction after the merciful pattern of Horace and Thackeray rather than the merciless pattern of Juvenal and Swift. Like Thackeray, he removes all imputation of Pharisaism from his Books of Snobs by making it apparent that they are being set down by "One of Them-selves." It is the only tolerable recipe for the satirist who will also be a novelist. Snobbery becomes less rancid; it seems more like pensive nostalgia than snobbery.

His critics—and it is their second major error—have been strangely obtuse on this point. Sterling North accuses him of crafty urbanity, deliberate ambiguity, and split personality. He expostulates that "satire to be really great demands a wider base than pride, prejudice and private annoyance; it must rest upon an implied criticism of life." John Kennedy finds him "incapable of affirmation," and announces that he "can-not continue simply piling up particulars subacidly stated."

123

Thayer Bisbee assails his "curious combination of satire and apologia." Brendan Gill states that "if to be a satirist is to despise and hold up to ridicule the people one writes about, then Marquand, who pities and feels affection for his characters, fails to qualify."

Luckily Roger Burlingame and Bernard De Voto are more percipient. They know that the Thackerayan satirist strikes to correct, not kill. They realize with John Woodburn that Marquand's "irony springs from disapproval rather than contempt," that he attacks "the things which he hates best." If he is a necrophiliac, as Fadiman alleges, he is a necrophiliac because he is a lover. He must never leave off loving the sinner however he feels about the sin—and, to the Horatian satirist, sin wears more the motley of folly. But he is not really a necrophiliac; he loves the living thing in the dead tradition, not the dead thing in the living tradition. Nor is there real idolatry in his ancestor worship. His witty *pietas* would merely see to it that the *Lares* and *Penates* are kept in a place of honor on their shelves; and help make sure that the *Lemures* do not have to blush over-much for lemur-descendants. *Pietas* is the ultimate justification for the kind of social criticism Mr. Marquand writes. But *Pietas* is not ancestor worship at all. As Chesterton so nicely put it:

> A man belongs to the world before he begins to ask if it is nice to belong to it . . . The point is not that this world is too sad to love or too glad not to love; the point is that when you do love a thing, its gladness is a reason for loving it, and its sadness a reason for loving it more . . . one must somehow find a way of loving the world without trusting it; somehow one must love the world without being worldly.

As for Mr. North's demand for an "implied criticism of life," and his strictures on the insufficiency of "pride, prejudice and private annoyance," it might be said both that Mr. Marquand is not nearly so devoid of a philosophy as Mr. North seems to think, and that the Miss Austen, who wrote *Pride and Prejudice,* was luckier in that her day better supplied her

124

with that satiric indispensable, a fixed background of ethic
and of convention arising from ethic. Even at that Mr. North
ought to be prepared to allow Mr. Marquand *Pride and Prejudice*'s minimal and very patrician standard as enunciated by
Mr. Bennett: "In his library he had been always sure of
leisure and tranquillity; and though prepared, as he told
Elizabeth, to meet with folly and conceit in every other room
in the house, he was used to be free from it there."

Since *The Late George Apley* made its belated appearance
in 1937, there is a temptation to think of Marquand as a comparatively new writer. Actually, his first title (*The Unspeak-
able Gentleman,* 1922) is only a year later than Dos Passos'
Three Soldiers and three years earlier than Hemingway's
In Our Time. But, in that fifteen-year interim, he had served
a long and immensely lucrative apprenticeship to the half-
gods of the "slicks." When the half-gods went, the gods arrived with a vengeance; and still keep on arriving. For, except
for marking time in *B. F.'s Daughter,* Mr. Marquand's art has
continued to develop, to mellow, to mature. Nevertheless, it is
never safe to neglect the sorcerer's apprenticeship. The *Moto*
melodramas and costume novels ought not be overlooked—not
even for their own sakes.

If, in the *Moto* melodramas, Mr. Marquand boiled his
pot, he boiled it with the best China tea. Here is the same
technical *expertise* and beautifully stylized dialog. Here are
the same themes as in the greater novels: time and tradition; love and family; and the same moral problems that
bedevil George Apley and Harry Pulham, Jeff Wilson and
Charles Grey. *No Hero* (1935)—another archetypal title—
concerns itself with the moral imperative of patriotism. *Thank
You, Mr. Moto* (1936) studies the issues of expatriation and
commercial ethics. *Think Fast, Mr. Moto* (1937) deals with
family pride. These are all capital melodramas; but they are
something more than melodramas, too. They have, in embryo,
the maturer Marquand's interest in social milieux and in the
springs of human action. Emotionally speaking, the Confucian
Mr. Moto, who is part Colonel Haki, part Hercule Poirot and
part Charlie Chan, is a suitable *persona* for the equally Confu-

cian Mr. Marquand. Mr. Marquand, too, is so sorry for every one and every thing.

Again, emotionally considered, these melodramas permit Marquand the experience of having his cake and eating it, too. For once he can allow romance to best the Roman in him. He can arrange and contrive his endings as he chooses, though even here he prefers a Confucian stratification of society. Finally, technically considered, the *Moto* thrillers compel a kind of temporal tightness missing in the flashback tempo of the social novels. There is apparent in them a change of narrative muscle stress. Melodrama demands the consecutive; and, when he needs to, Mr. Marquand shows himself a master of the consecutive. It is almost as if he feels he can get his own back at time here. And not only at time. We see him, in the words of another Puritan, triumphing "over Death, and Chance, and thee, O Time."

He is not quite so happy with the suaver Zenda of his costume romances, such as *The Black Cargo* (1925) and *Haven's End* (1937). Nonetheless, these relatively inferior romances adumbrate the basic themes of the later, greater thrice-told tales that are the social novels. The pivotal Marquand book had come in 1930. It was *Warning Hill,* wherein Mr. Marquand first served notice that Howells was beginning to edge Hawthorne out. Beginning here, the voice is still the voice of Hawthorne, but henceforth the hand is the hand of Howells. Here, with the character of Grafton Jellet, Marquand for the first time enters his proper milieu; first approximates the specific kind of social "density" that will later be his unique cachet. From this time on—allowing, of course, for the two interludes of *Haven's End* and the slight *Repent in Haste* (1945)—he begins to touch excellence on every page. One of his recurrent themes—the recovery of the inheritance— emerges clearly in this book. Tommy and Marianne are the quintessential Marquand boy and girl in the archetypal Marquand situation. The process of distillation has gone so far that the end-product is in danger of turning into viscous treacle unless it somehow manages to get blended, cut and stiffened by the stronger liquor of non-nostalgic immediacy.

126

The *Apley* cut-glass, ancestral decanter, without in any way impairing nostalgia's delicate bouquet, supplied that liquor. 1937's *The Late George Apley, A Novel in the Form of a Memoir* initiates the six novels which go to make up Marquand's American *Comédie Humaine* of our century—a seventh, *Melville Goodwin, U. S. A.,* will appear in the fall of 1951. They are introspective family chronicles told neither by a Hamlet nor an "attendant lord," but by a compassionate Horatio—one, moreover, who stands in both an avuncular and a trustee relationship to his material, so that the reader is not surprised by a prevalent tone of tolerant irritation, the irritation of one intimately involved through family connection. Cool exasperation might be an even more accurate term.

The Late George Apley is an exquisite *tour de force* that refines upon the narrative devices of *Haven's End.* It exploits, with the utmost audacity, the eighteenth-century epistolary method, but one woven on a far subtler time-shuttle than Richardson knew how to operate. As perfect a pastiche as *Henry Esmond,* it draws heavily on the dry tentativeness of one of the New England scriptures, *The Education of Henry Adams.* It is a difficult trick to combine irony and pathos so unfailingly as Marquand manages to do here, especially the lambent and gentle irony of *Apley*'s perfect understatement. As befits his New England origin, George Apley is a more stiffly formal gentleman than Newman or Thackeray envisioned. There was never anything of the Corinthian buck about him. One of his letters to son John declares the Apley credo which Marquand makes no bones about letting the reader know is also his own: "At any rate, it will please you in later years to know that you have always been a gentleman, and, believe me, that is something." It is not enough, undoubtedly, but the great Cardinal would be the first to acknowledge that it is something.

Mr. Marquand's Brahmin does not always keep the fires banked in his furnace on the water side of Beacon Street. He has his moments of revolt. "I wonder," he writes, "will I ever walk up any road alone?" And again, a wry leit-motiv: "By and large, I have seen a great deal of Boston since I was born." Marquand's gift for satiric set-pieces, executed with a nonchalant flick of the wrist, is seen in the faultless underplaying of the "horsy" Brecking home. Where his mariner ancestors teased ships and rigging into bottles, Marquand creates miniature satiric *tableaux vivants* within the flawless blown glass of his larger narratives. Mary Monahan is the first of the Annabelle Lees to drift, wraith-like, through the greater novels. They grow more vivid and less shadowy in the succeeding books until, in *Point of No Return*'s Jessica Lovell, more a talisman than a person, Mr. Marquand gives some evidence of having finally exorcised his obsessive *princesse lointaine*.

Like Babbitt, Old Man River, Uncle Tom and Uncle Remus, George Apley has suffered the folk-lore fate of translation into a symbolic dimension. *Wickford Point* (1939), the most thoroughly brilliant and least read of the major Marquand novels, did not enjoy the same experience. It is an extraordinarily interesting book. With Allen Southby begins Marquand's thematic trick of satiric sub-plot, already adumbrated in the epistolary personality of Willing, *Apley*'s narrative point-of-view. Allen Southby also doubles in brass as the first satiric butt of what will be, book by book, Marquand's specialized assaults on American pedantry: Harvard professor; foreign correspondent; New Deal bureaucrat; radio columnist; sociologist. The "intricacies of Wickford Point . . . where every small thing was of importance and where the mind wandered languidly to this and that with a strange midsummer's madness," is American Chekhov, with the advantage of Marquand's wryly humorous resignation. The Brills swing gaily in a cherry orchard of the mind—or, rather, since this is New England, in an apple orchard, "too old to bear much any longer." The Brills infuriate cousin Jim, but, as he tells Pat, " 'I'd always come back here, and you couldn't stop me and I couldn't stop myself.' " It is a disarming enough confession of the satirist's affectionate ambivalence.

Wickford Point is Marquand's only pure comedy; and, as befits a classic comedy, it has a happy ending. But its net impact is not at all happy. It is a relentlessly tender vivisection of the contemporary New England essence which, to Mr. Marquand, is full of "an inexorable sort of gentleness, a vanity of effort, a sadness of pre-destined failure." The Brills are as ineluctably decadent as Faulkner's Sartorises; note, however, that decadent does not necessarily imply degenerate. For the Civil War slew New England as irrevocably as it did the ante-bellum South.

But there always remains love. For all his veneration for King Solomon's melancholy canticle, Mr. Marquand never reaches the point of sad satiety which cries aloud: "Stay me with apples, for I am tired of love." The furthest he is willing to go down the path of disenchantment is to confess with Jim Calder: "Surely love made marriage dangerous, since neither contracting party was in a normal state." It is during this same Henry Adams sort of soliloquy that Jim Calder indicates his dissatisfaction with his age's intimate investigations of the love relationship: "All the really good writers of my time had explored this field at length and with conspicuous success, but had they gone any further than Tolstoy? Had they even said as much as Jane Austen, who said exactly nothing?"

H. M. Pulham, Esquire's (1941) inquisition into the tender passion follows more in the footsteps of Trollope and Turgenev than of Tolstoy or Jane Austen. Along with *Point of No Return, Pulham* remains to date Marquand's most solid novel; and by all odds his most poignant. It is, in fact, so unutterably poignant at times that it threatens almost to deliquesce. When Marvin asks Harry on the telephone, " 'Harry, are you happy?' " the reader's heart stops. Then Miss Rollo enters with the cross-word puzzle, and the situation is saved. As in the case of Apley-Willing and Calder-Stowe, Marquand again dichotomizes himself into Harry Pulham-Bill King. Bo-jo Brown and Bob Ridge, insurance salesman *redivivus,* are capital comedy.

But in the end one finds oneself returning to *Pulham* as a novel of love; to its insights into the pitiful, divided human heart; to the great emotional authority Marquand is able to exert over the well-nigh intolerable pathos here. There is something quietly, desperately dreadful about Kay's joyless adultery with Bill King—one remembers the peaked face of Brenda Last in Waugh's *Handful of Dust*. In the end Kay learns that kindness is not a bad substitute for the ecstasy which is rarely for sale in the booths of Vanity Fair. " 'So we have to be kind to each other always, don't we?' " she says to Harry. Bill King had learned the even harder Thackerayan lesson which Hardy also learned but never the James whose theme was the death of innocence: that, when all is said and done, innocence remains the greatest shield of man in this vale of sorrow, the world.

> "I don't know why it is you make me laugh," Bill said, "because, frankly, you've always been a straight."
>
> "What's a straight?" I asked.
>
> "A straight," Bill said. "Don't you know what a straight is? A straight's someone in a skit who has all the jokes thrown at him. I start to tell you a joke. I say, 'I was walking down the street the other day,' and you say, 'Yes, you were walking down the street? Go on.' And I say, 'I met a dame,' and you say, 'Oh, you met a dame, did you?' That's what a straight is."
>
> Bill always had something to say that was new and interesting.
>
> "I see," I said. "I guess I've always been a straight."
>
> I thought Bill would laugh, but instead he finished his drink and poured out another one.
>
> "Maybe, but maybe it's better than being the smart man. He's mighty lonely and there're lots and lots of straights."

All through *So Little Time* (1943) Marquand remembers the Duchess of Richmond's ball on the eve of Waterloo. It is his richest and most ambitious novel to date, but not so perfectly integrated as *Apley, Wickford Point, Pulham,* and *Point of No Return*. The topicality clogs a little, too; it is too cluttered, too rich, too pell-mell. Time is Mr. Marquand's alembic; and not enough time separates him from the events he writes of here for the true sea change to have worked its spell. But the *reportage* approaches the miraculous. Never

130

were his eye and ear more faithful, or his historical sense so uncannily precise. Jeffrey Wilson, as protagonist, is the usual Marquandian counterpoint of dying man and living ghost; of reluctant present and vivid past. The Fred and Becky ménage, as a satiric set-piece, equals the Jaeckel comedy in *Wickford Point*. Marquand's mastery of the normal American idiom never flags, not even when it is filtered through the protagonist's consciousness. His sensitive assessment of small-town social gradations is as impeccable as ever. Jeffrey's map case with the rusty catch offers an occasion for one of the more exquisite Marquand fugues in time. Like all Marquand no-heroes, Jeffrey is a well-bred *homme moyen sensuel* with a habit of meeting up with Kismet in the drawing room; beset by the realization that "wars were all the same and that he was living in history, and he wished to God that he were not."

Polly Fulton, the heroine of *B. F.'s Daughter* (1946), feels just as desperate in her time-trap, but, being a woman, she does not philosophize so much about *la condition humaine*. Marquand's men are invariably handled more skillfully than his women, and his experiment here in speaking through a woman's mind and personality is not carried off nearly so well as Christopher Morley's *Kitty Foyle*. By way of compensation, perhaps, he splits Polly into herself and Bob Tasmin, and Bob Tasmin into himself and Tom Brett; the result is the central situation of *Pulham* in reverse. The mnemonics are more perfunctory; the metronomics too rapid. For the first time since *Apley* one feels that a Marquand novel has failed to advance in technique. It still moves the emotions, though, for if Mr. Marquand makes the mistake of coming forward too far in time, he is very careful to go back far enough. Polly herself tells us what is wrong with the book " 'Oh, God, darling,' " she says to Bob Tasmin. " 'Everything is so—so contrived.' " It is. For once the Montague-Capulet chess-board is a set up. Malcolm Bryant might have arranged it for a lecture. Or, better, it all reads too much as if Jeff Wilson, in his capacity as play carpenter, had clapboarded in becoming period décor a suburban variety of a social drama by Sardou.

But if *B. F.'s Daughter* seems over contrived, *Point of No Return* (1949) does not. It is Marquand's most three-dimensional novel to date, possessing as it does his old mastery of reproduction and criticism of life, together with a deepened power over creation of life in John Grey, who is drawn more in the round than any previous Marquand character under the rank of protagonist. (Incidentally, this faculty of continuous growth is another thing which sets Mr. Marquand apart among his contemporaries, most of whom are either standing still or else have already retrogressed.) His coolly supple prose is more modulated and less scintillant than usual; but deliberately so. More than ever in this volume is Mr. Marquand the Thackerayan novelist of personal memory, the laureate of the sick, throat-filling, despairing ecstasy of first love. He understands the mystery and the magic of the human personality with a mellower comprehension than before. In the realm of the Cyprian goddess the Marquand mixture is no different. Charles Grey loses his first love and succeeds in his second job. But this time the frustrate lover wears his rue with a difference. Jessica Lovell, ghost-like, fades down the winds of memory. Man is still alone, even in love; perhaps above all in love. Nothing is certain. But there are compensations between "the morning that separates" and "the evening that brings together for casual talk before the fire." Charles Grey, for example, "felt contented and at peace doing nothing but raking leaves on the lawn, he and his two children."

Mr. Marquand, like every other artist, has his limitations. He repeats himself. But it is still the mark of a first-rate writer to repeat himself rather than to repeat others. His invention is fairly slight; so was Thackeray's and that of *l'aimable* Jane; and, even now, the combinations on his chessboard are not yet exhausted. His satire lacks one dimension Thackeray's possessed. There is a good funeral in *Wickford Point;* but the death drums do not roll so majestically in Marquand as they do throughout his archetypal, seminal model, *Vanity Fair*.

A more serious limitation is, perhaps, his not possessing

Mrs. Wharton's consciousness of what *The House of Mirth* calls "the volcanic nether side" of the social surface. His heroes, it is true, scuff their polished shoes on the hardened lava; but no more. The saga knife is never unsheathed in his prose; the Eumenides do not lurk behind his draw-curtains. He does not know at its fullest *The Age of Innocence*'s "mysterious authority of beauty," nor will he permit himself to gaze for long on *Roman Fever*'s "accumulated wreckage of passion and splendour." But there is, after all, little in common between Mrs. Wharton and Mr. Marquand for all that he is her successor as historian of upper-middle-class American manners. He is New England blood and bone, and her superior in style and art, if not in passion. She is New York aristocrat. His sense of caste is what the English call "county"; hers smacks more than a little of the gilt épergnes of the Second Empire. As a matter of fact, their only real point of contact is the fortuitous circumstance that a supernumerary in *The House of Mirth* bears the name Melville Stancy and a quite different one in *Point of No Return,* the name Melville Meader.

It is a good critical principle always to measure a man for what he is, and never for what he isn't. Nevertheless, considering him purely as a novelist of love, one misses in Marquand the Greek dimension that invests Maurice Baring's great love trilogy: *Cat's Cradle, C* and *Daphne Adeane.* In Marquand, Cupid is always either checkmated or checkmating; but not quite in the sense of Belloc's couplet:

> The Love of God which leads to realms above
> Is *contre-carréd* by the god of Love.

For all his Roman *pietas* and *gravitas,* Mr. Marquand's sense of *hubris* is limited to some such premonition as Charles Grey's foreboding that all "the elements of his life were moving as they should that spring and he did not have the sense to pray that eventual compensation should be light."

But there! A critic's primary task is to criticize novels, not to find chinks—or Confucian principles instead of Christian ones, either—within the armor of a writer's personal philosophy. A novel is a novel is a novel, to ape the echolalia of Gertrude Stein. It is not a drama or a symphony or a theological tract. And, as novelist *qua* novelist in the high Victorian tradition—the highest yet for the novel in English—Mr. Marquand leaves little to be desired. He once, as Jeffrey Wilson, ruefully evaluated himself as "an important piece, too, like one of the Georgian armchairs by the fireplace, a piece with grace, with good finish, without anything new added, a piece that fetched a good price even when business was bad." But he is really more than that; much more.

During Charles Grey's last supper with the Masons in Clyde, Mrs. Mason served the same cracked cocoa, clear and bittersweet, he remembered drinking as a boy. They had had to do without it during the war, she told Charles, but Mr. Mason had found some in Boston recently. He was going to write a paper about cocoa for the Confessional Club.

"It's a funny thing to be writing about with the world the way it is," Mr. Mason said, "but it might just as well be cocoa as communism." Surprisingly enough there was quite a lot about cocoa and chocolate in the public library and it would start right with Cortez and the Aztecs. Their ruler, Montezuma, drank cocoa, and he ate small babies, too, that were cooked in a kind of chafing dish.

"Now, Virgil," Mrs. Mason said, "you're not going to put that in about the babies, are you?"

It might just as well be cocoa as communism? It might much better be cocoa than communism. Mr. Marquand is closer to the matter of the central novel than any other writer of our period. He does well to leave anthropology as well as anthropophagy to those of his fellows who prefer these subjects but are not, thereby, necessarily greater writers. Or, in the last analysis, as great.

F. Scott Fitzgerald:
The Touch of Disaster

RILEY HUGHES

"THERE NEVER was a good biography of a good novelist,"
F. Scott Fitzgerald decided, because the novelist is "too
many people." Yet in another sense, as Fitzgerald was also
aware, the novelist is nobody at all; he has no life when he is
writing. Art is the event for him then, not his own life. But
whence comes art, if not from life? It derives, as it imme-
morially has done, from such fruitful sources as introspection,
from non-participating observation, and from the novelist's
ability to project his own sympathy and awareness. These are
the bootstrap ways: by combinations and disjunctions in the
author's thought and experience they can be arrived at.

But there is another way, a leap—which cannot perhaps be
wholly contrived or willed—into insight. "I kindle, I vibrate,
respond to suggestion, imaginatively, so almost fortunately, so
generously and precipitately, easily," writes Henry James. Insight is at the heart of the novelist's gift; it distinguishes him
from the reporter and the critic. "Now I SEE," writes James
in gleeful capitals of a situation he was puzzling out in his

notebook. Because he could not, for a long time, *see* the circumstances surrounding the "ultimate consolation" of Therese Desqueyroux, Mauriac refrained from writing of it. In neither case did the author expect actual personal experience to act as solvent. Or take Arnold Bennett. For all the experiential detail that went into *The Old Wives' Tale,* this novel was born of a flash of insight, from Bennett's noting a grotesque old woman in a Paris restaurant and reflecting that she was "once young, slim, perhaps beautiful." The novelist, in short, is many people not because of the disguises he puts on, but by virtue of the number of disguises he penetrates.

Scott Fitzgerald, however, was thoroughly persuaded that the meat, in the homely phrase of the early New England poet, must come out of the eater. In his egocentric world, the novelist, a kind of Boswell without a Johnson, can enter into situations only through the most thorough-going participation. Imagination is not only not enough; it is suspect. For the materialist—Fitzgerald was not entirely mistaken in classifying himself as "essentially Marxist," and his "Fitzboomski" periods were recurrent, early and late—must everywhere apply the test of quantity.

In a callow short story dating from his Princeton days, Fitzgerald writes of an unnamed Elizabethan lecher who, pursued by his victim's brothers, is given sanctuary in the house of a bookish friend. He repays his host's eager curiosity not by telling him of his recent escapade but by calling for foolscap and sitting down to the composition of *The Rape of Lucrece.* Fitzgerald never found—his story almost implies that neither did Shakespeare—the balance between art and life which is necessary for the artist's complete integrity. Though he might toughly resolve to be another Keats, sane-headed, practical and conserving of self, he romanticized himself far too long as "a sort of combination J. P. Morgan, Topham Beauclerk and St. Francis of Assisi." With disingenuous surprise he announced his tardy discovery: "I had become identified with the objects of my horror or compassion."

When Fitzgerald began to write, the Jazz Age was a subject new to itself and to the historian. He found it necessary, says

Arthur Mizener, Fitzgerald's first biographer, to proceed "like some kind of impassioned and naive anthropologist, recording with minuteness and affection and at the same time with an alien's remoteness." The anthropologist moved from the simple gothic jungle of *This Side of Paradise* to the tribal complexities and disordered undergrowth of *The Beautiful and Damned.* "Two persons to be expecting some occurrence, and watching for the two principal actors in it, and to find that the occurrence is even then passing, and they themselves are the two actors." So Hawthorne wrote in his *Note-Books;* and so found Scott and Zelda Fitzgerald as they came from the hinterlands of the Jazz Age empire to penetrate its "disordered mind."

Francis Scott Key Fitzgerald had been born in St. Paul in 1894, of a Catholic family of some means which was proud of numbering the author of "The Star-Spangled Banner" among its forebears. (Fitzgerald thought it worth recording that his great grandmother had visited Dolly Madison.) Scott attended the Newman School (faint impressions of which may be found in his short stories, notably "The Freshest Boy") and then, attracted by the Triangle Club, enrolled at Princeton. He was briefly in the Army, as "its worst aide-de-camp," and even more briefly in advertising. Then, after a few short months of "struggle," he was an established writer.

The author's short career as a "spiritually unmarried man" contributed the substance of *This Side of Paradise;* his reading and his experiments in verse and prose provided its several manners. *The Beautiful and Damned,* his second novel, carries the Fitzgerald story into an Army camp, where he was to send Jay Gatsby, and on into the early years of his marriage. Fitzgerald's experiences in Alabama—where he met Zelda Sayre, the original Jazz Age baby—were to confirm his conviction that he was, by virtue of his Maryland inheritance, a Southern aristocrat. During his "haughty" Army career he found time to work on his first novel. It was published, after much revision, in 1920; and in the same year Scott and Zelda were married in New York, in the rectory of St. Patrick's Cathedral. Then Paris knew them, the Riviera, and the cocktail country of Long Island and New York. To pay the bill, Fitzgerald "asked of his nerves" some two hundred short stories, most of them "cheap" commercial ones. Then convinced—or was he hopeful?—that the novel had been destroyed by the movies' "grosser power," he became a hack for Hollywood.

Here, if anywhere, the Jazz Age was likely to go on forever. Fitzgerald's last years were embittered by illness and frustration. "I had been a mediocre caretaker," he knew at last, "of most of the things left in my hands, even of my talent." He died in Hollywood in 1940, leaving his fifth novel unfinished. His era had died before him. It seems incongruous that F. Scott Fitzgerald, the Jazz Age laureate, should have been writing into the age of the New Deal and the Nazis.

Fitzgerald's writing career extended over two decades. Yet of the nine books he published in his lifetime, seven were written in the 'twenties. *This Side of Paradise,* the first (1920), was as revolutionary a document for its time as *Main Street* and *The Grapes of Wrath* were to be for theirs. The book is an individual manifesto, a kind of portrait of the artist as a young Princetonian. Its notes of decadence and protest and its salute to change announce that here is a generation born disenchanted.

Yet for all its reputation as the definitive work on the Jazz Age, *This Side of Paradise* is a tentative book, one dedicated not to being but to becoming. It takes its hero, Amory Blaine, through his years at preparatory school and Princeton, and through interludes, only faintly sketched in, of the world outside, to the point where he is free of the past and the future, and about to plumb the present. His life is a process, Amory's friend Monsignor Darcy tells him, of leaving off being a personality and becoming a person. But when the process is complete, Amory, "a fish out of water in too many outworn systems," knows at last that he knows only himself.

What an expensive, random education it was: books, friends, girls, and one or two adults provide its ingredients. All exist to show Amory new sides to his nature, to appear in his lists of categories, to serve as audience for his epigrams. They serve, too, to sweep him toward the choice, foredoomed, he will make between being "great" and good. A choice foredoomed because

Amory soon loses his power to "scent evil." The "Victorian war" of 1914 forever ended, he thought, the world of wise men and of heroes. Now that his faith, always tenuous, is gone, only a final irony remains: the need of giving others—though "his ideas were still in riot"—a sense of security. Unlike Stephen Dedalus (whose problems "puzzled and depressed" him), Amory will not cloak himself in the arrogance of art. Significantly, he is himself artifact, and here he will put his trust. The book comes to an ambiguous close, for as Mencken observed in his *Smart Set* review: "What, after such a youth, is to be done with the fellow?"

Amory Blaine, however much he was given to vanity and ranting, was never a whiner. The hero of *The Beautiful and Damned* (1922) achieves "being" and thirty million dollars, at the end of the book, in an overwhelming state of self-pity. Anthony Patch, like Amory, begins early to cultivate the graces. After some experience of Europe he goes to Harvard, then lives a life of becoming by waiting, in listless elegance, for the death of his multi-millionaire grandfather. He breaks off a dream-like, curiously "platonic" affair with Geraldine, a Shavian paragon of virtue from the lower classes, to marry Gloria Gilbert, a society girl, or, as an extremely coy passage in dramatic form has it, a "bogus aristocrat." Gloria, like all of Fitzgerald's heroines, possesses a masculine mind. Anarchic sentiments may vaguely haunt his heroes; his heroines are ruthlessly Nietzschean. The will to power, the will to immolation and to annihilation consume them. Eleanor, the willful descendant of Maryland aristocrats in *This Side of Paradise*, runs her horse over a cliff in a moment of defiance; Gloria munches gum drops.

The "war between the sexes," a dominant American theme, is fought with increasing bitterness in Fitzgerald's books. The attitude toward marriage in *The Beautiful and Damned*, for example, is a revealing one. Gloria admits to Anthony that she would have been "entirely his" before their marriage if he so wanted it, as she would be capable of taking a lover afterward without soiling her essential self; her mind. The night before the wedding, Anthony hears outside in the darkness the coarse, menacing sound of a woman's voice. "Life was that sound out there, that ghastly reiterated female sound." *The Beautiful and Damned* is the story of the hideous reality, punctuated by drinking and boredom, of their life together, of the marriage of a woman who wishes to be her husband's "permanent mistress" but neither a wife nor mother, and of a man who is a permanent child. Meanwhile Anthony has been disinherited, and there is a long, sordid wait as the will is being contested. Anthony has an inglorious career in training camp, drifting weakly into a passionate yet weary affair. He returns to New York, has a brief, drunken fling as a salesman, and suddenly inherits his millions. When we last see them the Patches are off to Europe. Gloria moves cold and "unclean" in her Russian sable; and Anthony, who has reverted to his childhood, has tears of triumph and self-pity in his eyes as he says: "It was a hard fight, but I didn't give up and I came through!"

In the years of his early novels of disillusion Fitzgerald was also producing short stories which embodied an abject surrender to what Edward J. O'Brien has called the Puritanical dance of the machines, to commercialism as the highest good. These stories first appeared in *The Smart Set* and also in the leading mass-circulation magazines before being collected in book form, and with memorable titles: *Flappers and Philosophers* (1920), *Tales of the Jazz Age* (1922) and *All the Sad Young Men* (1926). A final volume of stories, *Taps at Reveille,* appeared in 1935. Most of Fitzgerald's short stories are negligible as art, but they achieve significance in terms of the American myth of progress, for which he was, in his moments of acceptance, spokesman. But in spite of their surface approval of American life, these stories reveal a profound disquiet, and the serious and commercial ones have the curious effect of contradicting one another's premises. "All of the stories that came into my head," he wrote in his last years, "had a touch of disaster in them—the lovely creatures in my novels went to ruin, the diamond mountains of my stories blew up, my millionaires were as beautiful and damned as Hardy's peasants." In one of the stories Fitzgerald speaks of the millennial book to be written, the book patently of his own ambition. "It will be neither cheerful nor pleasant but will contain numerous passages of striking humor." This is a remarkably apposite characterization of the short stories. That it can be a disastrous formula is best illustrated by Fitzgerald's incredibly banal play, *The Vegetable, or From President to Postman* (1923).

The Great Gatsby (1925), the fable for which Fitzgerald's name will always be known, achieves—as *The Vegetable* does not—passages of striking humor and a delicate wit. Its wit arises not so much from new material as a fresh way of looking at the old. The book ties together themes Fitzgerald had used before—most memorably those of the outsider from the West and the penniless young man of promise who meets and loves the girl "safe and proud above the hot struggles of the poor."

There are but two kinds of hero in Fitzgerald: the man who had money and must now live without it; and the man who was born without money and who has, by one species of outlawry or another, come late to the acquiring of it. Jay Gatsby, born James Gatz, is one of the latter. He enters the Army, trains in the South, and meets a girl whose charm for him lies as much in the civilization of her upbringing as in her person. Gatsby then goes overseas. Meanwhile, Tom Buchanan has exercised a kind of *droit de seigneur* over Daisy, for he has money and position. Elaborately, on his return from the war, Gatsby sets the stage for the rewinning of Daisy, for recapturing the past, for making everything exactly as it was five years before. He acquires an estate directly across the bay from the Buchanans', and he enters into an intricate relationship with half the drinking population of New York on the chance that Daisy might stray into one of the parties held on his "overpopulated lawn." But he has no conception of the ruthlessness of the assured rich. They can break any number of parvenus arrayed against them, as they will use and discard Dick Diver and Monroe Stahr. No "value," Fitzgerald tells us again and again, has power against the moneyed and assured.

The story of Jay Gatsby's tragedy escapes triviality and sordidness through its allegorical power. The book is a juxtaposition of scene and symbol from beginning to end; it is "metaphysical" in the modern sense. Everywhere is the sign of contradiction. Brooding over a Long Island out of El Greco are the enormous billboard eyes of Doctor T. J. Eckleburg, eyes which "look out of no face, but, instead from a pair of enormous yellow spectacles which pass over a non-existent nose." These eyes do more than survey the dumping ground which separates the valley of villas from the city. They are, ambiguously, but certainly, Fitzgerald's symbol of value.

The book was written, his editor, Maxwell Perkins, told a perplexed reader, to assist people to "distinguish the good from the bad." The author, it is true, will not always assist them to the distinction, but the fixed eyes of Doctor Eckleburg, appearing from out the mists at significant moments of the action, remind that the distinction exists. Sometimes it comes through a vehicle with which Fitzgerald was not always successful, the mode of irony. Consider the scene in Wilson's office after Mabel Wilson, Tom's mistress, has been killed, as her husband will soon discover, by Gatsby's yellow car. Wilson's neighbor Michaelis has been urging Wilson, whose melancholy has been mounting to mania, to talk to a priest. Wilson refuses, but begins to babble about his wife's infidelity, recalling that he told her she could "fool me, but you can't fool God":

> Standing behind him, Michaelis saw with a shock that he was looking at the eyes of Doctor T. J. Eckleburg, which had just emerged, pale and enormous, from the dissolving night.
> "God sees everything," repeated Wilson.
> "That's an advertisement," Michaelis assured him.

In *The Great Gatsby* irony has a fulcrum. Not only are there the standards provided by Doctor Eckleburg, there are the judgments, mid-Western and therefore not decadent, of the narrator, Nick Carraway. For counterpoint there are the norms of Tom Buchanan, whose transformation from libertine to prig the book unfolds. Irony resides in the fact, too, that Gatsby is more truly an "Oggsford man," by virtue of his few weeks there, than Tom is a Yale man after four years in New Haven.

In *Tender Is the Night* (1934), the norm is not even ironically present. There are ironic touches, of course. The beach on the French Riviera is a "prayer rug" from which the protagonist takes his final leave by making the papal sign of the cross. But irony has become sick disillusionment, as when harlots wave pink step-ins at departing sailors: "Oh, say, can you see the tender color of remembered flesh?—while at the stern of the battleship arose in rivalry the Star-Spangled Banner." What Henry James called "the failure of fastidiousness" —the waste and disorder of modern life—has become corruption at the core.

Tender Is the Night is, once again, the story of the crack-up of a marriage. The marriage of Dick and Nicole Diver is yet another of Fitzgerald's doomed matings of narcissists. Nicole, we are told, "had been designed for change, for flight, with money as fins and wings." At our first glimpse of her she is sitting in her chauffeur-driven car, "her lovely face set, controlled, her eyes brave and watchful, looking straight ahead, toward nothing. Her dress was bright red and her brown legs were bare. She had thick, dark, gold hair like a chow's." That is Fitzgerald's own hostile summing up, but he also lets the reader see Dick and Nicole, the fortunate Divers as their friends think them, through the worshiping eyes of Rosemary Hoyt, a young American movie star, who will play an active part in the disintegration of the marriage. Around the Divers, serving as raw material for the parties they give, are a group of expatriates almost interchangeable for the amount of liquor they consume and for their talent for insolence and the *non-sequitur* remark.

As the situation unfolds, one learns that Dick had been a brilliant young psychiatrist (though Fitzgerald tried to be "careful not to reveal basic ignorance of psychiatric and medical training," he is naive about what constitutes scholarship in the field) and Nicole had been his patient. Nicole had been committed to a European sanitarium for a psychotic condition resulting from an incestuous relationship with her father. (This part of the story was omitted from the magazine serialization.) But it is Nicole's money rather than her unhappy past and neurotic present that causes the gradual but inexorable decline. "The manner remains intact for some time after the morale cracks," Dick tells Rosemary. In the end Dick surrenders Nicole to her lover, in the approved "civilized" fashion, apparently as a part of Dick's therapy for Nicole. Nobody wins. "The victor belongs to the spoils," as Anthony Patch had put it.

Fitzgerald was himself aware that *Tender Is the Night* is "the story of deterioration," but he could scarcely have intended it to be what Maxwell Geismar has pointed out it really is, a documentary on the novelist's own collapse. Once more Fitzgerald had identified himself, this time more thoroughly than before, with the objects of his horror.

His last novel, *The Last Tycoon,* which appeared posthumously in 1941, was to be "a new way of looking at certain phenomena" and "an escape into a lavish, romantic past that perhaps will not come again in our time." The past is the year 1933 as it was lived in Hollywood. This, too, is the story of a deterioration, here of an art form—the movies—betrayed by big business and big labor. Monroe Stahr was luckier than Jay Gatsby, for he did not have to live in an imaginary past purchased by a meretricious present; the dream world of Hollywood was his connatural kingdom. Stahr, a producer who can say with the grandeur of a Louis XIV, "I'm the unity," is described as the last of the princes, the last of the men of personal responsibilities and loyalty. Kathleen Moore, briefly his mistress (for the book's "immediate, dynamic, physical love affair" as Fitzgerald saw it), tells him she has been a king's mistress and that Stahr is more of a king than her lover was. But this sick Hamlet in a Denmark of ambiguous and shifting loyalties has little at his command save the "private grammar" of Hollywood.

The end Fitzgerald planned for Stahr, which oddly enough he considered neither morbid nor tragic, was death in a plane crash, death before he could countermand the order he had given for his partner's murder. The novel was to conclude on

144

a grand note of irony. The bodies of Stahr and his companions were to be found by children of a mountain village—an idea Fitzgerald culled from a newspaper story—who were to strip the bodies of their valuables, which were to be of symbolic importance. In the terms of the novel as we have it, irony was to reside in the contemplation of the incomprehensible. The "sense that life is essentially a cheat" was strong with Fitzgerald in his last years. In the settled dark night of the soul it was always, he complained, three o'clock in the morning. It is difficult to agree with those who see in the pages we have of *The Last Tycoon* the framework of a masterpiece. We know Fitzgerald's design for the entire book, and nothing from his execution would indicate that the finished work would have reconciled his dark despairs and his artistic patterns from them into a meaningful oneness.

Oneness continued to elude Fitzgerald, as it had the thinly disguised projections of himself, his characters. The profound dualities in the nature of this "spoiled priest" (as Fitzgerald thought of himself) could not be reconciled. Beyond such contradictions as his austerity and his "perfect craving for luxury" was the most commanding duality of his life, one still not fully explored, his attitude toward the Catholic faith he had abandoned. He saw his Catholicism, which he sometimes thought of as a "romantic Chestertonian orthodoxy," in terms of his Irish background, also a source of ambivalence. At times he seemed proud of his "Celticism," though he protests a bit too much; at others it gave him "a sort of hollow, cheerless pain." Yet it was as true of him as of Amory Blaine that there had been a time when his "Celtic traits were pillars of his personal philosophy." "Celtic you'll live, and Celtic you'll die," Monsignor Darcy says to Amory. In a letter to Edmund Wilson in 1920, Fitzgerald wrote: "I am ashamed to say that my Catholicism is scarcely more than a memory—no that's wrong it's more than that."

As time went on, Catholicism meant even less than a memory to him; in the depths of his disillusion he wrote that he would ask nothing of either God or Lenin. He had, it is clear, begun reading contemporary philosophers early and immersing himself in contemporary manners out of a deliberate search for a secular integration. Such a pursuit could only lead to a rejection of the past—and a false simplification of the present. Yet Catholicism left its mark on his work. *This Side of Paradise* is far from being a "Catholic novel," yet who else but one who had at least been a Catholic would have, in the self-conscious 'twenties, made a monsignor a central figure in a novel? In *Tender Is the Night,* Dick Diver, "my comparatively good brother" among Fitzgerald's fictional family, says his farewell to the Riviera by slowly making the papal sign of the cross over the assembled bathers and umbrellas. Nothing in Diver explains the gesture; everything in Fitzgerald does. The sign of Diver's rejection is precisely that which for Fitzgerald contains the greatest mockery of self.

Because Fitzgerald was essentially rootless—what use, in the 'twenties, were loyalties to Catholicism, to Francis Scott Key, to the mid-Western virtues?—he was powerfully attracted to contemporary currents, which he mistook for ideas. Often self-conscious and mistrustful of self, yet at times going to his own books for advice, he was painfully aware of the lack of substance in his work. Somewhere, he hoped, in the right books, in making the timely gestures, learning and wisdom could be stumbled upon. When he reached out for ideas, he was not likely to find them; but intuitively, brooding upon his deficiencies, his inchoate protests, and his feelings of betrayal, he happened upon many insights which were later to become truisms. Amory Blaine's harangue on socialism in the closing pages of *This Side of Paradise* is sophomoric. But it is portentous. Fitzgerald never entertained ideas purely, for their own sake; or pragmatically, for what they could do. Most of all, he wanted people to like his mind. As he says of Amory, if enough people liked his mind, "it might be such a nice place in which to live." Ironically enough, it was in Hollywood that he discovered that he was "not a rational type."

Writing of Stephen Vincent Benét's early career and its contrast to that of his friend John Peale Bishop, Fitzgerald attributed the success of the one and the comparative failure of the other to the fact that "people want ideas and not fabrics." Yet his own conflict, despite his concern for his paucity of ideas, was to be with fabric. The American novel, with the single transcendent exception of Henry James, has been the history of an unequal struggle with fabric. Hawthorne and Mark Twain were all but broken by it, and it hindered Melville more than most of his critics will admit. Our romantic impatience with form and our Emersonian feeling that the conscious stone will grow to beauty quite unaided account in part for our traditional inability to hammer the saying into meaning.

And for all that we think of him as, so to speak, a naturally mannered stylist, Fitzgerald spent most of his creative life wrestling with the problem of form. His first novel, indeed, is an instance of the triumph of form over the novelist. It is little more than a patchwork of skits and sketches sewn together with a large and random hand. Edmund Wilson, a friendly critic, calls it "one of the most illiterate books of any merit ever published." On the occasions, unfortunately rare in his total work, when Fitzgerald was successful with form, his meaning attained a clarity it did not otherwise have. It is true of Fitzgerald, as it is of all writers not absolutely of the first rank, that he could achieve idea, achieve the thing only through form. He had no other than oblique utterance.

Such is the indirection, the elevation of form into meaning which takes place in *The Great Gatsby*. Nothing Fitzgerald had done before really prepares one for this book. Some of its themes he had touched on before, and was to treat again. It derives, it is true, from his own life. But it is the only one of his novels to derive as well from his view of life. *Tender Is the Night* and *The Last Tycoon* present, as did the two earlier novels, the flat, mirrored surface of the author's experience. Only *Gatsby* is prismatic. For this effectiveness Fitzgerald is more beholden to literature than to life. Without his acquaintance with Conrad and Henry James, *Gatsby* would not be the book we know. For one thing, the Conradian device of the involved observer lends dimension. (Up to this time, in his life and books, Fitzgerald had striven for "an almost theatrical

147

innocence by preferring the role of the observed to that of the observer.") Without Nick Carraway, Jay Gatsby would not be in focus. Gatsby started out to be someone he knew, the author tells us, and then became himself, for Fitzgerald could not keep himself out of his fictions. In the first two novels the author's identification with the hero is embarrassingly complete; in the last two the identification is diffused: he assumes one mask after another. Only in *The Great Gatsby* is there disjunction between the author and the objects of his compassion.

The verdict of time on Fitzgerald's work will never permit it to be entirely lost to us. Much of it will be forgotten, of course, because Fitzgerald was a profoundly unoriginal writer, and his time had no enduring stamp. He himself felt that "the ennui of changing fashions" would "suppress" him and his books. Few of his writings, it would seem, other than *The Great Gatsby* and a handful of the short stories, will be remembered as anything more than period pieces. Historians will go to them for data on that era in our national life when frivolity was a prime social force. The student of our literary history will, it may be, turn to Fitzgerald to examine the personality of a man who wrote in half a dozen different styles.

For there were at least three Fitzgeralds: the allegorist of *This Side of Paradise* and *The Beautiful and Damned,* both with their morality-play characters and sermonizing; the fabulist of *The Great Gatsby* and "The Diamond as Big as the Ritz"; and lastly the impressionist of *Tender Is the Night* and *The Last Tycoon.* In the first two novels the clash of conventionality in style and form with the shock of new ideas is characteristic of the 'twenties. In the following decade form and matter merged into one another, and Fitzgerald caught the manner of it. In the last two novels, the very syncopation of the nervous 'thirties, the Angry Decade as someone has called it, has gotten into the author's bloodstream. His prose is a remarkable barometer of the sensibilities, of the very pulse, of the successive decades which produced it.

F. Scott Fitzgerald, the unrivaled poet of the thousand dollar bill, was the last of the romantics. Early and late he was perplexed with the dualities of life and the dream. Each was escape from the other. "His life was a sort of dream," he wrote in *The Crack-Up* (1945), "as are most lives with the mainspring left out." In Amory Blaine, the life-dream, with its essential ingredients of youth and money, had its first of many embodiments. When Amory's appendix burst as he was four hours out on a voyage to Italy, telegrams were sent and the great liner turned back. "You will admit," writes Fitzgerald, "that if it was not life it was magnificent." Life was the pursuit of the magnificent dream. For twenty years of worldly success, artistic fulfillment, and a growing awareness that somewhere along the tinseled way his personality had become lost, Fitzgerald looked sentimentally back on that rare time in the beginning "when the fulfilled future and the wistful past were mingled in a single glorious moment—when life literally was a dream."

The later novels and the bitter reminiscences of *The Crack-Up* are the charred remains of the career that failed to measure up to its bright promise. "There are," he had written, "no second acts in American lives." But *The Great Gatsby* is the dream made palpable, tender and lasting. There the ambiguities are resolved, fashioned into art out of failure and regret. And behind the book, finally unreached and perhaps unanalyzable, is the haunting figure of Scott Fitzgerald, self-dispossessed heir to all the ages.

John Dos Passos:

Technique vs. Sensibility

HERBERT MARSHALL McLUHAN

MOST ELABORATE of the many spoofs made by James Joyce was his obeisance to Dujardins as his "master" of the interior monolog. Only less elaborate have been the jokes played by Mr. Eliot, as in presenting to Harvard his copy of Jessie Weston with many pages uncut. To darken the counsel of those who choose to live in darkness has always been a form of light-bringing among the wits. But easily the most esoteric literary high-jinx of our time is the very formal debate, conducted far above the heads of Bloomsbury, between Wyndham Lewis and James Joyce. Lewis's "attack" on Joyce as a romantic time-snob, and Joyce's "counterattack" in *Finnegans Wake* are not just obscurantist trifling but a means of offering important insights of those readers who have acquired certain preliminary disciplines.

The reader of Dos Passos, however, is not required to have much more reading agility than the reader of the daily press. Nor does Dos Passos make many more serious demands than a good movie. And this is said not to belittle an excellent writer

151

who has much to offer, but to draw attention to the extreme simplification to which Dos Passos has submitted the early work of James Joyce. *Three Soldiers* (1921), *Manhattan Transfer* (1925) and *U. S. A.* (1930-'36) would not exist in their present form but for the *Portrait of the Artist as a Young Man, Dubliners* and *Ulysses*. It is as a slightly super-realist that Dos Passos has viewed and adapted the work of Joyce in his own work. And since his technical debt to Joyce is so considerable, one useful way of placing the achievement of Dos Passos is to notice what he took over and, especially, what he did not take.

As a young man in Chicago and at Harvard Dos Passos was much alive to the imagists, Sandburg, Fletcher, Pound, Amy Lowell and the French poet Cendrars. From them he learned much that has continuously affected his practice. Their romantic tapestries and static contemplation of the ornate panorama of existence have always held him in spite of his desire to be a romantic of action. The same conflict, between the man who needs to participate in the life of his time and the artist who wishes to render that life more luminous by self-effacement in his art, appears also in Whitman and in Hemingway. Hemingway's solution may prove to have been in some ways the most satisfactory insofar as he has succeeded occasionally in holding up the critical mirror to the impulse of romantic action, and not just to the action itself.

Dos Passos has been less sure than Hemingway of his artistic direction, though more confident in his politics. But everywhere from *One Man's Initiation* (1917) to the trilogy *U. S. A.* he has been conscious of the need for some sort of detachment and some sort of commitment. *Three Soldiers* is a portrait of the "artist" as G.I. in which, as in E. E. Cummings' *The Enormous Room,* the demand of the individual for some kind of intelligibility in a merely bureaucratic order is met by savage group-reprisal. That has remained the vision of Dos Passos.

For in recent decades the artist has come to be the only critical spectator of society. He demands and confers the heightened significance in ordinary existence which is hostile to any self-extinction in the collective consciousness. So that when the balance is lost between individual responsibility and mass solidarity, the artist automatically moves to the side of the individual. With equal inevitability, the less resourceful man, faced with the perplexities of planned social disorder, walks deeper into the collective sleep that makes that chaos bearable to him. The work of Dos Passos is almost wholly concerned with presenting this situation. His people are, typically, victims of a collective trance from which they do not struggle to escape. And if his work fails, it is to the extent that he clings to an alternative dream which has little power to retract the dreamers from their sleep, and even less power to alert the reader to a sense of tragic waste.

Born in 1896, John Dos Passos grew up in a milieu that had brought to a focus a number of discordant themes and motivations. The popularity of Darwin and Spencer had by then led to the profession of a doctrinaire individualism which got melodramatic treatment at the hands of a Frank Norris. Louis Sullivan and Frank Lloyd Wright were considerably affected by the spirit associated with the flamboyant extroversion and aggression of "frontier" Darwinism. Carl Sandburg's "Chicago" illustrates the curious blend of democratic lyricism and megalomaniac brutality that existed at that time. Robinson Jeffers has the gloomy distinction of representing today the then fashionable code of doctrinaire sadism which found a center in Chicago at the turn of the century.

Superficially it may appear odd that the cosmic humanitarianism of Whitman should have fostered such diverse expressions as the work of Sandburg and Jeffers. But as Sidney Lanier pointed out long ago, Whitman himself was a Byronic dandy turned inside out. Reared on the picturesque art of Scott with its preoccupation with the folk and their crafts, nurtured equally on the heroic panoramas of Byron with his vistas of world history, Whitman found no difficulty in transferring this aristocratic art to the democratic scene. Had not the aristocratic Chateaubriand earlier acquired in America the palette and the scenes which were to attract to him the discipleship first of Lord Byron and later of Stendhal and Flaubert? And the Jeffersonian dream of democracy was of a level-ing-up rather than a leveling-down process. An aristocratic dream after all.

Co-existing with the fashionable Darwinism of mid-West tycoons was the grass-roots populism which found an academic spokesman in the formidable Thorsten Veblen. Veblen is ably presented in *The Big Money*, the last of the *U. S. A.* trilogy, as are Henry Ford and Sam Insull. Taken together, Veblen, Ford and Insull are strikingly representative of the unre-solved attitudes and conflicts of the milieu in which Dos Passos grew up. Nor does Dos Passos attempt any reconcilia-tion of these conflicts. While his sympathies are entirely with the agrarian Veblen and the grass-roots, his art is committed to rendering the entire scene. And it is attention to the art of Dos Passos that the critic finds most rewarding. For Dos Passos is not a thinker who has imposed a conceptual system on his material. Rather, he accepted the most familiar tradi-tions and attitudes as part of the material which his art brings into the range of the reader's vision. It is by the range of his vision and the intensity of his focus that he must receive criticism.

As a boy in Chicago, Dos Passos was devoted to Gibbon's *Decline and Fall of the Roman Empire*. Artistically, Gibbon's late use of baroque perspectivism, the linear handling of his-tory as a dwindling avenue, concurred with the eighteenth-century discovery of the picturesque, or the principle of dis-continuity as a means of enriching artistic effect. So that the later discovery of contemporary imagism and impressionism by Dos Passos, and his enthusiasm for the cinematic velocity of images in the French poet Cendrars, corresponded pretty much with the original revolution in eighteenth-century taste and perception which carried letters from the style of Gibbon to Sterne.

Looking first at the technical means which he employs as a writer, there is the basic imagistic skill in sharpening percep-tion and defining a state of mind with which *Manhattan Trans-fer* opens:

Three gulls wheel above the broken boxes, orangerinds, spoiled cabbage heads that heave between the splintered plank walls, the green waves spume under the round bow as the ferry, skidding on the tide, crashes, gulps the broken water, slides, settles slowly into the slip.

Many passages of this wry lyricism counterpoint the episodes of the book. The episodes and characters are also features of a landscape to which these lyric chapter overtures give point and tone. The point is readily seized and the tone extends over a very narrow range of emotions: pathos, anger, disgust. But Dos Passos employs the impressionist landscape monotonously because he has never chosen to refract or analyze its components to zone a wide range of emotions. Open any page of Pound's *Cantos* and the same impressionist landscapes will be found to be presenting a variety of carefully-discriminated mental states. Pound does not accept the landscape as a homogeneous lump of matter. Even satire is managed by Dos Passos in a direct, lyric mode though the technique seems to be impersonal:

He's darn clever and has a lot of personality and all that sort of thing, but all he does is drink and raise Cain . . . I guess all he needs is to go to work and get a sense of values.

or:

The terrible thing about having New York go stale on you is that there's nowhere else. It's the top of the world. All we can do is go round and round in a squirrel cage.

Manhattan Transfer is full of such planned incongruities which achieve a weak pathos when they could more successfully have effected a robust guffaw. The author is sensitive to the ugliness and misery as things he can see. But he is never prepared to explore the interior landscape which is the wasteland of the human heart:

Ellen stayed a long time looking in the mirror, dabbing a little superfluous powder off her face, trying to make up her mind. She kept winding up a hypothetical dollself and setting it in various positions. Tiny gestures ensued, acted out on various model stages. Suddenly she turned away . . . "Oh, George I'm starved, simply starved . . . we've got to be sensible. God knows we've messed things up in the past both of us . . . Let's drink to the crime wave."

The effect is comparable to that of *The Great Gatsby*, which sustains this Hansel and Gretel sort of wistful despair to create a child-pastoral world. Out of the same situations Hemingway at his best—as in the first page of *A Farewell to Arms*—can obtain moments of tragic intensity—landscapes of muted terror which give dignity to human suffering.

But Dos Passos too often seems to imply that the suffering is sordid and unnecessary or that some modification of the environment might free his characters from the doll-mechanism that is their private and collective trap. Seeing nothing inevitable or meaningful in human suffering, he confronts it neither in its comic, intelligible mode, nor in a tragic way. It angers and annoys him as something extraneous.

The difference from Joyce is instructive. For in *Ulysses* the same discontinuous city landscape is also presented by imagistic devices. The episodes are musically arranged to sound concordantly. But Joyce manipulates a continuous parallel at each moment between naturalism and symbolism to render a total spectrum of outer and inner worlds. The past is present not in order to debunk Dublin but to make Dublin representative of the human condition. The sharply-focussed moment of natural perception in Joyce floods the situation with analogical awareness of the actual dimensions of human hope and despair. In *Ulysses* a brief glimpse of a lapidary at work serves to open up ageless mysteries in the relations of men and in the mysterious qualities of voiceless objects. The most ordinary gesture linked to some immemorial dramatic mask or situation sets reverberating the whole world of the book and flashes intelligibility into long opaque areas of our own experience.

To match Joyce's epiphanies Dos Passos brings only Amer-

ican know-how. And, indeed, there seems to be no corner of
the continent with whose speech and cooking he is not familiar.
There is no trade or profession which he does not seem to
know from the inside. Joyce contemplates things for the being
that is theirs. Dos Passos shows how they work or behave.

Earlier, Joyce had opened the *Portrait* with an overture
representative of the stages of human apprehension, which
with Aristotle he held to be a shadow of the artistic process
itself, so that the development of the artist concurs with the
retracing of the process of poetic experience. By a technique
of cubist or overlayering perspectives both of these processes
are rendered present to the reader in an instant of inclusive
consciousness. Hence the "portrait" claim of the title. The
very setting side-by-side of these two operations is typical,
therefore, of the level and extent of symbolic implication in
Joyce. (The Oxen of the Sun section of *Ulysses* fused both
these processes with both the human biological and civilized
processes, as well as with the parts and totality of the book
itself, and yet has been read as a series of parodies of English
prose styles.)

The difference between this kind of art and that of Dos
Passos is that between one of univocal, psychological and one
of properly analogical effect. Joyce constantly has his attention on the analogy of being while Dos Passos is registering
a personal reaction to society.

It is not a serious criticism of Dos Passos to say that he is
not James Joyce. But Joyce is his art master and the critic
is obliged to note that Dos Passos has read Joyce not as a
greater Flaubert, Rimbaud or Mallarmé, but as it were through
the eyes of Whitman and Sandburg, as a greater Zola or
Romains. This is negative definition which does not bring into
question the competence of Dos Passos or belittle the quality
of positive delight he affords. His *U. S. A.* is quite justly established as a classic which brought into a focus for the first
time a range of facts and interests that no American had ever
been able to master. But it is in the main an ethical and political synthesis that he provides, with the interest intentionally
at one level—the only level that interests Dos Passos.

Manhattan Transfer, which corresponds roughly to Joyce's *Dubliners,* cuts a cross-section through a set of adult lives in New York. But the city is not envisaged as providing anything more than a phantasmagoric back-drop for their frustrations and defeats. The city is felt as alien, meaningless. Joyce, on the other hand, accepts the city as an extension of human functions, as having a human shape and eliciting the full range of human response which man cannot achieve in any other situation. Within this analogy Joyce's individuals explore their experience in the modes of action and passion, male and female. The stories are grouped according to the expanding awareness of childhood, adolescence, maturity and middle-age. Man, the wanderer within the labyrinthine ways at once of his psyche and of the world, provides an inexhaustible matter for contemplation. Dos Passos seems to have missed this aspect of *Dubliners.* But in *U. S. A.,* while extending his back-drop from the city to the nation, he did make the attempt to relate the expanding scene to the development of one mind from childhood to maturity. That is the function of "Camera Eye." "News-reel" projects the changing environment which acts upon the various characters and corresponds to riffling the back issues of *Life* magazine.

But *Ulysses,* with which *U. S. A.* invites comparison, shows a very different conception of history in providing a continuous parallel between ancient and modern. The tensions set up in this way permit Joyce to control the huge accretions of historic power and suggestion in the human past by means of the low-current of immediate incident. The technological analog of this process occurs in the present use of the electronic valve in heavy-power circuits. So that Joyce does not have to step up the intensity of the episode or scene so long as he maintains its function in the total circuit. Deprived of this symbolic "feed-back" process implicit in the historic sense, and which is manipulated alike by Joyce, Pound and Eliot, Dos Passos is left with little more current or intensity than that generated by his immediate episodes.

Since criticism, if it is to be anything more than a review of the "content" of works of art, must take cognizance of the technical means by which an artist achieves his effects, it is relevant to consider some of the stages by which the kind of art found in *U. S. A.* came into existence. If there is anything to be explained about such a work it can best be done by noting the extraordinary preoccupation with landscape in eighteenth-century art. For it was the discovery of the artistic .possibilities of discontinuity that gave their form to the novels of Scott as well as to the poems of Byron and Whitman.

Whitman, a great reader of Scott in his youth, later took pains to bring into his poetry as much of the contemporary technology as he could manage. Whitman's poems are also camera-eye landscapes in which human tasks are prominent. In his numerous portraits which he strove to bring into line with the techniques of the impressionists' painting, he wove the man's work into his posture and gestures. His aim was to present the actual, and he took pride that in his *Leaves of Grass* "everything is literally photographed." As for the larger lines of his work, it is plain that he uses everywhere a cinematic montage of "still" shots.

It is not only in the details but in the spirit of much of his work that Whitman resembles Dos Passos. And it is hard to see how anyone who set himself to rendering the diverse existence of multitudes of people could dispense with the technique of discontinuous landscapes. In fact, until the technique of discontinuous juxtaposition was brought into play it was not even possible to entertain such an ambition. "Remember," he said of the *Leaves* to Dr. Bucke, "the book arose out of my life in Brooklyn and New York from 1838 to 1853, absorbing a million people, for fifteen years, with an intimacy, an eagerness, an abandon, probably never equalled." Taken in connection with his technical inventiveness, this enables us to see why the French were from the start so much more interested in Whitman than either his countrymen or the English. Hopkins, struggling with similar technical problems at a more serious level, remarked, however, that he had more in common with Whitman than with anybody else of his time.

From this point of view it is plain, also, why Tolstoy and Hugo could take Scott and Byron with the same artistic seri-

159

ousness with which Dostoevsky regarded Dickens. Dickens was probably the first to apply the picturesque to discoveries in technique, to the entire life of an industrial metropolis. And the brilliance of his technical development of this matter provided W. D. Griffiths with his cinematic principles seventy years later.

However, it was in Flaubert's *Sentimental Education* that the acceptance of the city as the central myth or creation of man first leads to the mastery of that huge material by means of the technique of discontinuous landscape. Moreover, Flaubert makes a continuous parallel between the fatuity of Frederic Moreau's "education" and the deepening sordor and banality of nineteenth-century Paris.

It is slightly otherwise in *U. S. A.*, where the development of political consciousness of the "Camera Eye" persona is not so much parallel with as in contrast to the unfolding landscape of the nation. And this again is close to the way in which the development of Stephen Dedalus in the *Portrait* as a self-dedicated human being runs counter to the mechanisms of the Dublin scene. The author's political and social sense unfolds without comment in the "Camera Eye" sections, with "Newsreel" providing the immediate environmental pressures which are felt in different ways by everybody in the book. Both of these devices are successfully controlled to provide those limited effects which he intends. But the insights which lead to these effects are of a familiar and widely accepted kind.

That, again, in no way invalidates the insights but it does explain the monotony and obviousness which creeps into so many pages. The reader of Dos Passos meets with excellent observation but none of the unending suggestiveness and discovery of the *Sentimental Education* or *Ulysses*. For there is neither historical nor analogical perception in the *U. S. A.*, and so it fails to effect any connections with the rest of human society, past or present. There is a continuous stream of American consciousness and an awareness that there are un-American elements in the world. But as much as in any political orator there is the assumption that iniquity inside or outside the U. S. A. is always a failure to be true to the Jeffersonian

dream. The point here is that this kind of single-level awareness is not possible to anybody seriously manipulating the
multiple keyboards of Joyce's art.

Dickens as a newspaper reporter had hit upon many of his
characteristic effects in the course of his daily work. Later,
when he turned to the serial publication of his stories, he was
compelled to do some of that "writing backwards" which, as
Edgar Poe saw, is the principle underlying the detective story
and the symbolist poem alike. For in both instances the effect
to be attained is the point at which the writer begins. The work
finally constructed is a formula for the effect which is both
the beginning and the end of the work.

It is interesting to note how Browning moved toward a
fusion of these interests in the *Ring and the Book,* turning
a police romance into a cross-section of an inclusive human
consciousness by the technique of the reconstruction of a
crime. Artistically he is more complex than Dos Passos in the
use he makes of the dramatic process of retracing or reconstruction. For that retracing reveals many of the labyrinthine
recesses of the human heart which the merely panoramic impressionism of Dos Passos cannot even attempt to do. And it is
also this profound drama of retracing the stages of an experience which enables the popular detective story to sound varied
depths of the greatest human themes in the hands of Graham
Greene. In the art of Eliot (as in *The Cocktail Party*) it permits the sleuth and the guardian of souls to meet in the figure
of Harcourt-Riley, as in Browning's Pope.

The failure of Dos Passos' insights to keep pace with the
complex techniques at his disposal is what leaves the reader
with the sense of looseness and excessive bulk in *U. S. A.* In the
equally bulky *Finnegans Wake,* on the other hand, which exploits all the existing techniques of vision and presentation in
a consummate orchestration of the arts and sciences, there is
not one slack phrase or scene. *U. S. A.,* by comparison, is like
a Stephen Foster medley played with one finger on a five key-
board instrument. There is that sort of discrepancy between
the equipment and the ensuing concert; but it is not likely to

disturb those readers who have only a slight acquaintance with Joyce.

Manhattan Transfer and the *U. S. A.* trilogy are not novels in the usual sense of a selection of characters who influence and define one another by interaction. The novel in that sense was a by-product of biological science and as such persists today only among book-club practitioners. The novel as it has been concerned with the problems of "character" and environment seems to have emerged as a pastime of the new middle classes who were eager to see themselves and their problems in action. Remove from these novels the problems of money and the arts of social distinction and climbing and little remains. From that point of view Flaubert's *Madame Bovary* was the deliberate reduction of the middle-class novel to absurdity. And Sinclair Lewis's *Babbitt* is, as Ford Madox Ford pointed out, the American *Madame Bovary*. But the *Sentimental Education* is a great step beyond this, and taken with *Bouvard and Pecuchet,* provided the framework for the symbolic epic of the commonplace which is *Ulysses*. The middle classes found romance and glamour in the commonplace, but they were not prepared for the profound existentialist metaphysic of the commonplace which Joyce revealed.

In such a perspective as this the collective landscapes of *U. S. A.* represent only a modest effort at managing the huge panorama of triviality and frustration which is the urban milieu of industrial man.

But the fact that a technological environment not only induces most people into various stages of automatism but makes the family unit socially non-effective, has certainly got something to do with the collective landscapes of *U. S. A.* Its structure is poetic in having its unity not in an idea but a vision; and it is cubist in presenting multiple simultaneous perspectives like a cycle of medieval mystery plays. It could readily be maintained that this method not only permits comprehensiveness of a kind indispensable to the modern artist, but makes for the intelligible rather than the concupiscible in art. The kind of pleasure that Dos Passos provides in comparison with Hemingway is that of detached intellectual intuition rather than that of sympathetic merging with the narrative and characters.

The current conception of art as vicarious experience, on the other hand, seems mainly to support the attitude of behavioristic merging with the lives of the characters portrayed. And since this tendency is geared commercially with the demands of an untrained reader mass, it is irresistible. It helps to explain why a Dos Passos is considered high-brow although he offers no more strain on the attention than a detective story. It is because of the kind rather than the degree of effort he invites that he is deprecated as high-brow by readers who accept the cubist landscapes of the newspaper, and the musical equivalent in jazz, without perturbation.

Although Dos Passos may be held to have failed to provide any adequate intellectual insight or emotion for the vast landscape of his trilogy, his themes and attitudes are always interesting, especially in the numerous biographies of such folk heroes as Edison and the Wright brothers, Debs and La Follette, Steinmetz and Isadora Duncan, Ford and Burbank. These sections are often masterly in their economy and point. The frustration of hopes and intentions in these public figures provides the main clue to the social criticism which underlies the presentation of dozens of nonentities. For it is usually pointed up that the great are as helplessly ensnared in merely behavioristic patterns irrelevant to their own welfare, as the crowd of nobodies who admire them.

The frustration and distortion of life common to the celebrated and the obscure is, in Dos Passos, to be attributed to "the system." No diagnosis as crude as this emerges directly. But over and over again in the contrast between humble humanity and the gormandizing power-gluttony of the stupidly arrogant few, there is implied the preference for a world of simple, unpretentious folk united in their common tasks and experience. It has often been noted that there is never love between the characters of Dos Passos. But there is the pathos of those made incapable of love by their too successful adjustment to a loveless system. Genuine pathos is the predominant and persistent note in Dos Passos, and must be considered as his personal response to the total landscape. Yet it is a pathos free from self-pity because he has objectified it in his analysis of the political and economic situation.

The homelessness of his people is, along with their individual and collective incapacity for self-criticism or detachment, the most obvious feature about them. And home is the positive though unstated and undefined dream of Dos Passos. In wandering from the Jeffersonian ideal of a farmer-craftsman economy in the direction of Hamiltonian centralism, power and bigness, Dos Passos sees the main plight of his world. Hamilton set up the false beacon that brought shipwreck. But out of that shipwreck, which he depicts, for example, as the success of Henry Ford's enterprise, we can recover the dream and create a reality worthy of it. That is an unfailing note. For those who are critically aware he prescribes the duty of selfless dedication to the improvement of the common civilization. And in three uninteresting, short novels since *U. S. A.* he has explored the problem of discovering a self worth giving to such a cause. The current need would seem to be for a historic sense which can resolve the Hamilton-Jefferson dichotomy.

There is, perhaps, little point in dwelling on these aspects of Dos Passos, in which without new insight he reflects the ordinary attitude of the great majority. Yet, there is great social hope in the fact that this common intellectual ground is so large and so admirably chosen. But it is outside the province of criticism, which is concerned with the means employed and effects obtained by an artist. By the time the critic comes to the point of confronting Dos Passos the Jeffersonian radical, he has moved into a territory shared by Frank Capra.

And Dos Passos may have lost his stride as an artist through the very success of those social causes which were the militant theme of *U. S. A.* To have a cause to defend against a blind or indifferent world seemed to give tone and snap to the artist in him who has since been overlaid by the reporter. But if this is the case, nobody would be happier than Dos Passos to have lost his artistry on such excellent terms.

William Faulkner:

Tragedian of Yoknapatawpha

ERNEST SANDEEN

The map of Yoknapatawpha County which appeared in *Absalom! Absalom!* in 1936 shows that this setting for most of Faulkner's fiction bears some topographical resemblance to the Lafayette County where Faulkner has lived since early boyhood.[1] Yet the legend on the map, "Jefferson, Yoknapatawpha Co., Mississippi . . . William Faulkner, Sole Owner & Pro-

---

[1] In view of the importance which "Jefferson" and "Yoknapatawpha" have had in his stories, the most significant fact of the Faulkner biography is his almost continuous residence in Oxford, Mississippi. Although he was born (September 25, 1897) in New Albany of the neighboring Union County, his family came to Oxford when William was still a child—a family with an illustrious past, counting governors, statesmen and military leaders among its ancestors.

Faulkner's most frequent and most extensive wanderings from his home town came in the period of his youth before his novels had begun to appear. In World War I he joined the Canadian Flying Corps, was transferred to the RAF and saw action as a flier in France. After the war he returned to Oxford, attended the State University there for two years (though he had never finished high school), worked as a housepainter and was postmaster at the University from 1922 to 1924. There were three more brief sojourns away from Oxford before he came back finally

165

prietor," seems to affirm that any similarities between this imaginary region and an actual region are purely coincidental, although it also suggests that the fictitious town and county are nevertheless situated in Mississippi.

Small red circles on the map, with labels lined in, locate the places where the most important events in Faulkner's various fictions occur: CHURCH WHICH THOMAS SUTPEN RODE FAST TO, SARTORIS PLANTATION, REVEREND HIGHTOWER'S WHERE CHRISTMAS WAS KILLED, BUNDREN'S, and so on. The map gives in graphic form a total view of Faulkner's major fiction, comprehending much of the work done up to 1936 and prophesying works to come. This bird's-eye perspective shows that Faulkner's stories, most of them, are all parts of one whole, but it shows further that the wholeness consists in more than a common physical setting. Unlike most maps, this one de-emphasizes topography, conveying an impression of community rather than of place merely.

One reason for this effect is that the map pictures not only an imagined region but an imagined history. For example, not far to the north and east of MISS JOANNA BURDEN'S is JOHN SARTORIS' STATUE & EFFIGY. The reader of *Light in August* remembers that Miss Burden's grandfather and brother were shot to death as carpetbaggers by the famous figure represented in the statue. Again, OLD FRENCHMAN PLACE, WHICH FLEM SNOPES UNLOADED ON HENRY ARMSTID AND SURATT, AND WHERE POPEYE KILLED TOMMY is associated with two other

to settle down to a serious writing career: a few months as a clerk in a New York City bookstore, an interval in the artists' and writers' colony of New Orleans where he came to know Sherwood Anderson who encouraged him to write, and an eight months' walking tour in Europe in 1925.

His early novels, especially *The Sound and the Fury* and *As I Lay Dying*, attracted serious critical notice but popularity and financial success did not come until *Sanctuary* was published in 1931. Since then there has been no diminution in his literary achievement or in his reputation, though of course there have been fluctuations in both. In January, 1939, he was elected a member of the National Institute of Arts and Letters, and in December, 1950, he was awarded the Nobel Prize in Literature for 1949. Thus Faulkner with his continued growth and success has not followed the all-too-common course of the American writer who in mid-career suddenly appears to have outlived his times or his inspiration—or both.

points on the map: VARNER'S STORE, WHERE FLEM SNOPES GOT HIS START, because Flem extorted Old Frenchman Place from Will Varner, and JAIL WHERE GOODWIN WAS LYNCHED, because Goodwin was lynched for Popeye's crime.

These few examples of the innumerable interrelations which the map diagrams may suggest the complex inner unity of Faulkner's fiction, the community of his characters. Living only by the creative fiat of their author, they do not form a real society and yet they are significantly related to a real society and their mythic history is related to a real history. To return to the legend on the map, Jefferson, Yoknapatawpha County, is located in Mississippi, and yet William Faulkner is its sole owner and proprietor.

Faulkner provides nothing so static as the phrase "a picture of the South" would imply. He furnishes rather a process in self-discovery, at once personal and social. What happens in his fiction is that the South is forced to face itself with a savage honesty, an impassioned detachment. The aristocratic Sartorises, Compsons and Benbows; the humbler folk like Wash Jones, Ratliff and the Bundrens; the Negroes, Simon, Dilsey and Lucas; the swarming parasites, the Snopeses and their kind; the criminals like Christmas and Popeye—all these Faulkner characters and the events they enact are the means by which a writer brings the region he is part of, painfully but with determination, toward self-awareness.

The state of mind which Faulkner explores is not simple and it is not worn on the sleeve. It means self-contradiction and inner conflict, an often seething mixture of pride and bad conscience, of exaltation and shame. One general effect which his work conveys is that to be a Southerner is something special, something strange and difficult; it is to find oneself in an unrelenting predicament, a privilege to be treasured and a curse to be borne. The typical Faulkner character is mysteriously at war with himself. For example, in *Absalom! Absalom!* Quentin Compson feels deeply implicated as a Southerner in the terror and the guilt of the Sutpen story which he tells his Harvard roommate. Yet when his listener at the end asks the

abrupt but logical question, " 'Why do you hate the South?' "
Quentin replies at once, " 'I dont hate it.' . . . *I dont hate
it* he thought, panting in the cold air, the iron New England
dark; *I dont. I dont! I dont hate it! I dont hate it!*"

To a large degree the mentality which Faulkner dramatizes
in order to know it, is a heritage. His predilection for situations in which (the flashback is the appropriate method for
developing plot and character suggests that he conceives of
story as imaginative history.) This habit of mythic-historical
perception is evident also in the innumerable thumbnail gene-
alogies scattered through his fiction. Only the *Iliad* and the
Odyssey offer adequate parallels in this respect and these
miniature pedigrees and biographies, as in Homer, are often
not necessary to the story but are relished for their own sake.

Many of his protagonists would appear incredible in what
they do if they were not related to a continuity beyond themselves: a family, a town or neighborhood, a region, a race.
When brought together on Faulkner's map of fiction these
various histories begin to suggest a single larger pattern in
which the Civil War is the central fact. This conflict Faulkner
recognizes as both the ruin of the Southern way of life and
its apotheosis, the destruction which rendered the history of
the South indestructible, the vanquished unvanquished. In
brief, the Civil War was the means by which the Old South
with all its emotional and moral ambiguities fastened itself
upon its descendants for their good and for their ill. This is
the heritage that gives to Faulkner's people their communal
character which is more important always than their character
as individuals. Even those who do not understand the historical situation are still a product of it and are governed by it.

One force which remains constant throughout the history of
the South as Faulkner reimagines it in his stories is the aristocratic sense of honor and pride.) As a source of motivation it
figures largely in Faulkner's discovery of what it means and
has meant to be a Southerner. Mark Twain when he returned
to the South in 1882 to revivify his memories of the Mississippi River, was struck by the universal addiction he found
there to the chivalric ideal, which he thought had been de-

stroyed some twenty years before. Judging what he saw from the point of view of his adopted Northern land where the *Zeitgeist* swept on unimpeded, this Southern loyalty to a lost and mistaken cause seemed to him an anachronism, a willful refusal to keep up with the nineteenth century, which he called "the plainest and sturdiest and infinitely greatest and worthiest of all the centuries the world has seen." In his opinion this outdated chivalry falsified everything: it encouraged in civil life the lawless violence of the duel and the feud; it reduced architecture to sham medieval castles and literature to sentimental rhetoric.

Certainly he oversimplified when he made Sir Walter Scott alone responsible for the "unprogressive" medievalism which he found in the South. Here he mistook an effect for a cause, the real cause being much more complex than he suspected. But his perception of the medieval connection was correct. The planter society, aristocratic and agrarian, was eager to discover and to emphasize a sympathetic relation to the landed gentry of the Old World, the only class in the nineteenth century which had inherited its values in a direct line from the Middle Ages. The planters liked to see the South as a timocracy superior in its cultural heritage to the raw plutocracy of the North.

Whatever might have been false about these aristocratic pretensions, either before or after the Civil War, Faulkner searches out and pillories as fiercely as Mark Twain. In fact his exposure is much more devastating because (he is at heart sympathetic) as Mark Twain was not and therefore he has more at stake. With a kind of desperate integrity he strips away the shams, brutalities, sentimental nostalgias and puerilities which surround the timocratic ideal in order to rescue what may be genuine at the core of it. One way of indicating Faulkner's scope is to say that in this process he becomes an anatomist of human pride through the whole gamut of its operation, from the derring-do of the Sartorises to the simple, sturdy self-respect of the sawmill worker, Byron Bunch.

A sense of honor is the one human value which is Faulkner's constant preoccupation. It provides the basis for his

169

tragic vision and it creates the mysterious psychological atmosphere in which his characters move.)It is shown in excess and in defect. In Thomas Sutpen it is the single obsessive idea of every waking moment; in Wash Jones and Anse Bundren, on the other hand, it rises up dimly from the unconscious life only under some extraordinary stimulus. In the Reverend Hightower it takes the form of nostalgia for a single glorious historic moment of thundering hooves, and it means arrested spiritual growth and decay. For Quentin Compson it is perverted into a love of death, but for the sewing-machine salesman Ratliff it blossoms into a serene, affable self-assurance. Even the convict who is the chief character in *The Old Man* has a jealous, injured sense of his own worth. From his frustrated train robbery he had not wanted "the crass loot; that would have been merely a bangle to wear upon the breast of his pride . . . a symbol, a badge to show that he too was the best at his chosen gambit in the living and fluid world of his time."

For Faulkner the delicate adjustments required on both sides between pride and shame, honor and dishonor, define the relations between whites and Negroes. Carothers Edmonds in "The Fire and the Hearth" remembers that after seven years of intimate boyhood companionship with his black foster-brother, Henry Beauchamp, "one day the old curse of his fathers, the old haughty ancestral pride . . . stemmed not from courage and honor but from wrong and shame, descended to him." On this day he refused to lie in the same bed with the Negro boy, and when he tried to make amends a month later by eating with the Beauchamps, he was served at the table alone. " 'Are you ashamed to eat when I eat?' he cried. Henry paused, turning his head a little to speak in the voice slow and without heat: 'I aint ashamed of nobody,' he said peacefully. 'Not even me.' "

Intruder in the Dust is essentially a competition in pride between the white boy Charles Mallison and the elderly Negro, Lucas Beauchamp. The boy finds that Lucas is a worthy antagonist who can fill him with "frantic shame and anguish, and need not for revenge, vengeance but simply for re-equalization, reaffirmation of his masculinity and his white blood." It is therefore not a humanitarian motive which impels him to save from lynching the old Negro who is accused of shooting a white man and who is too proud to defend himself openly. Charles is simply driven by self-respect and by pride in his race to steal out under cover of night with only a terrified Negro boy and an elderly maiden lady as his accomplices, in order to dig up the victim's body—a dangerous venture which ultimately exposes the real murderer.

In the person of mixed birth Faulkner sees the whole drama of racial relations, the attractions and repulsions, the pride and the shame, reduced to basic nonpartisan human terms. Both Joe Christmas and Charles Etienne Bon spend their lives in unceasing, fanatical violence, asserting their white blood against Negroes and their black blood against white men. But their struggle is a futile one. Like Sam Fathers, son of an Indian chief and a quadroon slave, each of them is "himself his own battleground, the scene of his own vanquishment and the mausoleum of his defeat."

It is precisely their tragedy that their ambiguous status severs these persons of mixed blood from race, community and family. Most of Faulkner's characters derive their meaning from the group to which they are bound by tacit loyalty and an unwritten code. Such is the intangible fraternity of barnstormers in *Pylon* (1935). Most important, however, is that large but distinct social entity, the South itself, whose integrating principle the Northerner Shreve McCannon tries to analyze in *Absalom! Absalom!:* "What is it? something you live and breathe in like air? a kind of vacuum filled with wraithlike and indomitable anger and pride and glory at and in happenings that occurred and ceased fifty years ago?" To which the Southerner, Quentin Compson, replies, "You can't understand it. You would have to be born there."

The family as the vehicle of this regional heritage is the most important social unit in Faulkner's fiction, and among the several families he has created, the most romantically conceived are the Sartorises. The novel *Sartoris* (1929), which introduced this line, also brought it to extinction, or at least narrowed it to the one male heir, the infant Benbow Sartoris. Young Bayard, the hero of the tale, and his twin brother John have served as fighter pilots in World War I; John has been killed in combat and Bayard returns as a heavily marked member of the Lost Generation. This post-war disillusionment is no more convincingly tragic in *Sartoris* than it was in Faulkner's first novel *Soldiers' Pay* (1926). In both, the self-pity beneath the callow cynicism is apparent.

Sartoris, however, marks an important early transition in Faulkner's career; it shows him finding his proper material, for the fatality which pursues the younger Sartorises follows the heroic Southern family tradition. John was shot down because he deliberately attacked the German Fokkers in an airplane which he knew was vastly inferior. Bayard, after flirting with danger in various guises through the course of the book, finds the destruction he apparently desires when he undertakes to fly an experimental airplane which no one else will fly. According to the aged Aunt Jenny (Sartoris) Du Pre, who ought to know, the reckless daring and violent end of these young men can be taken as typical of the male Sartorises in any period.

The Sound and the Fury (1929) traces the decay rather than the mere destruction of a family. Unlike the Sartorises, who suffer no decline in family honor, all the twentieth-century Compsons are cursed with moral failure, each in a different way. The father, a lawyer without a practice, sells off the Compson land bit by bit while reading the Latin poets and drinking himself to death. The mother is a petulant, self-made invalid who regards the failings of her children as maliciously calculated to make her suffer.

But the curse falls most heavily upon the son, Quentin, because of the terrible significance for the family which he finds in the moral degradation of his sister Candace. When he learns, first, that she is to be married to a man he thinks unworthy of her and then, later, that she is already pregnant with another man's child, he suddenly sees her as "the frail doomed vessel" of the family's pride "and the foul instrument of its disgrace." The incestuous dream she inspires in him is incest only in a figurative sense: the pride of family turning in upon itself, a pathological concern for the family purity. In him the Compson history is distorted into a narcissistic love of death, and he ends his life, not as a Sartoris would do it— by a deed of impossible daring—but by simply drowning himself. As for Candace, it is the measure of her doom that she can feel no family responsibility whatever for her behavior although she loves and respects her brother Quentin.

Jason (IV) Compson suffers the least, yet he is the most ignobly cursed of all. Because he lives only for his own material advantage, in him the Compson tradition is inverted: he views himself as a suffering hero, the persecuted victim of the family. He was not sent to Harvard as Quentin was; he has to support his mother, his idiot brother and a houseful of lazy, shiftless "niggers"; and the scandalous conduct of Candace and her daughter reflects on his good name. This paranoiac picture Jason transfers to the world at large. When he loses money on the stock exchange he is being cheated by New York Jews; he will not trust his painfully acquired savings to any bank; he believes that his employer is always taking unfair advantage of him and that his job as a store clerk is beneath him.

The youngest child, the idiot Benjamin, sums up symbolically the decay of the Compson lineage. All of the other children are brought into relationship with him, each in a significant way. When he is rechristened, it is Quentin who gives him his new name: "(Benjamin, our lastborn, sold into Egypt.)" The sale of Benjy's pasture provides money for Quentin's year at Harvard and for Candace's wedding. Candace is the one human being he deeply loves, and thus he duplicates, on a primitive level, the family narcissism of Quentin. Finally, it is Jason who, hating the Compson family, has Benjy gelded and after the mother's death has him at once committed to a state asylum. Therefore it is appropriate that Benjamin should suggest the title for the book: in his bellowing, described as "the grave hopeless sound of all voiceless misery under the sun,"

173

the Compson story becomes "a tale . . . full of sound and fury signifying nothing."

As I Lay Dying (1930), the novel that followed *The Sound and the Fury,* is complementary to it, for the Bundrens, simple pine hill farmers of the Frenchman's Bend region, with no illustrious line to live up to, exceed themselves as the Compsons fall below themselves. "I aint got no people," Anse assures Addie when he comes courting her; "so that won't be no worry to you." Addie has relatives in Jefferson, she says, but "They're in the cemetery." Yet after Addie's death, Anse and the children are determined to carry out her request that she be buried with her own people. As an individual, each retains his own measure of ignorance and folly, his own selfish interests. Only as a group, in their dedication to the family mission, do the Bundrens reach out beyond themselves, macabre and preposterous as the mission becomes before it is accomplished. The current of motivation runs deep; they do not talk among themselves about what they are doing and they cannot explain it to outsiders. "I give her my word," is all that Anse, the family spokesman, can offer.

Because one of the sons, Darl, trying to end the gruesome expedition, sets fire to the barn where the coffin is resting temporarily, the other Bundrens turn upon him and sacrifice him with scarcely a qualm. He is the most intelligent and articulate member of the family and it is therefore ironic that they succeed in having him committed to the insane asylum. To them, however, with their solemn single-mindedness, the irony is not apparent.

In *Absalom! Absalom!* (1936) a man who comes of humble people like the Bundrens tries to found a planter family like the Compsons and Sartorises. For Quentin Compson who tells it to his Harvard roommate, there is a terrible significance in this story of Thomas Sutpen who suddenly appeared in Jefferson in 1833, tore a plantation out of the nearby wilderness, married Ellen Coldfield by whom he had a son and a daughter, and then thirty years later found his "great design" frustrated by ironic coincidence. Quentin suffers this history of Sutpen's Hundred as a part of his very being, not only because there are parallels between it and the Compson story, but because it brings out the flaws, the cruelty and the presumption, of the whole Southern aristocratic pattern. The pride of family and of class which appears in the Sartorises under the appealing guise of Cavalier gallantry appears in Sutpen as demonic ruthlessness, as a cold, compulsive ferocity.

The destruction of the Sutpen family is synchronized with the destruction of the South in the Civil War, and there is a moral as well as a temporal connection. Like the Southern planter reviewing his failure to found and maintain an aristocratic society, Thomas Sutpen as he contemplates the defeat of his scheme to found a genteel family cannot see the irony as retribution. His failure is due, he believes, to "a minor tactical mistake," although he cannot discover what it was. His sister-in-law, however, has another view: "But that our cause, our very life and future hopes and past pride, should have been thrown into the balance with men like that [Sutpen] to buttress it—men with valor and strength but without pity or honor. Is it any wonder that Heaven saw fit to let us lose?" Wash Jones, the humble squatter who had habitually looked up to Sutpen and his kind as gods, was also disillusioned at last; "for the first time in his life," Quentin's father believes, "he began to comprehend how it had been possible for Yankees or any other army to have whipped them—the gallant, the proud, the brave; the acknowledged and chosen best among them all to bear the courage and honor and pride."

The Sutpen story compels Quentin to suffer his predicament as a Southerner but it cannot force him to repudiate his Southern heritage. The novel ends with Quentin's vehement declaration that he does not hate the South. As if to vindicate Quentin's assertion—and his own as well—Faulkner returned in his next book, *The Unvanquished* (1938), to the glamorous Sartorises. This is not actually a novel but a series of heroic episodes told by Bayard Sartoris (the elder) as his own eyewitness account of events during and immediately after the Civil War.

The Hamlet (1940), a kind of picaresque chronicle, is Faulkner's fullest account of yet another family, the Snopeses,

175

which he had introduced eleven years before in *Sartoris*. Although the Snopeses, too, have long been in the land, they remain outside the pattern which includes Faulkner's other families: there is not enough family dignity among them—with a few exceptions—even to be betrayed or distorted. All that moves them is their mean preoccupation with material gain, and they band together only to exploit the community. Individually they exploit each other as well. As Flem Snopes, the leader of the clan, gradually takes over Will Varner's control of Frenchman's Bend, and his relatives appear on the heels of his triumphs, Faulkner makes clear again and again that no genuine family feeling exists among them. However, the way in which Flem starts his own family most plainly indicates how greed has supplanted pride in the new aristocracy which he represents. When he learns that Will Varner's unmarried daughter Eula is pregnant, he offers to marry her—at his own price. This step is his final triumph in Frenchman's Bend, his "usurpation of an heirship."

A historical degeneration is shown in Flem's acquisition, through his marriage, of the Old Frenchman's Place, the ruins of a pre-Civil War mansion. Yet it does not reach its final degradation until the later period of *Sanctuary* (1931), when it is converted into the bootlegging establishment where Popeye commits two of his crimes. From Flem Snopes' greed to the gangster mentality of Popeye is but a short, logical step. Both men stand for a new order and an alien one, an order made possible only by the self-destruction of the Sartorises and the moral default of the Compsons. Neither Flem nor Popeye can understand what the Old Frenchman's Place is a relic of, because neither could have understood the Confederate Soldier, Charles Bon, when he said, "if you haven't got honor and pride, then nothing matters."

Much has been made, especially by his detractors, of Faulkner's "naturalism"—his alleged amoral attitude, his supposed interest in the sensational, the abnormal and the sensual for their own sake. But as the contours of his total intention have emerged more and more clearly with each new work, this question of his naturalism has become less and less relevant. All that can be said is that he has chosen to write of the South in a manner more like that of his best contemporaries and immediate predecessors than that of Thomas Nelson Page or of John Pendleton Kennedy. His serious attempt to create an image of the Southern situation with imaginative fullness and truth has required, in his view, a certain naturalistic emphasis. As one of Faulkner's Southern characters contemplates "that people from which he sprang and among whom he lives," he sees (in *Light in August*, 1932) that they "can never take either pleasure or catastrophe or escape from either, without brawling over it. Pleasure, ecstasy, they cannot seem to bear: their escape from it is in violence, in drinking and fighting and praying; catastrophe, too, the violence identical and apparently inescapable."

Faulkner has also been criticized for "romantic" excesses. In this perspective his work is seen as sensational melodrama, a twentieth-century chamber of Gothic horrors. But despite the lyrical subjectivity which broods over his scenes of violence, they are too concretely realized to be confused with the veiled enormities of the romantic imagination. There are many horrors in Faulkner's books and they are artfully managed to produce a maximum impression. But they do not occur in the vacuum of mere effects, whether romantic or naturalistic. In fact, his horrors are memorable exactly for the reason that they arouse the sense of moral outrage.

There are those characters in several of Faulkner's novels who are peripheral to the action but whose sensitivities register the burden of the story. These characters are as different from each other as Horace Benbow in *Sanctuary*, Quentin Compson in *Absalom! Absalom!*, Hightower in *Light in August*, Ratliff in *The Hamlet*, Gavin Stevens and his nephew in *Intruder in the Dust*, but the role they play is the same. Each acts not only as a center of consciousness but as a center of conscience. He not only is fully aware of the situation developed by the events in the story, he *suffers* it.

The moral intensity which gives to Faulkner's best fiction its distinctive esthetic quality brings it closer to classical tragedy than to any other literature. The fables which the Athenian tragedians used were certainly as sensational as Faulkner's. The Thyestean banquet, matricide, infanticide, suicide, incest—these were the "unnatural" matters around which their plays revolved. But to call their work, on this account, mere exploitation of the pathological and morbid would be to confuse raw material with subject, the particulars with the essence. Basing his dictum upon the practice of the best tragedians he knew, Aristotle urged the aspiring poet to look for the situation in which "the tragic incident occurs within the circle of those who are bound by natural ties." Perhaps one reason for the resemblance of Faulkner's matter to that of Greek tragedy is that "the blood relationship," in Malcolm Cowley's words, "is central in his novels." Like the plays of Aeschylus, Sophocles and Euripides, Faulkner's stories are arranged in mythic-historical family cycles, though unlike the Greek playwrights he has created his own legendary houses.

Faulkner has learned what every good tragedian knows, that sheer violence, if ethically conceived, can of itself attain a kind of sublimity simply because it reaches beyond the capacity for mere indignation. At this level the agent shrinks to insignificance before the chasm of evil itself which he reveals. What the motives of the monstrous Iago were or what happens to him have become relatively unimportant at the end of *Othello*. Only if he were a lesser villain in a tamer action would we demand to see his punishment with our own eyes. Similarly the violence depicted in *Light in August* and in *Sanctuary* defies the conventional procedures, legal or poetic, by which the desire for justice might be satisfied, and the reader is forced to gaze upon the inhuman essence of human evil.

The range and subtlety of Faulkner's literary art could be conveyed only through a detailed study of each of his major novels. Such a brief general review of his work as this can do no more than suggest his virtuosity. Almost every one of his novels shows something new in the way of technique. In nearly every instance the method of development is appropriate to the material. For example, it is probably his use of a series of testimonials by witnesses including the Bundrens as well as outsiders which saves the essentially preposterous story of *As I Lay Dying* from comic-strip caricature. His different ways of handling the problem of point of view, his recurrent images, even his proper names—each of these could be made the subject of an extended study.

Faulkner's most radical experiments belong to his earlier novels; in his later work he has become more simple and more direct. In this respect he is self-interpretative, his later stories constituting a gloss upon his earlier ones. As for style, *Light in August* marks a high point between ascending and descending tendencies. In his novels before this one his style seems too studied or self-conscious or imitative; in his work after this time he often seems too reckless, sometimes even contemptuous of style.

Through all the wealth of his technical experiments appear two elementary and time-honored virtues of the story-teller's art. One is his ability, as Caroline Gordon has observed, to create a variety of characters. Even his minor characters are clearly and distinctively personalized. Perhaps for this reason a minor character in one book is so easily and consistently converted into a major character in a later story. In addition, however, Faulkner has been able to amalgamate his individuals into a community. He has created the Sartorises, the Sutpens, the Bundrens, the Snopeses and the others, and out of them he has also created Jefferson and Yoknapatawpha.

Secondly, Faulkner is not only able but is willing to tell a story in the conventional sense. Apparently he does not feel that a well-wrought plot artfully contrived to induce and maintain suspense is a degradation of his art. Only one of his novels, his second, *Mosquitoes* (1927), is conceived of as an impressionistic "slice of life." It is not surprising that in his last book he has made a detective out of his county attorney, Gavin Stevens; most of his novels, like the greatest of Dostoevsky's, can be read on a literal level as mystery stories.

Appropriate to the heroic ideal which is a part of their Southern inheritance is the stoic virtue of many of Faulkner's characters, their will to endure. The Negro in Faulkner is consistently notable for "his capacity to wait and endure and survive." The Canadian Shreve McCannon believes "that in time the Jim Bonds [i.e., the mulattoes] are going to conquer the western hemisphere . . . and so in a few thousand years, I who regard you will also have sprung from the loins of African kings." Lucas Beauchamp, a Negro with a strain of aristocratic white blood in him, seems to anticipate this raceless race to come. In his serene aloofness he is a new type clearly distinguished from Faulkner's earlier man of mixed blood. "Instead of being at once the battleground and victim of the two strains" as Joe Christmas and Charles Etienne Bon were, Lucas "was a vessel, durable, ancestryless, nonconductive, in which the toxin and its anti stalemated one another . . ." He was *intact and complete, contemptuous . . . of all blood black white yellow or red, including his own."*

In his patience, his "desire to endure because he loved the old few simple things which no one wanted to take from him," the Negro has been a better Southerner than many of the whites. For it has been the peculiar mission and burden of Yoknapatawpha to preserve itself, bearing its guilt and shame as well as its virtue and honor, despite the Civil War which was intended to destroy it and the glittering rewards which have since seduced many of its citizens into betraying it. Out of the stubborn refusal to remain vanquished, out of the struggle and travail has survived something of unique value to "a mass of people who no longer have anything in common save a frantic greed for money."

This stone which the builders rejected is nothing less than Yoknapatawpha itself. As Gavin Stevens explains in *Intruder in the Dust* (1948):

We alone in the United States . . . are a homogeneous people . . . Only a few of us know that only from homogeneity comes anything of a people or for a people of durable and lasting value—the literature, the art, the science, that minimum of government and police which is the meaning of freedom and liberty, and perhaps most valuable of all a national character worth anything in a crisis . . .

But Yoknapatawpha transcends national as well as regional boundaries. When Faulkner depicts the Southern psyche with its moral obliquities, complexities and conflicting impulses, he dramatizes at the same time the whole cultural predicament of the twentieth century. Perhaps he is more thoroughly appreciated in Europe than in America because there the modern dilemmas have been more fully experienced and a longer historical memory gives deeper resonance to his heroic overtones.

Faulkner's only novel of romantic love, *The Wild Palms* (1939), follows closely the tradition of the grand passion which goes back to the Troubadours and the Courts of Love. The ardor which joins his lovers is illicit, irrevocable, at once erotic and transcendental. In other words, it is the dark passion of that orthodox kind described by Denis de Rougemont which leads logically to death as its consummation. Yet Harry Wilbourne after he has been sentenced to a long prison term at hard labor for the attempted abortion which killed his lover, refuses the invitation given him to join her in the union of death; *"between grief and nothing,"* he resolves, *"I will take grief."*

This is the same conclusion McCaslin Edmonds comes to in the story "The Old People":

> "Think of all that has happened here, on this earth. All the blood hot and strong for living, pleasuring, that has soaked back into it. For grieving and suffering too, of course, but still getting something out of it for all that, getting a lot out of it, because after all you dont have to continue to bear what you believe is suffering . . . And even suffering and grieving is better than nothing . . ."

Then Edmonds adds what Harry Wilbourne must also have believed: " 'there is only one thing worse than not being alive, and that's shame.' "

In Faulkner's writings, as in all tragedy, the worth of human life is grimly tested, but the final verdict is by no means

181

grounds for despair. His novels are probably not appropriate reading for children—"children" of any age. "For every one that is a partaker of milk, is unskilful in the word of justice: for he is a little child. But strong meat is for the perfect; for them who by custom have their senses exercised to the discerning of good and evil." [2]

Faulkner offers "strong meat" indeed, but for the practiced and the discriminating he provides such sustenance as it is hard for them to find elsewhere in modern American fiction.

[2] *Hebrews*, V, 13, 14. Those who have doubted the firmly ethical center of Faulkner's vision of life must have been puzzled by the speech he gave in Stockholm on December 10, 1950, when he received the Nobel Prize. "I decline," he said on that occasion, "to accept the end of man. . . . He is immortal . . . because he has a soul, a spirit capable of compassion and sacrifice and endurance. The poet's, the writer's, duty is to write about these things." But the reader should see the speech in its entirety. (Cf. *The New York Herald Tribune* "Books," Jan. 14, 1951, p. 5.)

Ernest Hemingway:
The Missing Third Dimension

MICHAEL F. MOLONEY

THE PUBLICATION of the slight and flaccid *Across the River and into the Trees* (1950) will not affect Hemingway's historic position as the most considerable figure in American fiction in the past quarter of a century. Even among those whose admiration is qualified there is no inclination to doubt the sharpness of his impact on the current literary scene. Reputations, of course, may be established by various means. The endorsement of the idols of the *coteries* can do much to win a hearing for a young writer, and this came early to Hemingway from two of the most legendary of Olympians—Gertrude Stein and Ezra Pound. The ability to hit off the popular taste before that taste has become quite aware of itself can be a weighty factor and the myriad synthetic Hemingways who have followed in the master's wake testify to something more than the extravagance of his success. Yet, beyond cavil, the severest evaluation of this writer, if it be honest, cannot be unaware of his formidable powers.

Here is neither the place nor the moment for a lengthy excursion into critical theory, but it is perhaps permissible to restate the ancient and unchallengeable truism that every art seeks to mirror the eternal in the temporal, the generic in the specific. It does not matter whether the writer be a classicist or a romanticist by conviction. It does not even matter whether he be an intellectualist or a sensist by profession. In every true artist the *daimon* will triumph over the limitations of faith. For the true artist is an indefatigable searcher for what W. K. Wimsatt, Jr. has called "the concrete universal," that is, for the graphic illustration of that experience which, while occurring in a particular time or a particular place, has a relevance that transcends these. Only by some such theory as this can art possess perennial value; only by some such supposition can the cultural heritage of one epoch be meaningful to a succeeding epoch.

What then are some of the universals to be found in Hemingway's writing? One characteristic note which links him with authors so various as Homer and Louis Bromfield is his love of the good earth, of cool streams, of clean air, of the fresh smell of woodlands, of the challenge of the long hike, of hunger bred in the open air. It is the tug of these primeval things which annually lures yearning tens of thousands from bench and desk to the forests of Maine, the trout streams of Michigan and Wisconsin and the mountains of Oregon. Without question, in this phenomenon there is testimony to the artificiality of modern urban life, a kind of instinctive admission that man is a creature of earth and Antaeus-like derives his strength and physical well-being from intimate contact with her.

Hemingway's treatment of the urge behind the phenomenon is, to be sure, never crudely sociological. Instead, he is a poet with fine awareness of the manifold impressions of sight and sound and smell and taste, a poet for whom the Michigan hemlock forests of his boyhood are forever at the tips of his senses. Nick Adams, in "Big Two-Hearted River," seeing ahead "the far blue hills that marked the Lake Superior height of land," smelling the crushed sweet fern under his pack straps, savoring "the juice syrup of the apricots," listening as the buckwheat cakes "sputtered in the pan," attests to the existence of what Wordsworth called the "grand elementary principle of pleasure" in the universe.

And Nick Adams is typical of Hemingway's later heroes. His bullfighters like "the smell of the stables about the patio de caballos" and Robert Jordan revels in "the clear night air of the mountains that smelled of the pines and of the dew on the grass in the meadow by the stream." This is, without question, Hemingway's basic affirmation. I am not concerned at the moment with its inadequacy as a philosophy of life or as an esthetic principle. As far as it goes it is a positive thing and it orientates Hemingway loosely with those romantics who place their faith in the illumined senses.

A second inescapable virtue of Hemingway is his tragic sense. This may well be the weightiest factor in his craft. To possess the tragic vision is not easy for the contemporary writer. As Joseph Wood Krutch has brilliantly pointed out, the tragic fall demands of the hero a largeness of spirit, a comprehensiveness of destiny, which the scientism of the twentieth century has denied to mankind. It has been eloquently argued that tragedy is equally impossible in a culture completely dominated by the Christian view—that since the Christian vision is of man's ultimate and certain triumph it was in the nature of things for the greatest literary monument of the Christian Middle Ages to be styled a *Commedia*.

To the proponents of this theory the great age of Greece and the sixteenth-century English Renaissance were as inevitably true periods of tragedy. In the first the accepted majesty of human endeavor was overshadowed by the unanswered questions of human fate; in the second, the serenity of the Christian synthesis had been thwarted by intestine defection and external assault.

It is a tribute to Hemingway that in so hostile a period he has kept his mastery of the tragic spirit. True, he does it at the expense of obvious strain. The "hard-boiled" atmosphere of the Hemingway fiction is there very likely because the author feels the futility of tragic differentiation in subdued colors within an experiential area so limited as that of modern man. Hence his palette frequently takes on a hard, if not nightmarish, quality. But despite this he is surprisingly consistent in suggesting and in maintaining the tragic tone.

In "The Snows of Kilimanjaro" there is tragedy of a high order which is only remotely connected with the gangrenous death of the hero. This story, though greatly admired, is, perhaps, on the whole, too contrived. If the dream of the rescue at the end is a trick which comes off well, the feverish recollection of snow on Bulgarian mountains, in the Gauertal, on the Madlener-Haus hints at too glossy a finish. But the dying hero's review of his wasted talents and wasted hopes is finely tragic in a way rare in modern literature. The heart of the matter is not that death has cut short a promising career. The true tragedy is antecedent to the hero's physical death. It is the tragedy of a man who lacked the courage to reject the world—symbolized by the life of ease he had been living—that he might save his soul—symbolized by his artistic gifts. Death brings him clarity of insight into himself and he realizes with something of the pathos of Marlowe's Dr. Faustus that the hour of repentance is past. Thus conceived, the story is a secular morality play.

Tragic, too, is the presentation of Manuel, the superannuated bullfighter in "The Undefeated," from the collection, *Men Without Women* (1927). What, after all, is the theme of this story but the man-against-time thesis which, with a thousand permutations, runs through Western literature from Homer to Herrick, from Horace to Housman. Manuel has known the great triumphs of the bull ring. He is old now. He retains the unquestioned style of the supreme artist but the coordination of hand and eye which youth alone can give has departed. Still, his is the high courage which will ask no favors and make no concessions. It cannot be very far wrong to find in Manuel's last fight Hemingway's symbol of man's endless struggle against the flux of circumstance.

For the most part, the sureness of Hemingway's tragic touch is in inverse proportion to the length of the work. In *To Have and Have Not* (1937), the end of Harry Morgan is scarcely tragic since tragedy demands awareness on the part of the protagonist and Morgan's awareness is on the instinctive rather than truly human level. In a *Farewell to Arms* (1929), likewise, there is no profound tragic appeal in the main plot. The relationship of Lieutenant Henry and Catherine Barkley in this, the most famous novel to come out of World War I, scarcely rises above the physical. Even in death Catherine is only the trapped animal. Her world is a world of two dimensions only—of muscular and nervous reaction. There is a poignancy in the famous conclusion of the book as there is in the scene where Catherine gives Lieutenant Henry the St. Anthony medal in the efficacy of which she does not believe, but poignancy is not to be identified with the tragic vision itself.

In *For Whom the Bell Tolls* (1940), the tragic tone is much better sustained. The description of the end of Robert Jordan is carefully and deftly done, but it is not the best thing in the book. And the presentation of El Sordo's last battle, marvelously good though it is in detail, strikes one reader—it may be unjustifiably—as somehow Hollywoodish in its over-all effect. But throughout the narrative there are numerous points of genuine tragic interest. The irreconcilable struggle between selfish and selfless impulses, between vanity and humility, between cowardice and courage, is of the essence of tragedy and Hemingway has portrayed that struggle vividly. His presentation of the deterioration of Pablo is one major triumph, that of the death of old Anselmo another.

Just as an enormous vitality and a grasp of the tragic dimensions of life are important elements in Hemingway's work, so his narrative gift, which like his tragic immediacy is best illustrated in his short stories, is not less significant. In an age where bad writing has been the rule rather than the exception, the contemporary short story has probably produced more sound craftsmanship than any other genre, and Hemingway has been among the most conscientious of its practitioners. Indeed, it is difficult to think of him at his best other than as a short-story writer. The longer works, on careful reading, tend to disintegrate into component parts. This is true necessarily of *The Sun Also Rises* (1926), which is picaresque in organization. It is true also of *To Have and Have Not*. *A Farewell to Arms* is likewise highly episodic. Only *For Whom the Bell Tolls* seems organically constructed and even here it is startling to see how many sections, when disengaged, can stand by themselves.

Certain peaks of Hemingway's narrative form stand out above the consistently high level of his achievement. "The Killers" has been widely anthologized, as well as adapted to cinematic treatment. "The Short Happy Life of Francis Macomber" has also drawn Hollywood's eye. "The Snows of Kilimanjaro" has been called Hemingway's "most accomplished" if not best piece of writing by Malcolm Cowley. "My Old Man" from *In Our Time* (1924) has been justly admired as has the companion piece, "Big Two-Hearted River." From the novels Cowley has included in the *Portable Hemingway*, Harry Morgan's last adventure from *To Have and Have Not*, the Caporetto episode from *A Farewell to Arms* and El Sordo on the hilltop from *For Whom the Bell Tolls*.

Several factors contribute to Hemingway's narrative power. One of the most important, unquestionably, is the clipped, athletic march of his sentences. The bare bleakness of the conversation in "The Killers" is an extreme example (here admirably adapted to the speakers) of this trait. But, in general, all of Hemingway's characters talk alike. The manner of their speech is the straightforward assertion or the simple question without syntactical qualification, whether they be gangsters or laborers or decadent aristocrats or Italian or Spanish or American soldiers. Psychologically, Hemingway is right. In real life the incipient poetry which shows beneath the speech of his Spaniards must occasionally break into circumlocution. But Hemingway's fictional world, whatever its locale, is the deadly, stale, monotonous world of modern positivism and modern industrialism from which all spiritual leaven has been removed and he is consistent in giving a universal flatness to the speech of his characters.

The simplicity of Hemingway's style, as numerous imitators have learned and as more than one critic has pointed out, is deceiving. His assumption of the illiterate pose is, of course, only a pose. Back of it lies a hard discipline which has forced intractible words to conform to a pre-conceived pattern. One may legitimately question the accuracy of his ear for the nuances of speech, but the fact remains that the kind of effect he wants he superbly achieves. And in passing it may be observed that when Hemingway deserts this style for Steinesque cadences, as notably in *Death in the Afternoon* (1932), or for the more ambitious roll of Ciceronian rhetoric, as in the *Green Hills of Africa* (1935), he loses his mastery. In the one his muscular muse has donned an ill-fitting dinner jacket; in the other his schoolboy oratory is rank fustian.

Closely integrated with Hemingway's syntax is his language. The assault upon poetic diction which the nineteenth-century romantics had led had been only a relative thing, for literature throughout the nineteenth century remained a matter of the genteel tradition. But World War I ended all that. For good or for bad there has since been no washing of the materials of literature through the filter of a traditional culture. The writers of today have not only decided what their own literary standards are to be but they have remade even the ancients, who have struck their fancy, in their own image. How else account for their admiration for the seventeenth-century metaphysicals so remote from them in learning, in ideals, and in technique? Hemingway as much as any other man has put the raw language of the street, the poolroom, the barracks and the brothel into modern literature. Again, on artistic grounds alone, his judgment has been admirable. The bareness of his sentences has been heightened by the starkness of his speech.

A final significant element in Hemingway's narrative appeal is his grasp of the essentially dramatic. By dramatic effect is meant his ability to keep the reader's interest steadily focussed on the central characters and on the great scenes not through technical manipulation but through the simple inevitability with which the narrative is unfolded. Every great novelist has this dramatic gift. Of the nineteenth-century English novelists it was pre-eminent in Meredith and this alone will almost certainly win Meredith a rehearing despite the low ebb of his current reputation. Hardy, too, possessed it in full measure but like Dickens, although for different reasons, he was apt to allow the dramatic to degenerate into the theatrical. Thackeray had an unerring dramatic instinct despite a temperament that led him to excesses. Of contemporary American novelists aside from Hemingway, Steinbeck and Faulkner are outstanding for this power.

With Hemingway this dramatic sense is always present. As a striking example of it, Chapter XXI of *For Whom the Bell Tolls* may be cited. The time is daybreak, the scene a mountain-side. The appearance of the cavalryman signalizes the end of the respite which Robert Jordan and his little band have enjoyed. What follows is recounted with superb economy. The shooting of the Navarrese, the preparations for the attack and, in the center of the scene, Robert and Maria: the man now concerned only with war and its demands; the girl unable to understand that the grim business of killing or being killed has displaced her in his thoughts. It is possible that Hemingway's insight into the mind of neither the man nor the girl is unexceptionable, but purely as a piece of technique the chapter is magnificently executed.

These then are Hemingway's solid assets: a poet's awareness of the beauty of the universe in which man's too fleeting hour is spent; an almost exaggerated consciousness of the unending struggle, both internal and external, to which man is committed; a mastery of syntax and diction which always reveals and never beclouds his other virtues; a sure eye for the dramatic scene and an unfailing ability to reproduce it. It will be immediately evident that these virtues are heavily weighted on the technical side.

And what of Hemingway's defects? They are many and obvious and, like his virtues, they are closely related to his age. The world of which Hemingway writes is the world which has experienced a final disillusionment with the promises of Renaissance humanism. We are still close enough to a dead era to smile understandingly at the eulogy of Francis Bacon in the *Dictionary of National Biography:* "He stood, like a prophet, on the verge of the promised land, bidding men leave without regret, the desert which lay behind them, and enter with joyfulness and hopefulness on the rich inheritance that was spread out before them." These words, written more than fifty years ago, show, by their phrasal mockery of the Scriptural promise of heavenly rewards, how superbly confident modern man then was of re-entering the earthly paradise. Amid the frustrations of the twentieth century they have an ironic ring. Yet they luminously call attention to the pitiless logic of history whereby the Christian humanism of More and Erasmus shaded in the course of three hundred years into the atheistic humanism of Feuerbach and Nietzsche, from the latter of whom Hemingway would seem unquestionably to derive.

For Feuerbach God was only a myth expressing the aspirations of the human conscience. To explain his theory Feuerbach had recourse to the Hegelian concept of *alienation*, though using it in a sense quite different from Hegel's. *Alienation*, he explained, involves the subtraction from man, for the benefit of an illusory reality, of certain attributes belonging to his essence. Human attributes such as wisdom, will, justice and love are objectified by man in a fantastic being, the pure product of his imagination, which he calls God.

Although Nietzsche referred contemptuously to Feuerbach, he was indebted to the latter through the mediation of Schopenhauer and Wagner. For Nietzsche, too, God was only the mirror of man. The objectification of man's noblest traits in an external Being resulted, he believed, only in the degradation of man and this degradation was pushed to the ultimate extreme in Christianity. For in Christianity all virtue, all greatness of soul, all truth are considered the gifts of grace. Nietzsche's own atheism, he insisted in his *Ecce Homo,* was instinctive, not reasoned. Be that as it may, there can be little doubt that his ecstatic enunciation of the "death of God" was an important agent in the quickening of the nihilistic forces which in two world wars reduced the old liberal world to ruins.

The philosophy of Hemingway scarcely suggests academic sources, although in such a writer—so strange a mingling of

191

the intellectual and the sensuous—one can never be certain. But whether directly or indirectly acquired, his works reveal a rather systematic application of Nietzsche's principles. The superman in action, the conflict of the Apollonian and Diony-sian ideals, the substitution of new myths for the old faith, all these find their explication in his writings.

Like the Nietzschean superman, the heroes of Hemingway live in a world beyond moral good and evil. An obvious aspect of this truth is found in the free sexual relations of his men and women. Lady Brett, of the early *The Sun Also Rises*, "common as the way between Saint Alban's and London," may be taken as a convenient illustration of Hemingway's atti-tude toward sex. She is a creature of appetites which she makes no pretense of controlling, indeed, seems unable to control. She passes from one man to another with a casualness com-plete and unself-conscious. Desired by many men, she is ap-parently incapable of deep attachment herself. The explana-tion of her thwarted relation to Jake Barnes, if it is meant to motivate her actions (I do not think it is so meant) fails of its purpose. Her sexual function (like that of all of Hem-ingway's women including the incredible Renata of *Across the River and Into the Trees*) has no deeper justification than to help while away the tedium of her possessor of the moment. It provides an instant of relief in man's all-enveloping ennui, but as such it is no more significant than the excitement of the bull ring.

Liquor fails equally to break down the emotional impervi-ousness of Hemingway's heroes. From Jake Barnes to Robert Jordan they are heroic drinkers in a singularly joyless man-ner. They are little moved either by their indulgence or by the impending cirrhosis which it invites. Life may be empty but death has no terror. "Do you know that in about thirty-five years more we'll be dead?" asks Robert Cohn in *The Sun Also Rises*. "What the hell, Robert," Jake replies. "What the hell."

This callowness, one of the identifying traits of Heming-way, derives unquestionably from his experience as an ambu-lance driver on the Italian front in World War I and from the subsequent years in Paris where in the 1920's a now famous group of American literary expatriates were attempting to put together the pieces of their shattered personal faiths. One of his admirers has pointed out that in no other author of this age is there "such a profusion of corpses." And Hemingway's characters, in the presence of death, observe admirably the Nietzschean, "Be hard." Lieutenant Henry's farewell to Catherine Barkley, El Sordo's last hours on the hilltop, Ole Andreson's awaiting gangland execution—these are confrontations of death which are not so much philosophically stoical as they are bestially indifferent. The Nietzschean lineage of the Hemingway supermen is clear but from them much of the Nietzschean lyric ecstasy has evaporated.

Moreover, while Hemingway's heroes have the overtones of the Nietzschean superman they also reveal the triumph of the Nietzschean Dionysus over Apollo. One of Père Henri de Lubac's good services has been to point out (in *Le Drame de L'Humanisme Athée*) that in the beginning, at the time of writing *Die Geburt der Tragödie*, Nietzsche did not see in Dionysus a symbol of a pagan religion specifically opposed to Christianity. "His perspective was then scarcely anti-Christian. It was anti-socratic." It is in this earlier version of Nietzsche's Dionysiac-Socratic antithesis that Hemingway follows the brilliant German. His heroes are men of action rather than thinkers. For Nietzsche the opposition of Apollo and Dionysus could be fruitful. Greek tragedy was the result of the prodigious synthesis of their opposing powers—the serenity of the one and the universal energy of the other. But the Socratic *daimon* was incapable of such compromise. Greek civilization was ruined because eventually Socrates had vanquished Dionysus.

Hemingway's rejection of the Socratic reason has, very likely, no such philosophical justification. Rather, since he came to maturity in the period of World War I, his attitude is, it may be conjectured, a result of the general disillusionment of that period. The political architects of European liberalism, buttressed by the all-embracing doctrine of evolution, had for three generations prior to 1914 confidently charted the course of the future brave new world. When the charts proved illusory and the new world began to come apart at the seams, the gaudy claims of their creators became a mockery. And if reason could be so fallacious, might not the glorification of instinct have much to recommend it? To be sure, at that particular moment Nietzsche was reenforced by Freud. So it is that Hemingway's males are what they are. "I was not made to think," says the hero of *A Farewell to Arms,* but the same is true of Nick Adams and Jake Barnes and Harry Morgan.

In a famous essay written thirty years ago, Mr. T. S. Eliot warned that it is not enough for the man of letters to look in his heart and write. He must also, Mr. Eliot declared, ". . . look into the cerebral cortex, the nervous system, and the digestive tract." That Hemingway has looked into the nervous system and the digestive tract is abundantly evident. He has not, as we have seen, been so concerned with the cerebral cortex.

But even literal adherence to Mr. Eliot's three-fold admonition would not have been enough. The philosophy and literature as well as the history of the past century and a half lead to two concomitant conclusions. First, even the most frenzied romantic exaltation of the ego must finally confess the insufficiency of an ego-centric world. Second, the most enthusiastic proponents of nihilistic doctrines must turn at last to some kind of affirmation. That is to say, wherever man, in the name of freedom, sacredness of personality, or whatever the catch-word of the moment may be, dethrones God to eternize himself, he eventually is forced to look outside himself for the sanction of his divinity. Thus Feuerbach, who declared that the turning point of history would be the moment when man became aware that he alone was God, also insisted that man could not achieve divinity of himself but only by identifying himself with the collective being of society. That affirmation of Feuerbach's more effectively than August Comte's somewhat parallel teaching—more effective because Engels and Marx were among his disciples—enthroned the sociological idol on the central altar of the modern pantheon.

It is interesting to note Hemingway's reaction to this *Zeitgeist*. The testimony of his earlier works fails to reveal any spontaneous social devotion. On the contrary, in most of his central figures prior to *For Whom the Bell Tolls* there is more than a hint of the anti-social. They are lonely personages who have suffered at the hands of their fellow-men and who nurse their wounds and their resentment in a kind of Byronic (or pseudo-Byronic) grandeur. Even Nick Adams, although not anti-social, scarcely yearns for social integration. But like Nietzsche his master who, to facilitate the escape from the Socratic reason, found it necessary to take refuge in myth-making, Hemingway, too, could not entirely escape the myth. Hence when he came to write *For Whom the Bell Tolls* he was caught up in the anti-fascist crusade which provided doctrinal affirmation for the liberals of the 1930's. The issue here is not Hemingway's personal devotion to the popular-front forces in the Spanish Civil War. But devotion to any cause outside themselves was something new for the creatures of Hemingway's pen and the reader may well find in the over-all effect of his most ambitious book something of the *tour de force*.

Here we touch upon Hemingway's basic dilemma. His delight in brawn and ganglion has been repeated with increasing shrillness and monotony. Yet death is never far away in these tales—all his longer works are monodies—and the harsh brittleness with which it is presented is meaningful. We have noted Jake Barnes' swashbuckling on the subject. What is meant to be a more perspicacious approach is found in the comment of the narrator to the old lady in *Death in the Afternoon:* "Madame, there is no remedy for anything in life. Death is a sovereign remedy for all misfortunes and we'd do best to leave off all discoursing now and get to table." Somehow this has a hollow ring as though the author himself were ill at ease with the subject. One recalls, by contrast, the mournful meditation in the *Green Hills of Africa* on the diuturnity of the Gulf Stream whose blueness the Havana garbage scows cannot violate and the conviction comes that here is a longing for something more permanent in human life than the refuse of its sewers.

The judicious reader will not censure Hemingway because the scent of garbage, real as well as metaphorical, invades his pages along with the clean smell of the north woods and the African hills and plains. For man is man, that is, an animal of animals, and he who would write truly of him cannot be unaware of his animality. But for the greatest masters of literature man has always been something more. He is also a spirit, although "a great lob of a spirit," as a philosophical friend likes to put it. The omnipresent symbolism in Hemingway's writing seems to be a confession that this is true. For the utilization of the symbol is an admission that the fact is more than a fact, that behind it lie other planes of meaning and reality. In a strictly logical system of materialistic monism there could be no symbolism.

Hence Hemingway's naturalism is always promising to break through its isolation and to link up with the world of spirit but the promise is never quite achieved. It is this failure which will weigh heaviest against him in the final summing up. He has written that a fourth and fifth dimension are possible in prose. His own prose not only lacks a fourth and fifth dimension; it lacks, for the most part, a third. The obliqueness of his characters derives from his refusal or inability (whether he is the unconscious or willing captive of his age is a nice question) to give evidence to that potential in man which either raises him above or sinks him below the rest of the animal world.

Thomas Wolfe:

A Legend of a Man's Youth in His Hunger

GERARD S. SLOYAN

THERE MAY have been some brief uncertainty in the editor's mind as to which novelists of this century should find a place between these covers, but before the century had run one fourth its course one nomination, at least, had been made, and the candidate chosen by acclaim. Let the victor hint at the genesis of the accolade. He does it in a letter to his mother:

> I think I am inevitable. I think nothing can stop me now but insanity, disease, or death. These are human risks. I am in full bud and this thing inside me is growing beyond control. I don't yet know what I am capable of doing, but, by God, I have genius and I shall yet force the inescapable fact down the throats of the rats and vermin who wait the proof. Well, they shall have it, and may they choke upon it.
>
> Let who will call it conceit:—I will do it or die in the proof. Nothing else matters to me now; the world's my oyster and I will open and know the whole of it.

Should the reader find the objectivity of this judgment unpalatable, or gracefully wish to disqualify himself from among those upon whom the proof is to be forced, let him excuse himself now. But he should in fairness be reminded that Thomas Wolfe has achieved the doubtful eminence of this essay, along with such small tokens as a shelf of literary criticism and the conversion of his boyhood home into a museum, all in the dozen or so years since the dark side of his oyster opened to receive and acquaint him with a part he had not known. It seems doubtful that any of this was done on the strength of his Harvard period chest-thumping alone, from which the above is quoted. Besides, as a sheepish postscript penned to his mother the morning after admitted, some homemade wine had fortified his convictions. *In vino vanitas*, it would appear, when the wine is ill digested, even in such a citadel of truth and good digestion as Pleasantville, New York, whence came the letter of proud boast.

What Wolfe was capable of doing, not all agree. There is, however, the minimum accord exacted by the evidence. The latter consists of two lengthy novels, *Look Homeward, Angel* (1929) and *Of Time and the River* (1936), two more carved posthumously from the carload of manuscript turned over to his literary editor before his death in 1938, *The Web and the Rock* (1939) and *You Can't Go Home Again* (1940), and a fragmentary third member (although chronologically first) of what might have been a trilogy, given the title *The Hills Beyond* (1941). Besides this basic pentateuch there was published in 1936 an honest piece of literary self-examination, *The Story of a Novel,* and in 1935 a collection of short pieces and incidents entitled *From Death to Morning.* The catalog ends with *The Face of a Nation,* a compilation of some of his more lyrical passages, an arrangement of his prose in verse form called *A Leaf, A Stone, A Door,* and a thick volume of letters to his mother, Julia Elizabeth Wolfe, edited by John Skally Terry (1943).

The first two novels came into being as a result of the skillful midwifery of Maxwell Perkins, literary editor of Scribner's, whose faith in the youthful giant never flagged.

He it was who decreed that what had begun as *The October Fair* and grown to twice the length of *War and Peace* was ready—half of it—to break Wolfe's seven lean years of silence since first publication. In the earlier instance, Perkins had said, "All I know is that they cannot let it go, they cannot ignore it. The book will find its way." To Edward C. Aswell of Harpers goes the credit for having given form to the amorphous saga of George Webber, alias Eugene Gant, alias Thomas Wolfe.

The chief drawback to literary criticism is that there has been so much of it. This multiple assay, in turn, has been thoroughly read by some and thoroughly ignored by others, with endless possibilities in between; similarly with the writing it describes. In the light of this diversity of reader background, to whom should the critic's remarks be addressed? Momentarily, to the person unaware that Thomas Wolfe consistently showed himself incapable of any genre save autobiography. He wrote millions of words, not one of them unrelated to the sensations he had experienced, the people he had known, the aspirations he had conceived. While it is a canon of sound writing to tell of what one knows, avoiding all that one is ignorant of, the point to be made about Wolfe is that he seems never to have created a character or contrived a plot.[1] God made the people and things happened to them. Wolfe recorded them, first in his mind and then with his pen. The way in which he did it comprises his art. He reveals in his letters to his mother:

> I find I have become an eavesdropper. I listen to every conversation I hear, I memorize every word I hear people say, in the way they said it. I find myself studying every move, every gesture, every expression, trying to see what it means dramatically.

[1] The one exception to this, and it is a notable one, is the supplying of a full set of maternal ancestors for George Webber in the first 150 pages of *The Hills Beyond*. What it gains in objectivity and restraint, it loses in interest. Some also say that the young Indian hero of Webber's boyhood, Nebraska Crane, had no counterpart in life.

It may come as a surprise to some that the drama was the first art form he attempted. And yet his true ear for conversation betrays an earlier schooling in this discipline. Wolfe exercised no effort whatever in disguising the identity of his characters.[2] A few were composites—very few. The rest appeared as large as life in a Wolfe's-eye view, so much so that Asheville, North Carolina, could complain bitterly that it had all been put in a book, no foible spared, no harshness modified or weakness glossed over. He would change a name here and bestow a characteristic there, but for the most part Tom called them exactly as he saw them, chafing uncomfortably all the while in his third-person role.

There is little problem in determining how the author thinks. His soliloquies, chants and fulminations are on every page, untroubled by the literary niceties that forbid identification of the author with any of his puppets. There is a big company of players and Wolfe takes all the parts, but especially himself as the hulking protagonist of "six feet six in a world of five feet eight." At one time he grew conscious of the jibes of critics concerning his limitations. He countered with the claim (in an author's note to *The Web and the Rock*) that he had undergone a genuine spiritual and artistic change. This novel was a departure from the past, the most objective he had ever written. He struggled through the business of giving George Webber a family background somewhat more checkered than Eugene Gant's or his own, but after two score of pages he is back once more in the realms of introspection and apologia. The "release of inventive power which the more shackling limitations of identifiable autobiography do not permit" never saw the light.

This is not to say that Wolfe underwent no process of maturation. There is in his work a clearly observable movement toward spiritual adulthood, though not many would care

[2] He never ceased to deny this. "I can only assure you that my book is a work of fiction, and that no person, act, or event has been consciously described . . . The world a writer creates is his own world—but is molded out of the fabric of life, what he has known and felt—in short, out of himself." Letter to Mrs. J. M. Roberts, *The Atlantic Monthly*, Jan., 1947.

to say unequivocally that he had achieved it by the time of his death at thirty-seven. He remained always incurably boyish in certain aspects of his thinking. "I suppose I am a greater surprise to myself than to anyone under the sun," the seventeen-year-old could write. "I am changing so rapidly that I find myself an evergrowing source of interest. Sounds egotistical, doesn't it?" Egotistical not only in the sense of self-centered but self-enamored. As the end came on, he deserted the latter preoccupation in good measure but was irrevocably wedded to the former. Page upon page of *The Web and the Rock* is of this mirrored sort:

> This flesh had not betrayed him. It had been strong, enduring, and enormously sensitive within the limitations of its senses. The arms were too long, the legs too short, . . . but they belonged to the family of the earth, they were not deformed. The only deformity had been in the madness and bitterness of his heart. But now he had learned, through a wisdom of the body and the brain, that a spirit which thinks itself too fine for the rough uses of the world is too young and callow, or enamored of the beauties of its own artistic soul and worth to find itself by losing itself in something larger than itself, and thus to find its place and do a man's work in the world—too fine for all of this, and hence defeated, precious, fit for nothing.

The self-analysis is deadly. Yet like his sure touch in dissecting his literary virtues and frailties in *The Story of a Novel,* it led to no notable change. A scrupulous apothecary was Wolfe who mixed the right ingredients in the right way, and then could not find the courage to take the dose. He can hardly be blamed. The sole remedy for his deep-seated unhappiness was to live outside himself, to pursue his happiness in the one only Good, and there is no evidence that he was ever effectively taught that the heart's love is to be found there. He spent thirty-five years multiplying lesser goods, in the expectation that by some sort of magic the sum of finite things might be totted up to infinity.

One of his fictional selves, in the same novel, cries out in a frenzy that he is already old and worn out at twenty-seven, whereas once he had the strength of twenty men, working and reading and traveling with the energy of a great dynamo:

> I wanted to eat the earth, and feed myself with all the books and men and countries in the world. I wanted to know about the lives of all the people, to be everywhere, to see and know everything like a great poet, and I walked and roamed about the streets feeding on everything that the people did or said with a furious hunger that was never satisfied.

His bodily appetites were as limitless: food and drink in Gargantuan supply; the short span of his life measured out in coffee spoons enough to tax the mines of Hidalgo; intimacy with women (the conclusion is escaped hardly) in staggering proportion with all the rest. Yet they failed him. Did he ever come to know why? Or is it restricted to the Christian to gain all by renouncing desire itself?

Another man who drank twenty cups of coffee a day (dead at fifty-one and this the cause, or so his doctor said), a man who deserted love often but never lost faith, was Honoré de Balzac. In his *Pensées et Maximes* a surprising profundity appears. Witness:

> When things in ordinary life have failed to give us happiness, we have to look for it in a superior life, and the key to this new world is the imitation of Jesus Christ . . .

Now what access, if any, Wolfe had to this key is hard to ascertain. In *You Can't Go Home Again* he identifies himself with the great tragic writers of all time whose cup was loneliness. Ecclesiastes epitomizes for him the entire sensitive, brooding clan; the Spokesman, in turn, is embedded in a Testament that is "the most final and profound literature of human loneliness the world has ever known." Christ's way he recognized as far better, a way of love—hence one of joy— and perhaps for that reason not for him. Once there was a brief

202

meeting for him on Calvary. Without attaching too much significance to it, since the rebuff might have been as much the work of third-rate art as of the dying Christ, we can examine the reflections of George Webber, a prisoner and angry, on the Standard of the Nations hanging over him on the hospital wall:

Above the door there was a wooden crucifix, nailed with tormented claws, the splayed, nailed feet, the gaunt ribs, and the twisted thighs, the starved face, and the broken agony of Christ. And that image, so cruel in compassion, so starved, so twisted, and so broken in the paradox of its stern mercy, the fatal example of its suffering, was so alien to Pine Rock, to Joyners, and to Baptistry, to all the forms he knew, that it filled him with a sense of strangeness and uneasy awe.

Its suffering was alien to a few things besides, but to insinuate a connection with Webber's uneasiness is without warrant.

How is one to set down the influences that had a bearing on the peculiar genius of Thomas Wolfe? He found the thing hard to do in five volumes, wherefore five paragraphs may be expected to accomplish nothing at all. The beginning will serve as a convenient starting place.

On October 3, 1900, the boy was born of William Oliver and Julia Elizabeth Wolfe in Asheville, North Carolina. The father was of Pennsylvania Dutch stock, the mother of that pioneer race absurdly known as Scotch-Irish, a term without meaning except that everyone knows what it means. He was the youngest child, Frank and Effie, Mabel, Fred and Ben (for Benjamin Harrison) comprising the family that survived beyond childhood. They are described in *Look Homeward, Angel,* so intimately and with such detail that to read the volume is to live in the house that hard-reared them. This big, cheaply constructed frame dwelling of "eighteen or twenty drafty, high-ceilinged rooms," the place of the boy's youthful "exile" was known in its pre-museum days as "The Old Kentucky Home," in the novels "Dixieland." Asheville, the Altamont and Libya Hill of the fictional State of Old Catawba, was in those days a new-blown Mecca of phthisic-ridden or health-minded "guests," and where an extra dollar was, there was Julia Wolfe also.

Wolfe, senior, was a stone-cutter, a huge fellow with a penchant for declaiming in long pericopes the works of the literary masters. If the boyhood of Eugene Gant is a trustworthy source by one half, life at the "O.K.H." must have been a wretched experience. For W. O. Gant was a drunken lecher (the kind of man the family has to hide the new servant girls from), and to put it thus is to praise him.

Eliza Gant for her part was a mountain woman who never learned anything and never forgot anything, parsimonious and a pharisee. For the sake of gain she peopled her home with every sort of moral bankrupt, and affected surprise as she discussed with her (inexplicably chaste) daughter what might be going on upstairs between her sons as yet unshaven and certain female boarders of morals far from dubious.

Eugene knew evil early—in his own home, at school, as a paper-boy in Niggertown. He learned of God from his father's imprecations, his mother's pious wishes, and a series of shadowy Protestant ministers. Education and the world of ideas were opened to the hulking young Gulliver by a private school master and his wife, John and Margaret Leonard, he a propounder of the letter and she a spark of the spirit.[3] A misfit because of his undoubted genius, Gant after a bout of tortured adolescent love makes his way to the state university at Pulpit Hill. The graduate school at Harvard is next, after a brief war interlude; by this time the father is dying of grim cancer and the "buried life" is at an end.

The persevering reader has come to the second volume of Gant's odyssey, "the legend of a man's hunger in his youth," as the sub-title to *Of Time and the River* runs. The intellec-

---

[3] In real life, Mr. and Mrs. J. M. Roberts. He addressed her, in a lyrical letter dated May 30, 1927, as "mother of my spirit who fed me with light . . . I shall use the last thrust of my talent—whatever it is— to put your beauty into words." *The Atlantic Monthly,* December, 1946.

tual growth of the country boy among the Cambridge esthetes is done, like most of Wolfe's encounters with literary pretenders, in a broad and painful irony.

There is a European trip at the end of his graduate study: London, Paris, and a love affair with a large person affectionately addressed as a "Back Bay bitch," understandably ending in Gant's rejection. On the boat going home he encounters a comely young Jewish woman ten years his senior. She appears soon again in the life of George Webber, where as Mrs. Esther Jack she takes incredible abuse in the role of mistress and muse to the flailing madman. This affair, and Webber's instructorship in the School for Utility Cultures, Inc., are the burden of *The Web and the Rock*.[4] *You Can't Go Home Again* finds him lost in the sounds and smells of Brooklyn for four years, writing furiously to prove to himself and the world that his early success was no freak.

To multiply details is both needless and irksome, else what are "brief histories of American literature" for? It were well to get on with the man's qualities as a novelist. For that to be done adequately some further insight is required into the threefold matrix of his life in which every idea and passion was conceived. The first consideration might be of his relation to his family, the second to society, and the third to his own genius, which we shall temporarily equate with his peculiar mental endowment.

Wolfe thought himself an ugly duckling from the start, and was maddened that the rest of the brood should be blind to the cygnet in their midst. "You little freak," Helen Gant jeers at Eugene, "wandering around with your queer dopey face . . . Everybody's laughing at you. Don't you know that?" He knew it, and was resolved to throw the laughter back in their teeth. The one great bond of his life was with his mother, yet one would hesitate to describe it as love. Brothers and sisters all came in for his scorn at various times, which makes it particularly refreshing to see him inquire mildly upon occa-

[4] Wolfe taught at New York University from 1924 to 1930. He had a friend named Aline Bernstein, who exonerates largely the nameless hero of her novel, *The Journey Down*.

sion after the well-being of Mabel, Fred or Frank. His letters often end in words and inquiries indicating affection, yet an awareness of the jealousies and incredible rudenesses that tore them apart was never absent from his mind.

> Let us all be decent and fair and generous to one another; let us not talk over-much of our generosity and nobility; let us not curse and revile and abuse one another; let us not be torn by jealousy and ill-feeling.

It was the penny-pinching of his mother, so much despised by him, that was responsible for his education in college and graduate school. The sense of obligation and his inability to make a quick or ample return colors all his judgments. "You are the only one who ever writes me from home now and you have about deserted me," he complains. He sees in her failure to correspond a reproach aimed at his complete dependence.

> You didn't want me at home, you said nothing about my returning and I shall see that your desires and those of the family are realized . . . I have heard nothing from you. You are the only one with whom I can discuss my plans and you have denied me even that connection . . . I am no gold-digger, no parasite. I have had more than the others but I won't deprive them of a single penny. I never took sides in our family. I never took part in that wretched factionalism, the pairing off into . . .

Here the letter-fragment ends, but not by any means his burning and irrational resentment. It was not entirely unreasoned, of course, for Tom knew that the good dame with the snapping black eyes was a hard mistress who liked to reap where she had not sown. "For God's sake, all of you must watch your health . . ." he pleads at one moment but again, "It has taken me twenty-seven years to rise above the bitterness and hatred of my childhood . . . As for you all, I shall continue to remember you, and to be loyal to my blood even when, as usual, no answer comes to me."

The point of this sufficient sampling, which could be continued uninterrupted from the novels, is to try to determine if there was love in the man's life. It does not seem so, nor any depth of charity in his writings. One must go slowly here. Passion there is in plenty; absorption in individuals; fellow-feeling with his mother above all. Any of these might be the concomitant of love, but love is not to be identified with a particular one. The high point of heart-sharing seems to come in the tender portrait of Margaret Leonard whose virtues Gant-Webber presumably sought in women all his life. Once more the question arises how much of otherness there is in this. It is impossible to say. The suspicion that her role is one of discoverer with the genius of appreciation is not easily lost.

The endless tirades of old W. O. Gant (in *Look Homeward, Angel*) were calculated to drive from the home whatever of love his paternity might have engendered. His example seems to have accounted for little enough.

> "Woman, you have deserted my bed and board, you have made a laughing stock of me before the world, and left your children to perish. Fiend that you are, there is nothing that you would not do to torture, humiliate and degrade me. You have deserted me in my old age; you have left me to die alone . . . There is no ignominy to which you will not stoop if you think it will put a nickel in your pocket."

The whole Gantian epoch is interpreted by Wolfe as the search for a fatherhood that Eugene had never known. Cleaving to a Christian rather than a Freudian view, we recognize as most natural a youthful hunger for the protective, all-embracing love which mirrors that of God our Father. Eliza could not supply it, neither a multitude of harlots, nor the learning of a thousand books. The quest gives every appearance of going unsatisfied, and so the entire output of Wolfe can be charged sterile of this deepest of human emotions. There is the appearance of love on every page, but it proves to be no more than desire; gratitude, but always with the obstrusive question, Who is loved here?

Compassion? . . . Compassion! That is another matter.
The colored man suffers injustice over his innocent mongrel.
Death, the proud brother, sidles up to a little nobody on the
subway platform to make him equal with the mightiest. A
chaste girl of two years ago brazens it through when confronted at her place of employment with a boy from home.
It is no good to shrug these incidents off as sentiment. They
are a man suffering with men, or the word compassion has no
meaning. These are the places, not in his quires of introspection, where Wolfe awakens momentarily to the love that made
the Selfish Giant ask the little child, a strange awe fallen
upon him, "Who hath dared to wound thee?"

No work of art is done in a vacuum. A man lives and labors
among other men, usually with the degree of proximity of his
own choosing. Thomas Wolfe was a man of his age and time.
A rural Protestant from an area not unfairly termed culturally
undeveloped, he came to know ancient cultures and classics,
far places in his own world, literary trends and esthetic striv-
ings of the contemporary period. They did not change him so
much as they made him adhere more closely to his own soil.
He quotes the Greek tragedians and intimates that once he
knew their language, he lists German composers in long se-
quence without a slip, he gives a cross-section of his hero's
reading habits that amazes by its inclusive sweep. Each time
he does so there arises in the reader a new feeling of surprise.
Can this be the same man writing? Undoubtedly it is. Granite-
like, he goes unchanged, all contact with great minds and
hearts leaving him with a deep affection for the coarse and the
low.

Provincialism of the mind is inexcusable in the man exposed
to broadening. He takes his education out from time to time
and strikes it like a shiny new watch, as Lord Chesterfield
once warned one never to do. Perhaps it was for Wolfe a
defense. Perhaps his apparent non-absorption of what is genuine culture was begotten of all the hours spent in academic
"digs" and literary salons listening to the hollow chimes of
similar watch-strikers. "Whatever George Webber was, he
knew he was not an 'intellectual.' He was just an American

who was looking hard at the life around him . . . trying to extract some essential truth out of this welter of his whole experience." Yet Wolfe desperately thought of himself as an intellectual in the sense that he was convinced his intellect was constantly, productively at work—as it was, if not at the pace and level he imagined.

He seems to have gone entirely uncorrupted by wealth. Briefly he knew something of opulence but in the main Wolfe's was the genius fed by starvation. His student days were an epic of having not, as were his instructorship days and his rabbit-warren existence in Brooklyn.

> A man should live in a garret aloof,
> And have few friends, and go poorly clad,
> With an old hat stopping the chink in the roof
> To keep the Goddess constant and glad.

That was he, all right. And in reward for his fidelity She dwelt with him night and day, sat at his table, haunted his bed. As an epic of devotedness to purpose the man's story is not easily rivaled. The price he paid was bitter loneliness. Some men are voluntary exiles in Paris or Rome; to have left Old Catawba was expatriation enough for Thomas Wolfe. Old Catawba was just right. Its people were humble people, not going to set the world on fire, not intending to. It had no Charleston, no empty pretense, no look of fear, no cruelty in its people's eyes as in South Carolina, where they "cut off a nigger's fat lips with a rusty knife before they castrate and hang him." Yet in a state of revolt and siege against a society he professed to love, Wolfe lived his adult days.

He confessed that he loved North Carolina more than anything else in the world, but asked what it had to feed his spirit, his mind. He nourished a vigorous, long-distance hatred for Asheville's Four Hundred. "If any of them patronize me," he counseled his mother, "telling you I am a bright boy—for God's sake, don't look grateful or humble. Tell them I am pleased to hear of their interest, and that I should be glad to give them a few moments of my time when they're in New

York. This last is meant humorously—none the less seriously."

The naive adoration in the boy of literary personages and "name" professors was quite understandably distilled to a never thoroughly mature scorn in the man, sometimes amused, more often virulent. He had no use for critics in general and his own in particular, a revulsion explainable in part by the acidulous criticism (the term "barbaric yawp" was resurrected against his first novel), that seeks the rise of the critic by beating the other man down with one's bootstraps. Wolfe dissociated himself early from a Southern regional literature nascent in the 'twenties. In his view, its vanguard either pretty-prettied an essentially drab and unhealthy picture, hanging moss and old family retainers around for backdrop material, or else the coterie could not possibly know the South as he knew it. They were tributaries trying bravely to act the main stream.

The essential Babbittry of American life made Wolfe retch, and the vomit is found scattered through his pages looking no prettier than it ought to. His chief complaint was that Lewis and all the rest saw so little and were attributed with having seen so much. Here you have the great bulk of a nation (of half a world, for Europe fared no better) portrayed as stodgy, petty, mean, satisfied, whereas actually the wild diversity yet unity in littleness of men had scarcely been caught. *Babbitt* strong meat? A Christmas story, a child's tale. "The man who suggests the strangeness and variety of this life most is Sherwood Anderson. Or was. I think he's got too fancy since he wrote *Winesburg, Ohio*." Set it all down. Every foul breath and lewd laugh and October afternoon and work of art and ignorant sally and climbing nobody. It does not add up to much but it is life. And you have not captured anything until you have captured it all.

Wolfe was in perpetual revolt against power and position and posturing. Money did not interest him; its more obvious manifestations sickened him. The Jews came in for particular censure at his hands. Baited in the crudest way in Old Catawba where they were an odd phenomenon rather than a part of life, this nation of ancient, unforgiven wrongs took concrete form in the truculent figure of Abe Jones during the period of Gant's instructorship. Abe's was the "dreary gray face of the man-swarm cipher," his character as yet unformed from out the "glutenous paste of obscure yearnings," "grim, gray, unsmiling, tortured-looking . . . a picture of Yiddish melancholy and discontent."

At the opposite pole from this "painful Jewish and involuted intellectualism" was the tribe of perfumed apes, as portrayed in *The Web and the Rock*, that hung on the theatrical skills of Mrs. Esther Jack. Big, beak-nosed Jews with moons of oily faces and sensual nostril volutes, lit with a blaze of diamond studs and emerging from the lavish acres of their evening shirts, gushing flattery and pawing women simultaneously, they corrupted all they touched. There is nothing pretty about the picture nor is there much validity to his generalizations. Literary force has unimpassioned fact brow-beaten and cringing. The ledger is balanced, in Wolfe's clumsy way, by glowing tributes to the fairest of her race, that Esther whose beauty of form and face outshone the garments of her gladness. Hers is a morality manqué but she nonetheless a creature capable of loving and being loved, until Webber turns on her in fury as a traducer who can love only her people. This is the segment of the nation more than half gone over to Persian ways, however. Acting on his supposition that he misses nothing, Wolfe catches Abe's mother fairly, in *Of Time and the River*: "a great broodhen of earth rooted in the soil of two devotions: the synagogue and the home, and all that happened beyond the limits of this devotion was phantom and remote: this soil was ageless, placeless, everlasting."

Was there a population in between, made of Arimatheans and Farbsteins, Perlmans and Zacharys, normal, religious people of their own world and time? One cannot tell. Wolfe did not know them so they were not.

With Negroes it is the same. Their crowded shacks on streets of mud and staves he knew; their frying fish along the banks of a Lethe running high with white mule; their sweating, stinking, casual infidelities and boughten bodies; their bricks-without-straw existence and their patience without end. All these he knew, and he imagined that he comprehended the

211

Negro—this man who said "there is nothing that I do not know about Paris."

The novelist's conception of his own genius colored his work more than family or society could ever do, for through this glass all else was seen. A searcher always, the labyrinth of self entranced him. With something of humility and awe he approached the sanctuary of soul in the great temple of his body, shoes in hand. It was alternately a place of veneration and of disgust, filling him now with the assurance that no one such had lived, now with terror that it was not so or that men should not account it so. Revision was a fetish with him; because he saw ever more in the deep pool of his mind, composition had been a mad compulsion and delight, but the publication process was a shameless exhibitionism wherein the soul was voluntarily stripped for all to see.

It was a perfect agony, yet the words he all but let be torn from him he went on to defend with impassioned breath. Call it satire—a sample without significance—but there is a master key to the man in the boy's lament in *The Web and the Rock* that his huge appetite should be sniffed at by dull, prosy womankind:

> And pray, what is there so remarkable in *that?* Of course he *eats*—more power to his eating too. Was Hercules a daffodil; did Adam toy with water cress, did Falstaff wax fat eating lettuces; was Dr. Johnson surfeited on shredded wheat; or Chaucer on a handful of parched corn . . . did Washington have prunes for breakfast, radishes for lunch; was John L. Sullivan a slave of Holland Rusk, or President Taft the easy prey of lady fingers?

> Noble George—Gene—Tom! Shy companion of the Immortals, had they expected a paid-up member from Old Catawba's hills?

> Before leaving him laureled on Olympus, a final observation seems necessary. While every second page of Wolfe is filled with chortles of glee, war-whoops, hoots and hollers of

amused delight, there is no scrap of humor—no trace of a smile for the reader—in all the millions of words, one ancient, quoted wisecrack excepted. That either argues for a huge disability in the chronicler of all life, or else confirms him in his chosen role of tragic man.

The question remains, then: how good is Wolfe? It is not easy to answer. The matter is complicated entirely by the fact that this age has lost faith. Philosophical stature he has none among a people that will take from God one answer, let Him address them just once, but in a city of the deaf this part-of-one-eared man is king. He has heard a faint echo of all the gravest questions asked by men of every time. Posing them, unanswered, in anguish of spirit and with groanings unutterable, he is a raging prophet of the bitter hope: that things may somehow not be as bad as they seem.

If fifty years see Christ enthroned, or even man as a being resembling man, oblivion has its niche prepared for him. Come deeper darkness, man the searching animal, sin an archaism for what must be, then Wolfe's star is set for further ascendancy. Does all hinge on whether or not he has the world right? Who has decreed that literature's fortunes be pinned to ultimates? Oh, a multitude of men, most of whose names are forgotten: the people who made it literature. Message and medium are one—Jacob's hands and Jacob's voice—for the blind old man called Time is not that easily fooled.

Wolfe is derivative here, he is pseudo-Joycean, he is Ecclesiastes uninspired. Off with his head! He is in another place the determined realist who identifies with total reality what he has been able to see and experience and accept as true. Off with his head! Here again he fancies himself to be thinking as profoundly upon life as has ever been done, and because he is a bore he must perish. In *this* passage, however, he is a mighty Tubalcain hammering out the lordly brass and iron of a descriptive or a self-fathoming prose. The material resists; sparks fly. Has ever language been asked to do so much as this? Yes, but there is so much language with which to do it!

And Wolfe, the unrelenting smith, achieves again and again what few have cared or dared attempt, he comes close to setting down the wild diversity of things. Torrential, repetitive, wearing, disgusting, indiscriminate, annoying, needless, inexact, prodigal, diarrheic—you may call his spate all that. But in doing so you will come closer to the truth that a succinct and clever phrase would not have half described. Words are the signs of ideas, and when the ideas are huge, sometimes disordered and endlessly ramified, none but the patient craftsman who cares naught for space or time will catch their meaning. Mark Twain, supposed author of a thousand quips, is credited with having said that the difference between the right word and the wrong word is the difference between lightning and a lightning bug. In Wolfe the two come side by side. For, having missed the point of the remark, while everyone laughed he was busy considering those times when the lightning does not flash. The bugs are all included.

Where can writing such as this be found?

   And he remembered as well all things and persons in the store—the aproned clerks, with cuffs of straw and armbands catching up their sleeves, with pencils behind their ears and a straight part in the middle of their hair, the ingratiating unction of their tone and manner as they took the orders of reflective housewives, as well as all the rich and spicy odors that rose upward from great bins and barrels in the store . . . There were the smells of rich and bitter chocolate and of tea; of new, ground coffee pouring from the mill; of butter, lard, and honey, and sliced bacon; of smoked ham, and yellow cheese, cut in thick wedges from a ponderous chunk; as well as all the earthy smells of fresh garden vegetables and orchard fruits . . . the solid plunk and promise, the strange, sultry thrill of big green watermelons.
   And this whole scene that day—. . . sultry air and inky light and spurting and torrential rain sweeping in gusty sheets along the gleaming and deserted pavements, as well as the steaming flanks of the old gray grocery horse . . . had awakened in his young boy's heart a powerful sensation of joy, abundance, and proud, welling triumph . . .

It can be found bedded deep in heaps of slag that tire the mind and disgust the soul; filthy, word-poor vituperation; blasphemies unconscious of Whom they smirch; caricatures of creatures given a transfused and temporary interest by the labored limning of their few idiosyncrasies; women lain with without concern; city mice and country mice whose worlds unlike are yet the same in the dark-holed minds of their little vanities. It is hemmed in on all sides by a false-mystic chant that strains to endow itself with significance, as when he intones in *Look Homeward, Angel:*

> O sea, I am lonely like you, I am strange and far like you, I am sorrowful like you; my brain, my heart, my life, like yours, have touched strange shores . . . There by the sea of the dark Virginias, he thought of the forgotten faces . . . Dead, too? Where? How? Why? Why has the web been woven? Why do we die so many deaths? How came I here beside the sea? O lost, O far and lonely, where?

It is surrounded on every side by uncertainty ("My God! My God! What is life about? We are all lying here in darkness in ten thousand little towns—waiting, listening, hoping—for what?"). There is nothing you might call supernatural faith. ("He did not believe in God, nor in Heaven or Hell, but He was afraid they might be true.") The hope discoverable is unconsoling, even chauvinist. ("I believe that we are lost here in America, but I believe we shall be found . . . I think these forms [of self-destructive life here] are dying, and must die, just as I know that America and the people in it are deathless, undiscovered, and immortal, and must live.")

Once in a while, though, the man is caught out in love—with words for ideas' sake; with God's world; with men, those twisted images of God that never cease to be lovable somehow—and then he is worth your while to read, this tortured Colossus who never quite grew up in the things a man should long for. Had he but known what things to hunger after, this boy who tried so desperately to play the man . . .

John Steinbeck:

Life Affirmed and Dissolved

JOHN S. KENNEDY

JOHN STEINBECK is generally regarded as the most versatile of contemporary American fiction artists. This distinction is not undeserved, for he has tried his hand at a number of forms. During the first decade (1929-1939) of his fame, he had ten books published, and it was only in the last of these that he returned to a mood and manner previously used. There have been other repetitions since. But his first nine works were markedly different one from another in matter and tone and style. He shifted sharply and with a show of ease from costume drama to fantasy at once earthy and lyric to knockabout farce to abrasive naturalism to argument none too successfully disguised as narrative, proving that he could do more or less creditably in a number of fictional forms, even if in none did he demonstrate the mastery and finesse of indisputable greatness.

But though his books might show contrast in form, pace and diction, they inevitably had certain things in common. For example, binding together the now rather extensive body of novels, short stories, sketches, plays, is the California setting, and specifically the Salinas Valley setting, of most of his productions.

Steinbeck was born in Salinas, the white town in "the huge green Salinas Valley," on February 27, 1902. He was of German-Irish-Yankee stock, his father being treasurer of Monterey County and his mother a school teacher. After graduating from the Salinas high school, he went intermittently to Stanford University, but his education for his career as a novelist was chiefly gathered in a series of jobs as agricultural worker, laboratory assistant, and manual laborer. He broke into print as a contributor to the Salinas high school paper, and, after leaving Stanford, came East and worked as a newspaper reporter in New York and at various odd jobs. It was only after his return to California, while still in his middle 'twenties, that he wrote his first published book, *Cup of Gold* (1929), an historical romance about Sir Henry Morgan, the English pirate. His second book, *The Pastures of Heaven* (1932), had a California setting, as have most of those which followed. Just now Steinbeck is reported to be finishing a long novel, which he is said to consider his *chef d'oeuvre,* and, appropriately enough, its tentative title is *Salinas Valley.* Willa Cather would generally be considered a less versatile writer, yet she has dealt tellingly with a wider range of places: Nebraska, Virginia, the Southwest, New York, Quebec.

Far more important than the common scene in Steinbeck is the common theme. Something of the sort is discernible, of course, in the output of any writer, however many-sided. In Steinbeck's case the common theme may be called "reverence for life." Albert Schweitzer, the Protestant missionary who gained international renown by burying himself in the African jungle, says that the core of his creed is "reverence for life." If Steinbeck were in the habit of giving interviews to explain his purpose in writing (the very reverse is the case), he might well say that he aims at expressing and inculcating "reverence for life." At least, the student of his work as a whole easily discovers this concern running through it. To judge the worth of the idea, one must know what Steinbeck means by life, and it will be the chief object of these paragraphs to try to find out. But first, it may be observed that Steinbeck's preoccupation with life and living is perhaps the main reason for his popularity and influence.

Dozens of his contemporaries write consistently better than he, with greater subtlety and polish, greater depth and force. He can produce pages of beauty and impact, preceded and followed by pages of sheer trash, the emptiness of which is only accentuated by the pseudo-grandeur or pseudo-primitivism of the diction. He can be acutely sensitive and true for a chapter, then embarrassingly sentimental and cheaply trite. He can write dialog with authenticity and bite, and go on to more dialog which is reverberant rhetorical noise. He can juxtapose a penetrating analysis of human feeling, especially of sense impression, and painfully artificial fabrication. In short, he has at least as many faults as he has felicities in his talent; his books are by no means rigorously weeded.

Still, he has won both critical and popular acclaim, largely, it would appear, because he is, within limits, an affirmative writer. So many novelists in the 'thirties and 'forties have followed Hemingway's example of necrophilia. Their violent narratives have culminated by forcing the protagonist into a cul-de-sac, death, quick, arbitrary, grim and final extinction, and thus have been a reflection and a propagator of bleak despair with meaningless overtones of defiance. Other artists in fiction have been wryly fastidious chroniclers of picayune but lethal futilities, arguing that life amounts to no more than a steady series of defeats which may be individually no more than pinpricks but which add up to slow, unavoidable bleeding to death.

Steinbeck is different. He does not fit into any of the categories of negativism prevalent in this age's fiction. He is no Pollyanna—far from it. He depicts human existence as conflict, unremitting and often savage battle. But he suggests that life is worth living, flagellant and baffling though it may be. When, as rarely happens, he produces a memorable character like Ma Joad, that character has an irrepressible will to live, even under heart-breakingly adverse conditions, is resourceful and indomitable before the hostility of a world apparently bent on his or her extermination. In a time when the prevalent note in creative literature is that of despondency and abandonment to malign fate, whether armed with sledgehammer or scalpel, Steinbeck's assertion of the resiliency and tough durability of life has set him off from the generality.

Moreover, his prepossession with life, rather than with ideologies, has made it impossible to pigeonhole him politically, which is not true of many another novelist.

He did run afoul of the critical habit, prevalent in the 'thirties and early 'forties, that rated fiction principally, if not exclusively, according to the political bias a man's work showed or might be tortured into showing, or the political capital which partisans might, honestly or dishonestly, make of it. Thus, *The Grapes of Wrath* (1939) was attacked by the politically conservative as out-and-out Communist propaganda. It was nothing of the sort, even if Communists, despite their distrust of Steinbeck, did use its stark picture of the plight of the dispossessed as graphic evidence of the crimes and the certain collapse of capitalism.

Steinbeck had written of Communists not unsympathetically and had hit at reactionary Red-baiters in earlier books, but had clearly demonstrated his critical awareness of the bad features of the Communist mentality and methods in the novel, *In Dubious Battle* (1936), dealing with an abortive strike by migrant fruit pickers of whom monolithically organized owners would take pitiless advantage. Mac, the veteran Communist who foments and manipulates the strike, voices the familiar propaganda about the Communists' love for all workers and their disinterested toil to assure to every last mortal a life worthy of a man. And the appeal which communism makes to the unorientated and destitute by manifestly doing something while no help for the suffering comes from any other quarter, is forcefully depicted. But Doc, the character who, it is manifest, speaks for Steinbeck, debunks the legend of the Communists' altruistic humanitarianism; and the Party's cold-blooded exploitation of misery, as well as its callous use of the most despicable means to its power-seeking

220

ends, is graphically shown. Steinbeck evidently rejected communism because communism throttled life.

Hence the accusation that Steinbeck was pro-Communist had to be doubted on the basis of what he had written, even before one read *The Grapes of Wrath*. And a careful dispassionate reading of the latter novel showed there was no justification for the charge that it contained solid chunks of undisguised Communist doctrine. The book said, at unconscionable length and with some resort to sensationalism and melodrama, something incontrovertibly true: namely, that thousands upon thousands of Americans were being cruelly victimized and heinously degraded by a system, crazily inept at least in part, which destroyed masses of ordinary people for the inordinate and socially unjust and detrimental enrichment of remote, impersonal corporations. Steinbeck, aroused over the trampling of human life, put this strongly in accents of burning anger and disgust. He did not have to be a Communist to do so, and indeed it was an appalling commentary on the inhumanity or stupidity of the comfortably circumstanced that his indictment of a reeking evil should be answered only by wholly irrelevant name-calling.

But it was not very long until Steinbeck was under fire for precisely the opposite reason and being styled a sort of crypto-Nazi. This happened when *The Moon Is Down* was published as a novel and produced as a play in 1942. The United States was then at war, the Axis tide was still running strong, and many influential American publicists had agreed to make a mockery of exact truth for the duration. Steinbeck was writing of occupied Norway (he had visited the country, as he had Russia, a few years before), and his Nazi characters emerged as something like human beings, by no means admirable, but by no means demoniac either. For not making them intrinsically and uniformly monstrous, at a time when some of our most celebrated writers were trying to whip Americans up to a frenzy of indiscriminate hatred, Steinbeck was pilloried.

The allegations first of Communist, then of Nazi, sympa-

221

thies would appear to cancel each other out. But then again, they could lead one to believe that there might be a certain paradoxical justification for such seemingly contradictory charges. Communism and nazism have in common a commitment to collectivism, differing though they do as to the auspices under which it should be conducted. Was Steinbeck in favor of some sort of collectivism? It is plain from his books that he does not favor the familiar forms of economic or political collectivism, be they controlled by foreign dictators or native capitalists. For example, he writes scathingly of the monopolist who thwarts the poor Mexican in *The Pearl* (1947). He hits hard, for another example, at that centralization which would make of American agriculture no more than a mass-production scheme for the aggrandizement of urban shareholders, and this precisely because life is demeaned and quenched in the process.

In *The Grapes of Wrath* he has a tenant farmer say something in which it is not preposterous to find a faint echo of Leo XIII's teaching on property in his encyclical letter *On the Condition of the Working Classes:*

> If a man owns a little property, that property is him, it's part of him, and it's like him. If he owns property only so he can walk on it and handle it and be sad when it isn't doing well, and feel fine when the rain falls on it, that property is him, and some ways he's bigger because he owns it . . . But let a man get property he doesn't see, or can't take time to get his fingers in, or can't be there to walk on it—why, then property is the man . . . , stronger than he is. And he is small, not big. Only his possessions are big.

Is it fantastic to see some similarity between this and the words of Pope Leo:

> When man spends the industry of his mind and the strength of his body in procuring the fruits of nature, by that act he makes his own that portion of nature's field which he cultivates—that portion on which he leaves, as

it were, the impress of his own personality; and it cannot but be just that he should possess that portion as his own, and should have a right to keep it without molestation?

Steinbeck emphasizes the natural bond between life and productive property, the need that man has of a bit of earth to give him sustenance and dignity. He had touched on this earlier, as in *Of Mice and Men* (1937), in which Candy says:

> Everybody wants a little bit of land, not much. Jus' som'thin' that was his. Som'thin' he could live on and there couldn't nobody throw him off of it. I never had none. I planted crops for damn near ever'body in this state, but they wasn't my crops, and when I harvested 'em, it wasn't none of my harvest.

This is a legitimate complaint against a derangement which has contributed greatly to the dehumanization of man.

But later in *The Grapes of Wrath* Steinbeck seems to approve and recommend collectivism of a different sort, a collectivism which, according to him, would foster, rather than crush, life. The Okies have had their ramshackle but cherished homes and their small patches of earth snatched away from them by the insatiable behemoth of big-scale agriculture. What is wrong with this, it is suggested, is not the pooling of hundreds of family-size farms, but the fact of the alien ownership of the amalgam. Steinbeck does not oppose mechanized collective farming in itself. "Is a tractor bad?" he asks. "Is the power that turns the long furrows wrong? If this tractor were ours it would be good—not mine but ours. If our tractor turned the long furrows of our land, it would be good. Not my land, but ours." And there is much more in the same vein, urging a sort of popularly chosen and controlled socialism, which Steinbeck heatedly advocates without ever bothering to consider its pitfalls or its possible deleterious consequences.

This idea is not to be dismissed out of hand as absurd or pernicious. The social character of property, the legitimacy and desirability of social ownership of what is indispensable to the common good, the incomparable value and profoundly Christian character of voluntary cooperation and joint endeavor—these are not being called into question. But Steinbeck means something more, something different. Just here we are coming to grips with the central point in Steinbeck's concept of life: namely, that its fullness is found only in the group and never in the individual. While he regards with disfavor a superimposed collectivism, he believes ardently in the primacy of the collectivity. Permeating his works is this idea, which is the very heart of his philosophy of life: that the concrete person is in himself virtually nothing, whereas the abstraction "humanity" is all.

Consider some examples from books published over a span of years, and you will observe the persistency and growth of this attitude. In *To a God Unknown* (1933), Rama says:

> I tell you this man is not a man, unless he is all men. The strength, the resistance, the long and stumbling thinking of all men, and all the joys and suffering too, cancelling each other out and yet remaining in the contents. He is all these, a repository for a little piece of each man's soul, and more than that, a symbol of the earth's soul.

In *In Dubious Battle,* Doc tells Mac, "You might be an expression of group-man, a cell endowed with a special function, like an eye-cell, drawing your force from group-man . . . Yes, it might be worthwhile to know more about group-man, to know his nature, his ends, his desires." Later, he asks another character, "Can't a group of men be God?" In *The Red Pony* (1937), the westward migration of the pioneers is described as "a whole bunch of people made into one big crawling beast." In *The Grapes of Wrath* Tom Joad, quoting the ex-preacher Casy, declares:

> Says one time he went out into the wilderness to find his own soul, and he foun' he didn' have no soul that was his'n. Says he foun' he jus' got a little piece of a great big soul. Says a wilderness ain't no good, 'cause his little

piece of soul wasn't no good 'less it was with the rest, an' was whole.

It might be said that Steinbeck is doing no more than asserting, in a rather vaporous way, the solidarity of the human race, the continuity and interdependence of the species, the indubitable fact that all men are brothers and members one of another, or referring to the workings of mob psychology. But it is none of these things that he is getting at. Rather, he is ever more strongly affirming that, in the last analysis, man has no individual identity, that the human person as such, separately created and distinct from all others, does not in fact exist. Commitment to this idea may well be reaction against the unbridled, atomistic individualism which has wreaked havoc in society as a whole and in innumerable lives, and which, as his books indicate, Steinbeck recognizes as disastrous for mankind. But he has swung to and remains at the opposite extreme, that amalgamism which deprives the individual of initiative, responsibility, value, and even metaphysical being, and makes him no more than a cell in a supposititious monstrosity called "group-man" or an inextricable aspect of a pseudo-mystical entity called the "great big soul." It is the "great big soul" which, for Steinbeck, is life.

Indeed, he goes further than blotting out the boundaries of personality which mark off one man from another. He declares that, for man to be whole, he must be indistinguishably at one with all that exists. Casy, in *The Grapes of Wrath,* says: "There was the hills, an' there was me, an' we wasn't separate no more. We was one thing. An' that one thing was holy." Here again, one might dismiss objections, on the ground that all that exists, whether organic or inorganic, is interrelated and should be in harmony. There is an intimate interrelationship of all the levels of a universe made through, and bearing the mark of, the one Eternal Word. But Steinbeck is nowhere clear as to the essential, qualitative difference between man and the rest of created beings.

This can be plainly seen in what Edmund Wilson has called Steinbeck's "animalizing tendency." Wilson says that "constant in Mr. Steinbeck is his preoccupation with biology" and points out "his tendency in his stories to present life in animal terms." The tendency is one which Wilson applauds in Steinbeck as in Erskine Caldwell. Discussing the latter's *Tragic Ground* in the *New Yorker* in 1944, Wilson observed that its evaluation of man was "one symptom of a change in attitude which Western man is in our time undergoing in regard to his role on the earth." He went on:

> Even thirty-five years ago such books would hardly have been written. Today we read them for their humor and charm (e.g., a twelve-year-old girl working in a brothel), accepting incest and murder as quite innocent, and undisturbed by such casual cruelty as that of the hero of the present novel when he decides to go home by himself and leave his ailing wife alone, because it is made to seem as unconscious and natural as the self-preserving egoism of animals. The point is that we can read about all this today without anything more than a smile or a qualm because we are prepared, as our grandfathers were not, to study human behavior on the animal level.

Another critic, Alfred Kazin, says that Steinbeck approaches "the modern social struggle as a tragicomedy of animal instincts." And the same view was voiced by still a third critic, John Chamberlain. Reviewing *Cannery Row* (1945) for *Harper's Magazine,* he wrote:

> Cannery Row is an amoral place, and Steinbeck is amoral in his approach to it. Between the boys of the Palace Flophouse and the tomcats they catch for Doc there is little discernible difference, and the girls of Dora's Bear Flag bordello might be out of the Elsie Dinsmore books for all that Steinbeck cares. In Steinbeck's world whores are interchangeable with angels, and pimps with saints. From his marine biological expeditions Steinbeck has caught a naturalist's view of life as consisting of struggle, color, intensity, violence, feeding, and orgasm. Moral and ethical choices are merely man's way of making things difficult for himself; the animals know better.

226

. . . The Steinbeck attitude results in books that are devoid of human meaning. *Cannery Row* is exciting and pleasurable because it has salt, color and movement. But you can say as much for a circus or a zoo.

I quote these three critics at such length because none of them is likely to be taxed with religious fanaticism or moralistic narrow-mindedness, as is the case when someone like myself says that he finds in certain books a reduction of man to the merely animal level. A trio of leading non-religious commentators on letters agrees as to Steinbeck's concept of man's stature and status, and two of them rather like the novelist's appraisal of our species.

The reader of Steinbeck's works is always coming on plainly stated parallels between men and animals. In its most blatant and hideous form, this can be seen in that story of nightmarish horror, *The Snake*. In *The Pearl*, just after describing how the greedy bourgeoisie gang up on their peasant victim, Steinbeck writes:

Out in the estuary a tight woven school of small fish glittered and broke water to escape a school of great fishes that drove in to eat them. And in the houses the people could hear the swish of the small ones and the bouncing splash of the great ones as the slaughter went on. . . . And the night mice crept about on the ground and the little night hawks hunted them silently.

In *The Red Pony*, dogs hunting mice are compared with troops hunting Indians. In *Of Mice and Men*, the shooting of a decrepit old dog and the shooting of a decrepit old man are linked. In *In Dubious Battle*, the killing of a dog and the killing of a Negro are similarly linked, as are dogs fighting and men fighting, the slaughtering of men and the slaughtering of sheep. In *The Grapes of Wrath*, there is the same pairing of behavior and treatment between dogs and men, horses and men, and other forms of animal life and men. Examples could be cited from book after book, but the foregoing are enough to give substance to the statement that habitually and

227

characteristically Steinbeck sets human conduct and animal conduct side by side, on the same plane, not simply as commentaries one on the other but as indications of the same nature in the two apparently disparate sorts of creature.

Man is, of course, an animal. But he is an animal with a difference. He is a rational animal, a moral animal. Steinbeck seems to agree to man's rationality when he says, in *The Grapes of Wrath*, "Fear the time when Manself will not suffer and die for a concept; for this one quality is the foundation of Manself." And yet he incessantly presents man as a creature, indeed a captive, of instincts and appetites only, blindly desiring and striving, not reasoning, judging, choosing but automatically responding to impulses and attractions.

As for man's being moral, Doc (who, to repeat, is Steinbeck's spokesman in *In Dubious Battle*) says: "My senses aren't above reproach, but they're all I have . . . I don't want to put on the blinders of 'good' and 'bad,' and limit my vision." In *The Grapes of Wrath*, Casy says of sexual promiscuity: "Maybe it ain't a sin. Maybe it's just the way folks is . . . There ain't no sin and there ain't no virtue. There's just stuff people do. It's all part of the same thing." Pa Joad echoes this with, "A fella got to do what he got to do." And Ma Joad says, "What people does is right to do." As John Chamberlain suggests, this idea represents a conclusion Steinbeck has drawn from his observation of marine life. Reporting on one of his expeditions, he states in *Sea of Cortez* (1941):

> The true biologist deals with life, with teeming boisterous life, and learns something from it, learns that the first rule of life is living . . . He knows that morals are too often diagnostic of prostatitis and stomach ulcers. Sometimes he may proliferate a little too much in all directions, but he is as easy to kill as any other organism, and meanwhile he is very good company, and at least he does not confuse a low hormone productivity with moral ethics.

And so in man, according to Steinbeck, what counts, what

alone matters, is life, its preservation, its transmission. In his latest work, *Burning Bright,* which appeared both as a novel and as a play in 1950, Joe Saul suspects he is impotent and desponds. He is over the threshold of middle age, and he has not done the one capital thing—passing on physical life. His second wife, much younger than he, seeks to allay his self-contempt by getting a lusty youth named Victor to father a child which she will tell Joe Saul is his own. This she does on the advice of Friend Ed (plainly another Steinbeck mouthpiece), who is a model of wisdom and natural goodness. Thinking his manhood is vindicated, Joe Saul exults. But then Victor threatens to tell him the truth and is promptly murdered by Friend Ed. Joe Saul gets from a doctor conclusive proof that he is impotent, and upbraids his wife for deceit and infidelity. But Friend Ed persuades him that what his wife did was fine and beautiful and, when the child is born, Joe Saul greets it as his own, declaiming that every man is the father of every child and every child the offspring of every man. Life is vindicated, life goes on, and whatever violence is done the moral code is of no moment alongside that fact.

The thoughtful reader is appalled by the complete severance of man from morality which the book's argument represents. He reflects that fundamentally what is amiss with these characters is failure or refusal to recognize and accept God's will and word: as regards physical defects, the exclusiveness of marriage, the disposition of life. And this leads one to inquire about the novelist's attitude to religion.

We have already noted the idea, mentioned in *In Dubious Battle,* that the human collectivity, men *en masse,* may be all that is meant by the term "God." Several times in Steinbeck's works one finds the idea that a character has outgrown prayer because, with enlightenment, he no longer knows what or whom to pray to. This is the case, for example, with the scientist in *The Snake* and the ex-preacher in *The Grapes of Wrath.* "No, I can't pray to anything," says the first, and the second says, "I don't know . . . who to pray to." On the other hand, the ignorant, superstitious people of whom Steinbeck is writing in *The Pearl* and *The Long Valley* (1938) pray because it is part of an immemorial behavior-pattern which, quite as uninformed as their forebears, they unquestioningly accept.

These benighted men and women, incidentally, are Catholic, and it is interesting to see how Steinbeck treats Catholicism. It is not understandingly or sympathetically. In *The Pearl*, the Church is a symbol for obscurantism and the unscrupulous milking of the poor. Kino, an indigent fisherman, finds an enormous pearl, perhaps the greatest the world has ever known. Immediately everyone is scheming to get it away from him. Among the lusters after it is the priest. Up to now, Kino and his wife have not been able to be married in Church because they never had enough money to pay the fee; likewise, their baby has not been baptized because they could never meet the "cost" of the ceremony. Kino is bitter about this, as he is about the priest's preaching which, in effect, is no more than a browbeating attempt to keep the people shackled in their poverty, since its drift is that God's clear and immutable will for them is the squalor and hunger of the subhuman existence in which the upper classes have them imprisoned. But now that Kino has the pearl, the priest comes, smiling and reptilianly wily, to the fisherman's wretched shack —for the first time.

From a different racial background and a somewhat different social stratum is Jim Nolan, the tormented young man in *In Dubious Battle*, who, in revolt against the system which, he says, has ruined his whole family, joins the Communist Party and goes to his death in the fruit pickers' strike. His father abominated religion and would not hear of his worn-out wife's going to the Catholic church. He prevented her from attending Sunday Mass, but sometimes during the week, while he was at work, she would slip into the church for a few minutes' prayer. In the end, however, she turned away from the Church, refusing the priest on her death bed. The only religion that Jim knows is the Catholic, and this he knows very imperfectly. But he detests it. It might be parenthetically remarked that Steinbeck and his Jim Nolan are both unaware of Pius XI's strictures on a system which so cripples human nature as to deter it, if not alienate it, from the practice of religion. When, alight with enthusiasm over the strike, Jim talks to Doc, the latter says to him, "You've got something in your eyes, Jim, something religious." Jim furiously replies, "Well, it isn't religious. I've got no use for religion," and later, "I don't believe in religion."

It may be remembered that, a few years ago, Steinbeck published in *Collier's* magazine an article retelling the story of the apparitions of Our Lady of Guadalupe. This he related with every evidence of reverence, and he lavished upon it all the resources of his best poetic style. A reader unfamiliar with the rest of his writings might possibly have considered the piece the work of a Catholic. But, taken in the Steinbeck context, it was merely his presentation not of an historical fact, but of a lovely myth to which simple people in whom Steinbeck is interested and whom he has again and again used as subjects for his fiction, give credence. This, he is saying, is what such folk believe. Thus, the bus driver in *The Wayward Bus* (1946) always has a likeness of Our Lady of Guadalupe in the vehicle as a kind of amulet or fetish; his life shows that he does not conform to the code which the image symbolizes.

Nowhere does Steinbeck give evidence of adequate knowledge of the Catholicism on which he touches with evident disfavor in his various productions. He seems much more familiar with the cruder sort of evangelical Protestantism, and this is acidly treated in his books.

For example, there is an indictment of it in *To a God Unknown*. Again, there is Casy in *The Grapes of Wrath,* once an evangelist holding rambunctious revival meetings, half glory-shouting and half sexual orgies, throughout the hinterland. When, at the beginning of the book, Tom Joad is returning home after a stay in prison, he meets Casy by the wayside and is surprised to hear that the preacher has given up that work. "I was a preacher," Casy tells him. "Reverend Jim Casy—was a Burning Busher. Used to howl out the name of Jesus to glory. And used to get an irrigation ditch so squirmin' full of repented sinners half of 'em like to drownded. But no more . . . Just Jim Casy now. Ain't got the call no more. Got a lot of sinful idears—but they seem kinda sensible."

He further explains his abandonment of the ministry:

> I love people so much I'm fit to bust, sometimes. And I says, "Don't you love Jesus?" Well, I thought an' thought, an' finally I says, "No, I don't know nobody name' Jesus. I know a bunch of stories, but I only love people" . . . I figgered about the Holy Sperit and the Jesus road. I figgered, "Why we got to hang it on God or Jesus? Maybe," I figgered, "maybe it's all men an' all women we love; maybe that's the Holy Sperit—the human sperit—the whole shebang."

Casy gave up baptizing because nobody seemed to feel any different as a result of it. He had once baptized Tom and now asks him, "Well—did you take any good outa that baptizin'? . . . Did you take any bad from it?" And Tom answers, "No-o-o, can't say as I felt anything." Casy has also come to discredit the notion of sin. "Maybe we been whippin' the hell out of ourselves for nothin'." His apologia for withdrawing from religious endeavor goes on for paragraphs and pages, but perhaps the point is just as strikingly made by the single gesture of Pat Humbert in *The Pastures of Heaven* (1932), when, seeking to disengage himself from the dead hand of the past which has always kept him from enjoying life, he picks up the old family Bible and hurls it out into the yard to rot in the rain.

Steinbeck may justly be said to belong to that populous group of contemporary novelists who, rejecting as procrustean and unlivable a peculiar, diluted blend of Calvinism and Lutheranism, think that, in exposing such freakishness, they are refuting authentic Christianity. They look upon what is a caricature of authentic Christianity, find it wanting, repudiate it, and suppose that they have thereby pulled the props out from under the real article, whereas in fact they have left this untouched. Casy's ramblings are a case in point. They reveal that what he thought to be essential Christianity was, in fact, no more than an inorganic agglomeration of bits and tatters torn away from the original, and inoperative and incapable of standing searching scrutiny. The privativism which Casy, Pat Humbert, and other Steinbeck characters find and disavow in what they take to be integral Christianity is actually a disease at the heart of a faint and fragmentary copy of genuine Christianity. Thus, the notion of grace which Casy scorns, is a travesty on the Christian doctrine of grace. The former holds grace to be entirely subjective, no more than an emotional impulse, a nervous compulsion, muscular response to stimuli, while the latter holds it to be objective, a distinctively spiritual power and presence. If you ridicule the first because, in practice, it leads to grotesque and sometimes disastrous doings, you still have not rebutted, indeed you have not even considered, the second.

Steinbeck, therefore, nowhere comes to grips with the basic, pristine Christian religion. Hence he never takes into account what it has to say about human nature, human life, human destiny. He is not conversant with its moral code as a whole. He is not familiar with its bearing upon the human predicament, the light it casts upon it and the resources it brings to mortals for managing and solving it.

His last book, *Burning Bright*, harshly highlights all that is weakest in Steinbeck as a philosopher and a writer of fiction. Even if one could do the impossible and agree that adultery is no more than an outdated word so long as life is propagated, there is the question of Victor's fate. Friend Ed, goodness and wisdom personified, recommends that Victor be used and then coolly kills the young man when convenience calls for that. There is no slightest hint that the murder is a wicked injustice. The brutality, the icy amorality of this is one of the most shocking things in all Steinbeck's output, the more shocking because it comes from a supposedly mature man and is surrounded with resounding generalities about the sacredness of life. Yet it is scarcely surprising in view of the sophistry in which, in his succession of works, Steinbeck has become ever more tightly entangled. And, by the way, one might here stress the fact that it is the sophistry, rather than the foul speech, which is most regrettable in Steinbeck's fiction. *Burning Bright* is almost entirely free of the vulgar, obscene, or blasphemous dialog which characterizes so many of Steinbeck's books. It is only the coarse Victor who recalls, and that but faintly and briefly, the profane and filthy language of the figures which dominate, and are constantly articulate in the idiom of lewdness, in several of the other novels. The rest of the principals use no offensive words, indeed their talk has an exalted ring to it, and yet the ideas they express are far worse than mere lurid utterance. To reproduce verbatim the gutter language of people who are virtually mute unless they resort to lascivious lingo is hardly to be compared with the communication of a philosophy of life which is totally fallacious. The reporting of the sordid does not begin to do the harm stemming from a false interpretation of man. Two such dissimilar writers as T. S. Eliot and Somerset Maugham have both emphasized that the novelist and playwright are primarily commenting on life in terms of a certain set of postulates and principles. Too often the reader does not advert to this fact, does not sift out and assess the author's concept of life, but is content to praise or blame on the basis of, say, what he considers the decency or indecency of speech used.

In *Burning Bright*, too, may be seen at its worst Steinbeck's failure with characters. He has written about fifteen volumes of fiction by now, yet given us almost no memorable characters. Ma Joad is a possible exception, but it is hard to name even half-a-dozen more. For the most part the men and women in Steinbeck's narratives are hazy, faceless, pithless. They are not sharply drawn, clearly projected, unmistakably themselves, or recognizable from one's experience however catholic. They have no forms, in the philosophical sense, which is but another way of saying that they have no souls. There are about them certain superficial peculiarities which make for a measure of material individuation, but almost nothing making for personality. They are heavily documented types, not living people. Nor is this merely a deficiency in imagination or technique. It springs from Steinbeck's conviction that a man or woman is just "a little piece of a great big soul." It has been said of Steinbeck that he is not a creative artist; if this is true, it is to be attributed to his missing the point of God's several creation of humans, each a separate entity, each a microcosm and a mystery which cannot be wholly fused or confused with any other. There is not anything abstract about God's attitude toward men, but there is about Steinbeck's.

Also in *Burning Bright* there is on display Steinbeck's tendency to cause his characters to speak in bombast. This novel abounds in the most stilted, overblown, porous talk that a reader is likely to encounter anywhere. It is hardly more than an accumulation of big, empty words through which an aimless wind blows, making unintelligible noises. Here Steinbeck is manifesting his penchant for the amorphous notion orotundly uttered. Imprecision in thinking is matched by imprecision in expression. The gutless abstraction emerges as a vapor of speech.

This is the irony of John Steinbeck's work: that, in his concern for Manself and Life, he has dissolved both for want of exact and plenary knowledge of what they are. He who would affirm the dignity of man, deals that dignity a shattering blow by denying man the dimensions and the personality which alone confer a dignity that is intrinsic and not an accident of circumstance, the attributes of sovereign intellect and unforced free will which alone make man more than the beasts that perish. He who would extol Life and win its reverence, strips it of whatever differentiates it from mere biological existence. And yet, over and over again in Steinbeck's writing, there are crude intimations of something beyond what, when he is being definitive, he sets as the terms of man's being. One could wish that the novelist would rigorously examine these, for it is only from apprehension and appreciation of them that there can come the clarity and strength which his work lacks.

Earlier in this paper there was reference to the resemblance which might be found between Leo XIII's doctrine of property and the ideas which Steinbeck expresses on the subject. It would be excellent for Steinbeck, both as a thinker and as an artist, if his concept of man were not so wholly at odds with that set forth by the Holy Father in his discussion of property. "Beyond the appeal of their instincts," says Pope Leo,

> the brute creation cannot go, for they are moved to action by sensibility alone, and by the things which sense perceives. But vastly different is the nature of man. He possesses, on the one hand, the full perfection of animal nature, and therefore enjoys, at least as much as the rest of the animal race, the fruition of the things of the body. But animality, however perfect, is far from being the whole of humanity. . . . It is the mind, or the reason, which is the chief thing in us who are human beings. It is this which makes a human being human, and distinguishes him essentially and completely from the brute.

The judgment one must pass on Steinbeck is this: that he is a sentimentalist. This may seem the wildest sort of misstatement, but it is literally true. Clifton Fadiman once said that the classification of Steinbeck as a hard-boiled writer is incorrect; if there must be a comparison with eggs, Steinbeck is soft-boiled. Fadiman was referring to the maudlin note sounded habitually in Steinbeck's work, as, for example, in the mawkish pages of *Of Mice and Men* or in the sickly conclusion of *The Grapes of Wrath*. But Steinbeck's sentimentality is something that goes beyond the facile tear-jerking which Fadiman decries. It is a way of regarding humanity, the way of feeling rather than of reason. "Steinbeck the realist" is a misnomer, for the flight from reason which, in common with so many of his contemporaries, he has indulged in, has prevented him from seeing reality as it is, in its entire fullness and proportioning and significance.

James T. Farrell:

Two Twilight Images

FRANK O'MALLEY

THE FICTION of Farrell is likely to bring immediately to mind a well-known figure imagined by the literary historian Taine: in this figure men are seen as field-mice being trampled to death by elephant herds, which portray the brutal forces of nature and civilization. Surely the people who stir about in Farrell's books seem as weak and small and helpless as field-mice, crushed in fear, blinded by poverty and debased by their own wild, unbridled instincts (instincts vaster than will or mind or soul, it would appear) and by the impact of a dark, dangerous, industrial and commercial civilization. In this respect, the work of Farrell draws us back to such nineteenth-century writers as Zola, the Goncourt brothers and George Gissing (a kind of Victorian Farrell)—to mention but a few—writers who took experience not from the salons of the old world but, one might say, from the sewers of the new.

Yet it is understandable that the plight of man in an urbanized, industrialized civilization could scarcely have been ignored, that the sensibilities of serious artists would have been

237

lacerated by the very life they experienced, that they would have to incorporate it into their fictions. This is a most unhappy, sad, suffering civilization—and writers, in the face and feeling of it, could not be expected to show themselves as sentimentalists or optimists. That they should have become materialists or Marxists or naturalists is no matter for wonder, for they were the heirs and products and observers of a highly secularized civilization, in which the destruction of faith and of the traditional philosophical and theological sources of value had been all but accomplished. They lived—and they made clear that they lived—in the twilight of civilization.

It is abundantly clear that Farrell, whether he be described as naturalist or materialist, is important for his expression of his sense of the twilight of civilization. This is what comes out most lavishly and painfully in his stories and novels: he offers a gruesome image of civilization—and within that civilization he establishes another image, his image of the Catholic Church, or rather of the Church as affected by the particular circumstances and pressures of modern, urban, secular existence.

In this essay I shall be chiefly concerned with these two images of Farrell. Appearing throughout his work, they are ground out, with the greatest interest and vitality, in his first (and from a literary, intellectual and sociological standpoint his "last") work, *Studs Lonigan* (*Young Lonigan*, 1932, *The Young Manhood of Studs Lonigan*, 1934 and *Judgment Day*, 1935). There is, contrary to the view of Joseph Warren Beach, little or no development in Farrell's universe after *Studs*. Undoubtedly Danny O'Neill (*A World I Never Made*, 1936, *No Star Is Lost*, 1938, *Father and Son*, 1940 and *My Days of Anger*, 1943) and Bernard Clare (*Bernard Clare*, 1946 and *The Road Between*, 1949) are types dissimilar from Studs, dissimilar, too, from those hardy vulgarians, Gas-House McGinty (*Gas-House McGinty*, 1933) and Tommy Gallagher (*Tommy Gallagher's Crusade*, 1939). But all of them move in essentially the same world, a world that does not change; it simply renews, reiterates, regurgitates itself.

For it is a *world*, the world as he absorbs it bitterly and honestly, that Farrell creates; it is not fiction that he has written so much as a transcriptive study of civilization—a lightless, despiritualized, chaotic, crushed and crushing civilization. The lightlessness and the chaos he understands and embraces with desperate thoroughness. This understanding and this embracement are complete in *Studs Lonigan* and remain, quite unchanged, down to his most recent work. Note, as evidence, the short story published in 1950, "The Fastest Runner on Sixty-First Street" (from *An American Dream Girl*). The boy of wonderful promise, Monty Aiken, is, at the story's end, "dead in dirt and in his own blood in the center of the alley" —just another victim, an epitomized Studs Lonigan.

In Chicago, "at two o'clock in the morning, Studs Lonigan walked breathlessly along Fifty-eighth Street"—after an attempted robbery. Moments like this abound in Farrell. And there are the other common sights concretized in Farrell's rather stale language: the bouncer jerking out a blackjack, the jazz blaring, the "nigger" kids twisted together, wrestling in the street, the inevitable elevated station, the guys around the fireplug talking, the tall and old flat-sided office-buildings, the strikes, the slayings, the milk-riots, the imitation marble counters of restaurants, schoolteachers demanding their pay, oil trucks rumbling over railroad tracks, the dance marathons, "all those foreigners come here to take jobs away from Americans," the drab apartment houses, the line of darkened stores, the vacant lots, the grassless plots of dirt, the automobiles backing away from the greasing tracks, iron-grilled elevators jerking and rattling upward, the waiting in the city rain, pay-no-bills announcements, for-rent signs in dirty windows, the cellar-entrances barricaded with refuse, the poor bars and the closed banks, machinery rusting and crowds roaring. Such are the images taken at random from the pages of *Studs Lonigan*, images that fuse into a single horrid image of civilized desolation.

The most appropriate and stimulating location for Farrell's young men, "the flower of the community," is the poolroom, the very heart of life on the city nights. Sharply in *Young Lonigan*, Farrell arranges a characteristic episode: in the hot July night, Studs and his older friends, the guys, foregather

239

in front of Bathcellar's Billiard Parlor, with its narrow, slitted entrance. Studs, "ashamed of his size, age and short breeches," anxiously tries to win the favor and confidence of the racy, dressy, loud-mouthed hangers-on as they shout jibes at and play practical jokes on the people passing in the street. Now at the beginning of his sorry wisdom, Studs injects wise-cracks of his own and is let in on the tricks of the guys. He finds himself feeling good in this society, for the attitude of the guys has "stamped him as an equal." A few minutes later, Studs is introduced to the poolroom itself, a smoky furnace of affliction but to him, in his youngness, a place of arcanal sacredness: he is thrilled by the experience, anticipating "the time he could come in and play pool and call Charley Bathcellar by his first name"; and he is exhilarated as he washes his hands in the foul poolroom lavatory.

When Studs returns to the street, he sees a ghostly, consumptive old man and other "dopey-looking" passers-by—and reflects upon how they, in their stupor and senescence, must envy the poolroom gang: "They were young and strong, and they were the real stuff; and it wouldn't be long before he'd be one of them and then he'd be the real stuff." The guys with the real stuff continue to hang around and talk of "the passing gals" until they decide to visit some of them and, cramming into a hack, are off. Young Studs is described as watching them go, "wide-eyed with admiration and envy" and looking out to "the time when he'd be able to pile into a hack and go with the lads" and feeling again that "it wouldn't be long now before he'd be the big-time stuff." Thus do the ambitions of Farrell's adolescent in the dismal city start to rise and extend themselves.

And there is another night—a misty autumn night created in *The Young Manhood of Studs Lonigan,* a night on which an older Studs, matured in civilization, walks about, worried about his health and full of nostalgia for the vanished places and faces of the old neighborhood poolroom world:

He stopped under the elevated structure, just south of Fifty-ninth Street. A train rumbled overhead. Sometimes they'd play shinny, or had fights here. He moved on past a row of apartment buildings. In his time they'd looked new and modern, with lawns and trimmed bushes in front of them. Now they seemed old. The niggers, all over again, running down a neighborhood.

Stopping, in something of a trance, by his old school building, he thinks of the innumerable times he had run through the yard, "stiff-arming anybody who came near. They were afraid of him. Damn tootin', they were. Studs Lonigan had been something to be afraid of." To cross a street, Studs rushes out recklessly in the traffic but arrives safely—and breathlessly—on the opposite side. He is pictured as proud of this action, for "it had been taking a chance. His guts were still there, and he was still the old Studs Lonigan, ready to run risks. If he hadn't had guts, he wouldn't have taken the risk of his life, dashing in front of the cars. Damn tootin', he was." Wandering through a park, he encounters some of his old friends—"a bunch of guys like him"—and the talk is of other guys, one in a sanatorium with a bad heart from the "bum gin he'd been guzzling," another dishonorably dismissed from the service and now "dying by inches" from his excessive carousing, another "in the nuthouse," still another just discharged from the hospital and looking bad: "lungs."
But Studs asserts that he feels good enough, expressing only his concern that "things are changed" in the old neighborhood, that "the boys are getting separated." After they all go to a saloon, Studs, in a seizure of melancholy, suddenly leaves the guys:

He staggered back to the park, and over onto the wooded island. He looked for the tree where he and Lucy had sat that afternoon so long ago. He couldn't find it. He staggered about frantically, and finally got out of the park at Cottage Grove. He fell asleep on the car and rode out to South Chicago. He didn't get home until three o'clock. He felt lousy.

One is reminded of a line from Robinson Jeffers: "remember that civilization is a transient sickness." Farrell's man of the real, the big-time stuff is now decomposed or decomposing (even though he tries to reassure himself to the contrary), a sick transient of civilization.

Here and there in his work Farrell betokens at least a faint sort of sentimental primitivism—in delineating the plight of his people of the cities, struggling to be human again, his people of the vacuum, sucked out and dehumanized by their endurance in civilization. For example, in the short story, "The Benefits of American Life" (*Guillotine Party,* 1935), the sturdy Greek shepherd boy who comes to America and "that tremendous paradise known as Chicago," becomes a dance-marathoner, winning the super-marathon for a prize of five thousand dollars only to ruin his health in the strain of the contest. And the prize-money is used, on his return to Greece, to pay for his remnant of life, "with his lungs rotting away on him," in a tuberculosis resort of his native mountains. Farrell would here suggest, I think, the virtues of the simpler, humbler, more primitive life as opposed to life in the urban American civilized paradise. So he allows his lonely Greek boy in the huge city to remember "his homeland and his Grecian mountain" and "the long, slow days with the sheep."

In another story, "Clyde" (*Callico Shoes,* 1934), a drug-store clerk is sketched off as having entered willingly into "the alienness of the enormous city, sentimentalizing his deter-mination to fight out its loneliness." But his point-of-view alters, since in the strange, sprawling city he is stifled. There is no community among men, none of the really human con-tacts he longs for; he suffers from the disease of homelessness: "The unconcern of the crowds, the impermanence of the ac-quaintanceships he formed, the crushing noise, the shouts of a ceaseless, merciless dollar struggle, all attacked his dazed nerves and his bucolic naiveté." Farrell shows him as yearning for home, for "that lazy, dead, Indiana village" where he had once known certainty of life and where he did have a sense of belonging:

His imagination repeatedly fixed and caressed images of his beloved Indiana earth, beloved earth and foliage and woods withering through remembered but dimming distances. At home there, life, the universe, all those images, objects, associations and events which adolescence links into the abstraction called life, had seemed friendly, saturated with amiability. Back in Indiana, everything, even stray stones, seemed to have had personality to the young man, Clyde—as he recalled them in his urban isolation.

This element of primitivism or sentimentalism in Farrell is, however, pretty well dissipated in the attitude of Studs who, at the opening of *Judgment Day*, remains thoroughly impervious to the appeals of the Indiana plains and the solitary farmhouses glimpsed from a train window on the way back from Terre Haute where he had gone to the funeral of one of the guys with the real stuff:

Winter had never seemed so dreary to him as it did now, not even on some of those sunless days, when, as a kid, he had walked alone through Washington Park with the ground hard and chunky, the snow dirty and crusty, the trees and bushes stark and bare. From the train, the land here looked harder, the patches of snow dirtier, an ugly sight. He wondered how the people in these parts, cut off from the rest of the world, could stand looking at the earth on such days as this one, hearing nothing but silence or the wind, except for the passing trains and automobiles. He thought of how his father and mother would so often sit home in the evening, and not have a word to say, and asked himself how the farmers and their wives ever had anything to say to each other. Living like they did out here, their minds must, he felt, always be on such things as death.

And Studs laughs softly realizing "how glad he was that he lived in a big city like Chicago." Clearly Studs cannot fancy himself as a "pilgrim from civilization"—even though it kills him. And kill him it does.

Strikingly, it is in the very last part of *Judgment Day* that Farrell manages the most pathetic—and quietly horrible—experiences of his victim-character: Studs, with two weeks be-

243

fore his marriage, sick and wandering and lost in his job-hunting. The entire scene is gloomy to the extent of nightmare: Studs, nervous, afraid, undecided, scanning want-ads, assembling shreds of self-confidence to brave the bureaucracy of personnel-managers ("he wasn't a dummy, either . . . if they'd only give him a chance, he'd show them. He saw himself, getting the chance, working himself up, becoming a big shot in the Nation Oil Company. But things had gone too far for him to be kidding himself with such dreams") and, after leaving the hopeless and unreal "proposition for live-wires," drifting in the rain, "wondering where to go and what to do next."

He encounters—realizes that he must—defeat after defeat, turning away and slamming the door behind him, bucking himself up with the "sneer from the old days, the old Studs Lonigan sneer of confidence" and throwing back his aching shoulders. The scene, accumulating, reaches its lowest level in his obscene experience of the burlesque show on South State Street and ends, as he staggers home, utterly sick and dying, the rain beating down on him until, at last, he crawls up the stairway of his house to throw himself in and, while his mother screams, to crumble down at the door. Here, with relentlessness of detail, Farrell describes the dissolution of the young hopeful, "with the frank and boyish face," he constructs in the first part of the trilogy: the low, furtive, fearful, animalized movement of the creature overwhelmed by the ponderous power of a civilization he can neither confront nor comprehend.

Broken and writhing victim-character that he is, Studs, nevertheless, is a more convincing and moving character than Danny O'Neill or Bernard Clare. Danny O'Neill is too much of a set-up: Farrell prepares his situation too obviously. He is a healthier human being than Studs—and one whose ambitiousness is steadily before him. But he lacks the genuine anxiety—no matter how inarticulate—of Studs. His star is too sharply pointed and shines a little too mechanically. Early, in *Father and Son,* he deliberates upon what he might become when he reaches manhood: he might become a "soldier of Christ"; still he feels that he doesn't want to be a priest; he

244

thinks that he would rather be a stellar baseball player than anything else. At any rate, he is later represented in the school yearbook as "one of the best all-round athletes ever turned out at St. Stanislaus."

I think that it is somewhat interesting that the Danny O'Neill of *Gas-House McGinty* day-dreams himself into being the "sixteen-year-old find of the White Sox," taking part in the pennant fight between the White Sox and the Yankees before forty thousand frenzied fans in Comiskey Park. He has, of course, a phenomenal success but remains throughout everything "modest, calm, unaffected, handling himself like a veteran campaigner," even though, in the sight of the extraordinary performance of one who had "still to shave himself for the first time," women faint, strangers pound one another on the back and people crowd around to shake the new hero's hand.

This element of what might be called athleticism in Farrell is worth commenting on. It is reported that Farrell is an immoderately enthusiastic baseball devotee—and, in this light, there can be some speculation that he might have written the great baseball novel, if he had so directed his powers. Joyce, we know, had an unusual talent as a tenor which he did not develop; and, it has been pointed out by L. A. G. Strong, that in Joyce's "championship" of the tenor O'Sullivan there may be recognized "an act of penitence for the buried talent." Conceivably, Farrell's "championship" of the baseball player may be a similar act. One wonders, too, about any possible link between the pain of Farrell's frustrated athleticism and the transfer of his devotion to literature as an arena in which he has become indeed a "veteran campaigner."

In any event, the vocational frettings of Danny O'Neill are brought out in rather wooden fashion: "Would he advance in life in the coming year? Would he get to college? Would it lead him on the road to where he would be fixed so that he could be somebody? . . . And would his name ever mean anything in Chicago, in cities all around the country?" At commencement, Danny's doubts about the future are presented with equal dullness: he is sure, as he listens to the class oration,

245

that he is "no match for life," that he lacks the brains and perseverance, that he has already shown himself a goof and a failure.

Farrell's handling of Danny's self-pity and fear of life is very external, lacking the acuteness and the sometimes overwhelming pressure of his portrait of Studs. It seems as inevitable as it is obvious that, when Danny goes to work in McGinty's office, he will (in his desire for the education that will liberate him) concentrate utterly on literature and be oblivious of the office-work. Equally inevitable and obvious is the patronizing, leering reaction of the office muckers: "Hey, did you fellows hear that? He's readin' Shakespeare." With exceeding ungainliness Farrell has laid out Danny's (and his own) course, the course that is "indispensable for literary fame" and success:

> Success! Sometimes riding home in a crowded train, he wondered if people seeing him thought that they were looking at a young man who had a destiny. Success! Every day he answered telephones and people sometimes complained and said they didn't want to speak to a clerk, they wanted to speak to somebody, somebody in authority. *Somebody*. To be somebody.

Consonant with his nature, Bernard Clare achieves success. He actually becomes *Somebody*. But in his narration of Bernard's rise from the ranks, Farrell is considerably more externalized and awkward than he is in manipulating the career of Danny O'Neill. He introduces an unlimited and confused batch of reflections and incidents involving social justice, left-wing politics and Communist agitation. The exultation of Bernard at one moment, over the party's cause, in *The Road Between*, is clumsily and tritely managed: Farrell describes Bernard marching in the May Day parade, "linked in the bonds of solidarity," with his head held high and tears welling in his eyes and believing that "there was pathos, sorrow, death, joy and hope in this parade, and that it was all symbolized in the song, *The Internationale*, which was being sung today in many lands and in many languages."

But if Bernard Clare's exultation is impersuasive, his an-

guish is even more so. His fervent desire to write to end injustice is heavily indicated: "He'd throw this, all of this, back
in the face of the world. . . . he would not think his pen was
futile. He would use it, use it. Damn it, he would. He would
try to drive shame so deeply into people that they would wince,
wince and never forget it." Correspondingly banal is the description of Bernard's "great agony" upon reading of the execution of Sacco and Vanzetti: "He leaned against the stone
fence facing Fifth Avenue, trying to check his tears, blowing
his nose vigorously so that strangers might not see him crying.
. . . How petty were his own despairs, his own angers, his own
irritations, his own complaints!" There follow the quite foolish
rhetorical questions:

> Would humanity remember this, remember in anger?
> Humanity? Was this humanity walking on Fifth Ave-
> nue? Or had it been humanity last night in Union Square?
> Or was it humanity he saw in the lavatory at the Willis
> every morning? Or Tommy Stark and Cassidy at the
> store where he worked day after day? Himself and Al?
> And the whore in Harlem that time?

Farrell lamely answers the lame questions: yes, "all, all were
humanity." Throughout the Bernard Clare books, there are
other flat rhetoricals and similarly flat conclusions: "Yes,
today America, this entire country, was like one lump of uncertainty." And Bernard, at the close of *The Road Between,*
with the prospect of Paris before him, considers whether he
will find in Europe, in Paris, even in Russia, what he had
been unable to find in Chicago, in New York, in America.
Then his thoughts suddenly return to Chicago:

> What was happening in Chicago now? Chicago! He
> had once been a boy there, a frightened and ordinary
> boy, and somehow that boy had grown into this Bernard
> Carr,[1] an American writer, standing here and looking

[1] The Bernard Clare of the book by that name becomes Bernard Carr
in *The Road Between.* It seems that Farrell received the serious objections (even to the extent of lawsuit) of a person actually named Bernard
Clare (whom, of course, Farrell never had in mind). So, in the next book
on the career of Bernard Clare, Clare becomes Carr. But Bernard is still
Bernard.

across at Union Square in the morning sunlight. How had it happened? How had he found his road and won the confidence he now felt? The seeds of this change were not here in New York. They had been planted back there, halfway across this American continent. His heritage was there, not here, and not in the cultured Europe he was about to see. And somehow out of that heritage he had developed this ambition to become part of the memory of mankind.

In the unbelievable bathos of this summary, Bernard Clare, critic (and no less a victim for being critic) of civilization surely comes forth as a fatuous character, a character much more meaningless than Studs, the scared sacrifice of civilization.

For the sordid suffering of Studs is real. Compared with him, Danny O'Neill—real enough, too—seems too conventionally fitted out for rescue from his untoward environment; and Bernard Clare, in his rebellion, is much too opaque, mousy and anemic, removed at least from the human pity and horror generated by the narration of the career of Studs. I believe that Farrell is more objective in his handling of Studs: with Danny O'Neill and Bernard Clare there is, perhaps, too much self-identification on the part of Farrell, who here may be creating merely his "voices."

The plight of soul or career in these later characters comes out, in excess, as an attitude, a point-of-view now associated with Farrell himself. In particular, there is his attitude towards the Catholic Church, for the Church is, as I have said, his second persistent—and maybe his more significant—image. The Church, as Farrell presents it, especially in the Studs Lonigan trilogy and in the Danny O'Neill tetralogy, is a dreary, sentimental and shapeless refuge for the impoverished or empty-headed superstitious; it swirls in and out of the chaos of life and degradation and death in which his characters move. But it has no real relevance for their lives: the characters recollect the dreadful catechetical lessons dinned into their brains, grim lessons of sin and hell and damnation; they are exposed to the vulgar-orotund and slick-dogmatic sermons; they swoon through the indulgence of the sweetest minor pieties and berate themselves, in maudlin conscience-pangs, for their prurient offenses against the law, the law from which they are never delivered by love or the faintest intimation thereof. Their highly-individualistic religious experience is part of their own terrible isolation within the dark world.

Altogether in Farrell's work religion, lacking any genuine dynamic, any genuine entrance into the lives of the people, is just an inconsequential retreat from discomfort and noise, despair and poverty: "And it was so quiet in the church . . . Ah, how pretty a thing Mary was"; and the eyes of the petitioner become "glued in fascination on the Italian features of the statue, the large red lips . . . the lovely reddish blush of the cheeks."

While the religious propulsion of Farrell's male characters appears to have as its highest goal the complacent security of membership in the "Order of Christopher," the religious drive of his female characters is towards satiation in what can only be called novena-antics: Lizz O'Neill, for example, turned in upon herself as she is, is expert in such things. But Farrell is nowhere more outrageous in the cast-irony of his treatment of religious experience than in the low-grade short story, "Two Sisters" (*Guillotine Party*).

Here the two harridans meet after attending Mass in St. Clement's Church: midway in their indecent barging and quarrelling, one of them expatiates on the virtues of devotion to the "Little Rose of Jesus Christ," on the advantages of joining the Society dedicated to her and on the wonders she would work for the members. Devotion to other saints, she piously and placidly avers, had fine results, too: praying to St. Anthony, for instance, for lost letters; to St. Joseph for domestic tranquillity; to St. Rita for the relief of colds, and so on. Still, she assures her sister, for any unusual crisis, no saint could compare with the "Little Rose." At the story's end, after the lascivious bitterness between the sisters has passed, they go

out to the Shrine of St. Jude, who, it is opined, is quite powerful—and remain there praying until the janitor sends them
along by locking up the church: "They parted in good spirits,
agreeing to meet and make the novena to the Little Rose which
was commencing on the following Tuesday."

This story is, even for Farrell, exceptionally tasteless, coarse
—in theme, style and execution—and it is a vast distance removed from the spirit and style of a story by James Joyce
which it brings to mind, at least because of a similarity of
titles: "The Sisters," from *Dubliners,* a story cheerless enough
in atmosphere but told with such kindness and with such
fineness of perception and feeling as to make Farrell's oppres-
sive coarseness and critical realism all the more repugnant.

It is true, as Robert Morss Lovett, Farrell's great mentor,
has said, that Farrell in his short stories is capable of pathos
as well as irony. It is also true that Farrell has written a number of fine stories. But I think that it is an extremity of exaggeration or mistaken enthusiasm to suggest, as Lovett does,
that Farrell's short stories have serious blood-relationship
with those of Joyce in *Dubliners*. Any "family" resemblance
that exists must be coincidental, flimsy, superficial. Farrell,
we know, has unstinting admiration for Joyce and has undoubtedly borrowed from Joyce (as he has from Proust), notably the technique of dream-streaming.

Even so, Farrell's admiration for and use of Joyce (whose
naturalism is subordinated and transmuted) do not dislodge
the fact that Joyce is, in essence and in effect, a writer entirely
different from Farrell. Joyce is inseeing, subtle, incessantly
compassionate. His humor for men and their errant ways is
cosmical, Dantesque. Contrastingly, the spleen of Farrell is
often narrow, odd, viscous, perverse and unnecessary, bearing
some relation to that of the anonymous vagrant who inscribes
the soul's putrescence among the exudations of a filthy urinal
wall. In dealing with the Irish Catholics of his short stories,
Joyce is incapable of Farrell's too frequently raw and resent-
ful excrescences; nor is he ever ready to heap Farrell's ver-
minous indignities upon the humanity of his sinners, of his
low Christians in civilization.

Positive action by Farrell's members of the Church consists in the perverse practices of a wickedly-prejudiced sectarianism, manifested in crimes and thoughts of crimes against the Negro and the Jew. It seems to come naturally to Farrell's Catholic citizen to say:

> Mother, you can never trust a nigger or a Jew. The Jews killed Christ, and the nigger is a Jew made black till the Day of Judgment as a punishment from God. The niggers are descended from Cain. Cain slew his brother Abel and God turned on Cain for killing his brother, and said that all the descendants of Cain would be black, and they would have to live in Africa where it is uncivilized. And to this day they are an outcast people, and their skins are black like monkeys. You can never trust them.

Now it may be true that Farrell, in his time and place, has discerned and been dismayed by some of the worst features of Catholic life in America—sentimentalism, Jansenism and sectarianism—features which have made even the staunchest and most knowing Catholic minds shudder. These are the conditions that once appalled the young James Joyce among the Dublin Irish and which contributed to his, no less than to Farrell's, rejection of the Church. But Joyce never lost his *feeling* for the Church, despite his apostasy (his profound interest in the liturgy, for instance, remained throughout his books and throughout his life). Joyce's Stephen assures himself: "In temper and mind you are still a Catholic. Catholicism is in your blood"; and his friend Cranly remarks: "It is a curious thing . . . how your mind is supersaturated with the religion in which you say you disbelieve."

Farrell's preoccupation with the Church in his novels—and it is, as with Joyce, a preoccupation amounting to an obsession —is repellent, harsh, bold, without any of the tenderness of the Joycean sense of the inner strength and deep rhythm of the Church's life. The human beings of the Church in the dark and imperfect city, whether Dublin or Chicago, cannot help being tainted, tormented and distorted by the earthy conditions of their existence. Farrell, however, could not realize that

251

"Catholics are not Catholicism," that the integrity of the Church's ministry, of its dogma, moral code and ritual is in no way whatsoever diminished by particular, local circumstances or by the defalcations of particular Catholics.

Farrell's Catholics, then, are as degenerate as the civilization about them. And their physical and social poverty is as great and piercing and demoralizing as their spiritual poverty: "Silently, he cursed. He glanced around at his ragged children, from face to face, at his wife, at the gleaming kerosene lamp. He god-damned his poverty, the poverty that had robbed him of one son. God, would he ever break through it into something better?" Totally unlike Dostoevski or Bloy, Farrell does not have the Christian's or the Church's insight into the meaning and dignity of poverty. He does not provide, as Bloy does, his wretched poor with any chance to arrive at their meaning: poverty is simply a terror, a disease and a curse, and its victims are not allowed their proper illumination as "God's legitimate heirs." That the Saviour, in Bloy's phrasing, "wanted preeminently to be called Poor man and the God of the poor" is no part of Farrell's wisdom or of the wisdom of his creations. There is only bitterness minus any vestige of nobility in the hearts of Farrell's blighted Catholic poor.

And Farrell's social thought and action are merely humanitarian and utopian. What he cannot conceive is that social revolution or alteration will not alter the mystery or the meaning or the possibility of poverty—of the poor man whom God has placed on a pedestal. It is interesting to note that Farrell's approach to the problem and resolution of social evil and injustice is based upon his acceptance of the philosophy of progress (the modern materialist belief in progress, both bourgeois and Marxist utopianism) along with its easy corollary, the philosophy of despair or absolute pessimism (the resort or submission to despair when history doesn't turn out as expected or intended).

Farrell cannot grasp the Church's sense of the *mystery* of human history and destiny, with its "relative pessimism," as Maritain describes it in his *The Twilight of Civilization:*

If twilight ushers in night, night itself precedes day. And in human history it often happens that the first rays of a dawn are mingled with the twilight. In my mind, the notion of the present trials endured by civilization was inseparable from that of a *new humanism,* which is in preparation in the present death-struggle of the world, and which at the same time is preparing the renewal of civilization even if it be only for the time that St. Paul predicts as "a resurrection from among the dead."

The Church that Farrell makes real, in his twilight of civilization, is not the Church of resurrection, with perennial prospects of generating an integral humanism. His Church is a church of miserable stagnation, of the deadly living and the living dead.

On another point respecting the Church, Farrell has expressed himself with blunt disregard of the truth of the Church's attitude towards art and literature. Referring to "functional extremism," in his *A Note on Literary Criticism* (1936), Farrell says that Roman Catholicism promotes one form of it, requiring literature to *serve* Catholic theology and dogma, to point up and propagandize for the truths of the Church. He declares besides that, when especially crude mentalities interfere, literature must "enforce Catholic moral codes, and even Catholic political and social policies; it would thus have to conform to the pernicious prejudices of the Legion of Decency, and fly the noisy banner of Catholic Action." There are available the well-publicized instances of the activities of churchmen, lay and clerical alike, falling under and apparently justifying this indictment. Undoubtedly there are Catholics who—in a state of benightedness honest enough, I suppose—do take such attitudes toward the art and literature of the Church. They see it as something hopelessly sectarian and evangelistic, the literature of a party rather than the literature of the Universal Church (the *ecclesia gentium*), the product of fiercely "denominationalized" mentalities and movements.

But such Catholics do not represent the traditional, essential and living attitude of the Church toward art and literature. As Christopher Dawson has observed, in his *Education and the Crisis of Christian Culture:* "The first Christian education was the initiation into the Divine Mysteries in the liturgical sense, and it brought with it a development of religious poetry and music and art which were the first fruits of Christian culture." And the truly great and serious Catholic poets and novelists of our civilization (Bloy, Bernanos, Péguy, Hopkins, Claudel, Mauriac, Undset, Greene, to list but a few), all initiated into "the Divine Mysteries in the liturgical sense," reveal sufficiently that a Catholic literature is not to be regarded as arbitrary, prejudiced and high-pressuring but rather as fully and universally Christian, that the right significance of the Catholic writer is never to be found in a moralism or dogmatism.

Farrell, of course, admits that at least some literature has been produced by Catholics in our time. But, to sustain his admission, he cites with approval the rather inferior poetry of Francis Thompson. And when he declares that "Catholic literature of value is . . . rather the exception than the rule today," he is clearly exhibiting his ignorance of the gravity, range and depth of the achievement by Catholics in art and literature for more than half-a-century. Many of these Catholics have dealt, with greater artistic and technical skill than Farrell displays, with themes and situations similar to those of Farrell: the misery, poverty and evil of man against the background of a devastating civilization. But they have transfigured the misery and devastation in the light of Christian love and hope and patience, in the Christian sense of suffering and innocence and sacrifice.

A world of important difference lies between Mauriac's compassionate, Christian and artistically brilliant unfolding of the life of his poisonous Thérèse and Farrell's callous, meaningless and artistically inept manipulation of the career of Ellen Rogers (*Ellen Rogers,* 1941), a sort of pallid female imitation of Studs Lonigan. In his attitudes toward the Church, Farrell clearly indicates that he does not comprehend, in Romano Guardini's words, from *The Church and the Cath-*

olic, "that stupendous Fact that is the Church," or that, in the midst of a murderous civilization, the Church "is once more becoming a living reality" or, finally, that the artist, the poet and the novelist "with a force that moves his heart to the depths, will experience in the Church the overwhelming transfiguration, the exquisite refinement, and the sublime transfiguration of all reality by a sovereign radiance and beauty."

In offering what appear to be his most persevering images, Farrell impresses upon the reader the force of his unflinching honesty and the rectitude of his zealous, if limited, social sense and social responsibility. His fictions do not advance, however; they simply intensify (or accumulate), with monotonous repetitiveness and generally with unboundaried crudity, the dim experiences that have wholly engrossed the author. With regard to his most important characterizations, he is best, I think, in detailing the confused and naked heart of his primitive hero, Studs, and its incoherent search for a nebulous center; less interesting and less vital in tracing out the effort of the more refined Danny O'Neill as frustrated writer to locate himself outside the traps of family, friends and environment; and quite unsuccessful, actually, in depicting the attempt of the "wildly rebellious" professional writer, Bernard Clare, "to know and discover himself" in, for a Chicagoan, the alien world of New York.

When Farrell, the artist as a young man, forsook his religion and his city, he did not really, like Joyce, find his new strength in art but in society as a kind of reporter or transcriber of the density of contemporary American society. Although he is an inveterately *serious* writer, Farrell, in ultimate appraisal, is an earnest sociologist rather than a very good artist. His attitude toward literature (and his sense of his task), expressed as recently as 1947 in his *Literature and Morality,* has not got beyond the conception prevalent in the later nineteenth and earlier twentieth century.

The tendencies current in today's literature, altering "the entire face of the novel," are not what Farrell thinks they are. The "progress of science" and realism and naturalism in literature, as we know these elements, have, I think, run their course, except possibly in this country. But, says Farrell, "the naturalistic movement has not died out in literature." While he may be right in saying that through naturalism and realism "untold possibilities have been perceived and utilized," this is, nevertheless, no longer the day of Zola or Hardy or George Moore or Dreiser—nor is it, any longer, the day of Farrell.

The novel, it occurs to me, has for a long time been taking another—and so far not too much considered—direction: it is now a kind of philosophical or poetical-cosmological endeavor. Hannah Arendt was infinitely more accurate than Farrell when she wrote in the summer of 1949 *(The Kenyon Review)* that the modern novelist reveals himself "in the last as a poet whose main concern is judgment and not reporting, and as a philosopher who wants not just to portray the course of events but to discover and demonstrate logically the laws of movement governing the 'disintegration of values.' " And, quite different from those of Farrell and of all the "after the lost generation" Farrellites, the novels of Proust, Joyce, Broch, Kafka and Faulkner (whom Miss Arendt mentions, a list to which I would add the names of writers as various as D. H. Lawrence, Aldous Huxley, Charles Williams, Elizabeth Madox Roberts, Georges Bernanos, François Mauriac, Ignazio Silone, C. F. Ramuz, Thomas Mann and Arthur Koestler) "show a conspicuous and curious affinity with poetry on one hand and philosophy on the other."

Yet Farrell's great energy never amounts to poetry (if the evocative *word* meant everything to Joyce, it means nothing to Farrell) and his consciousness of the evil of civilization never becomes a vision or grows into the stature of a cosmology. He is unable to transcend, by any affinity with poetry and philosophy, the old naturalistic mode to which he has doggedly and humorlessly devoted himself. His people remain for the most part like animals "creeping forward" from one ferocious frustration to another. His situations radiate but little light: "And there was nothing to see. The world was full of blackness."

Novelists of the War:

A Bunch of Dispossessed

ROBERT C. HEALEY

IN *THE NAKED AND THE DEAD,* Norman Mailer describes Americans departing for war as "a bunch of dispossessed . . . from the raucous, stricken bosom of America." This is not an isolated opinion. In various ways it recurs time and time again in the fiction of World War II, fortunately counterbalanced by an opinion of America and Americans which is more optimistic and hopeful. The representative major novels of World War II are at once a criticism and defense of American society and an effective commentary on the present state of the American novel.

War is sometimes considered an excellent proving ground for the writer. According to this theory, the writer grows by experience and is certain to be enriched by contact with the complex emotions engendered by modern warfare. Yet the two greatest war novels, *War and Peace* and *The Red Badge of Courage,* were written out of the creative imagination and not from direct experience. And of the three significant American novels of World War I, *Three Soldiers, The Enormous Room* and *A Farewell to Arms,* only the third is widely read today, and it was not published until 1929, eleven years after the conflict. War may produce trends or styles or even revolutions in art, but the mere experience of war, even as suffered by sensitive writers, does not in itself seem to produce good novels.

It is not surprising, then, that *The Wall,* by John Hersey, the most distinguished novel inspired by World War II, is the only one which is totally unrelated to the author's experience. The others are basically transcripts of experience, loosely autobiographical and differing only in the mastery of technique and the nature of the philosophy each writer brought to his work. It was as if each of the aspiring war novelists—and some of them were consciously gathering material—went off to war equipped with the sort of camera he wanted for the type of shot he preferred. Some used color film, others black and white. Some were capable of nuance and chiaroscuro; others preferred the stark outlines of elemental situations. Most of them were primarily journalists, sociologists or propagandists. Once out of uniform, they assembled their snapshots, mixing in, as fitted their taste, rhapsodies to democracy, songs of sex and weighty questions of race, creed or color.

The results are as varied as the armed forces these novels tried to depict. The fourteen million men and women who at one time or other served in the war were as complex as the face of America itself. The uniform was their only source of similarity, identity as Americans their only common bond of strength and weakness. This was the generation which had grown up during the bitter days of the depression, which had enthusiastically embraced pacifism and proclaimed the utter futility of war, the first generation to feel the general loosening of mental, moral and social standards during the 'twenties and 'thirties. This, moreover, was a generation which considered itself hardboiled, which thought it knew its way around. However begrudgingly, it put on a uniform with few illusions, dimly conscious that the war was a sort of crusade, but preferring to look upon it as an unwanted but necessary job to be done. The inevitable reaction during and after the war was directed not against war itself but against fellow Americans and the "stupidity" of those who gave the orders.

Here, indeed, were epic raw materials: millions of Americans scattered over the face of the earth, the stresses and strains of normal backgrounds in abnormal situations, the impact and counter-impact of diverse foreign cultures. The very immensity of the materials made the role of the war novelist all the more difficult. Too sprawling, too scattered and too long to be encompassed in any single work, the war had to be broken down into smaller segments for literary purposes. There was no single physical focus, like the France of World War I, no single source of unity except the fact of the uniform. The novelists, many of them rushing into print without digesting their materials, had to content themselves with sections of the larger action. Sometimes, finding it impossible to focus on a larger segment, they ended up with loosely related sketches or vignettes. *Mister Roberts, The Gallery, Tales of the South Pacific,* and to some extent *A Bell for Adano* and *All Thy Conquests,* are novels in a very inexact sense. Only *The Young Lions* attempted to handle the war on the grand scale, and then only in Europe and Africa.

Nor is it possible to create a composite picture of the war and American fighting men from these separate treatments. To judge from *The Naked and The Dead, From Here to Eternity, All Thy Conquests, The Young Lions* and *The Crusaders,* the ordinary American fighting man was sex-mad, unscrupulous and completely insensitive, the end-product of a vicious society, and his officers were either fascists or incompetents or both, though the fascists are usually depicted as very competent and intelligent in gaining their ends. In *Mister Roberts, Tales of the South Pacific, Guard of Honor* and *Bell for Adano* there is a strikingly different portrait of officers and men, a more rounded and certainly a more hopeful one.

Both schools agree on only one point: sex also wore a uniform as the fifth horseman of the Apocalypse. Like every part of normal human activity, sex was heightened in the abnormal situation of war. All the war novels reflect this, but with astonishing variations which arise from the author's conception of

259

the human person. For some of the war novelists, sex, even in an atmosphere of war, takes its place in a larger context of standards and discipline. For others, the part becomes the whole, and the result is a series of Freudian case histories, a sort of Kinsey Report in uniform which gives the impression that sex was the American secret weapon. Paradoxically, the women in the war novels are all pale and shadowy, with the single exception of Lisa in *The Girl on the Via Flaminia.*

In the same way, the war novels differ in degree of emphasis on vulgarity and obscenity. John Dos Passos' three soldiers would have been shocked by the frankness of their World War II counterparts, just as many civilian readers are dismayed by many aspects of the war novels. Only the prude will demand a false picture of Army and Navy life, which inevitably has a raw masculine tone, but anyone can and should question the artistic validity and moral dimensions of portraits which over-emphasize realistic language and behavior and rely on unrepresentative case histories.

Until the clangorous appearance of *From Here to Eternity,* by James Jones (1951), Norman Mailer's *The Naked and The Dead* was usually considered the most outstanding and sensational novel of the war in terms of sales and critical reaction. After its publication in 1948, it became the standard basis of comparison for all war novels. Both as a literary performance and as a symptom of the society which avidly accepted it, it cries out for extended examination. It is more than a mere story of men at war: it is a brutal criticism of American society with a very definite and very negative point of view.

In 1944 Mailer, then only twenty-one and still at Harvard, was represented in *Cross Section,* an annual collection of new, unpublished writing, by a novelette called "A Calculus at Heaven," which is essentially the embryo of *The Naked and The Dead.* It was the story of five men fighting a hopeless delaying battle in a futile rear-guard action in the Pacific. In a series of flashbacks, Mailer examined the men's backgrounds, their frustrations and their hopes. The key to the title and Mailer's philosophy lies in these lines:

In America, men live, work and die without the rudest conceptions of a dignity. At their death . . . well then they wonder what the odds are on a heaven, and perhaps they make futile, desperate bets on it, adding up their crude moral calculus, so that if the big team, heaven, comes through, and wins and therefore exists, they will. be able to collect their bets that evening.

By ordinary literary standards "A Calculus at Heaven" was a very respectable performance, all the more remarkable because it was a seemingly authentic story about the Army by someone who had never served in the Army. It must have been obvious then that Mailer was a young writer of considerable talent with more than a passing interest in sociology. It is obvious now that *The Naked and The Dead* did not spring spontaneously from Mailer's Army experience. He may have become more fond of four-letter words, which are curiously subdued in the novelette, and he may have gained a more telling sense of realistic Army detail. Fundamentally, however, his Army experience seems only to have deepened his pre-existing conception of American life as a desperate gamble, in which men are futile pawns on the giant chessboard of circumstances.

The Naked and The Dead is deceptively simple in outline and structure. An Intelligence and Reconnaissance platoon makes the initial landing at the island invasion of Anopopei and is later assigned to a dangerous patrol. Lt. Robert Hearn, ex-aide of the task force commander, General Cummings, takes out the patrol and is killed. After incredible hardships, his men stop short of their mountain goal and straggle back to find that their mission was futile from the very beginning. There are ten main characters, eight members of the platoon, plus Lieutenant Hearn and General Cummings. Mailer examines the backgrounds of these ten through a flashback device he calls the Time Machine. They have been carefully selected with almost mathematical precision, presumably as a microcosm of all Americans: a hard-bitten Texan, a Jew from Brooklyn, a Pole from Chicago, an Irishman from Boston, a middle-class midwesterner, an educated but confused upper-class liberal, a Swede, a Tobacco Road Southerner, a Mexican and an educated, determined conservative. For some odd reason, the Time Machine does not seem to operate for Italians, the only major group unrepresented in this extraordinary cast.

The Time Machine discloses backgrounds which are physically and spiritually squalid, with sex the only continuity and a sort of numb hatred the only emotion. For nine of the ten, life has been a series of rude buffetings, an insecure quicksand from which there is no escape. Only the villain, General Cummings, knows the security of controlling his own fate. Because Mailer hates the General so much more than his other characters, he makes Cummings the most fully-realized character in the book. From his own end of the political spectrum, he regards him as a dangerous proto-fascist and does everything possible to set him off from the rest of his "normal" characters. Thus Cummings has intelligence and free will, and there is even a hint of sexual abnormality in his background. *The Naked and The Dead* becomes more than a one-track sociological document only in the conflict between Hearn and Cummings, a conflict of will rather than of circumstance.

Mailer's own conclusions on the function of the American novel are of some importance in assessing his work. "There are really no such things as types in America," he has been quoted as saying, "and as a result an American writer has to spend a good bit more of his time in defining his characters down to the section in which they live, their speech and the particular prejudices they've assumed before he can be concerned with such abstractions as courage, humanity, good and evil, or any of the other philosophical postulates which have formed the basis of most of the great European novels." Up to the word "before," this is very realistic self-appraisal, but in defining his characters Mailer has completely ignored the "philosophical postulates," which are basic to any great novel, European or American.

"The book," Mailer himself says, "finds man corrupted, confused to the point of helplessness, but it also finds that there are limits beyond which he cannot be pushed, and it finds that even in his corruption and sickness there are yearnings for a better world." It is not a realistic documentary, he insists, but a symbolic novel, the basic theme of which is the conflict between the beast and the seer in man. The beast is all too obvious, and the seer seems to be represented by the inanimate, tantalizing mountain. As a writer of considerable technical power, Mailer has succeeded very well indeed in defining the corruption and sickness in man, but these yearnings for a better world seem to elude him. On the basis of *The Naked and The Dead,* he must be considered, not a major novelist, but a powerful literary sociologist with a particularly pessimistic and deadening view of humanity.

The picture of the Army in James Jones' highly-praised *From Here to Eternity* is no less bitter and depressing, but the approach is somewhat different. This super-realistic study of the pre-Pearl Harbor Army in Hawaii is probably the frankest and most brutal serious novel in American fiction, the ultimate projection of a plodding, impassioned and thoroughly confused realism. Though the war enters directly only into the last few chapters, it permeates the atmosphere and provides the excuse for a thorough airing of the Regular Army's dirty linen. Jones' glorification of the American as rebel belongs to a strong tradition in American writing, but with a significant difference. The classic rebels of fiction usually had firm artistic, social or political convictions which inevitably brought them into conflict with the established order. But this is the soldier rebelling for the sake of rebellion in a semi-masochistic fashion, not because of firm convictions but because he is the confused heir to democratic ideas of individual freedom which have lost their outward form and inward meaning. It is act divorced from motive and ending in tragic absurdity.

Private Robert E. Lee Prewitt, boxer, bugler and soldier extraordinary, literally knocks himself out to prove that he is a human being according to his own lights. He freely chooses to fight the system, right or wrong, at the same time that he loves the system. This ambivalent attitude of the Regular Army, the thirty-year men, provides much of the fundamental emotional conflict and whatever meaning there is in this document. The Army is both hero and villain. Prewitt and his buddies are presented as the lonely, restless children of the depression, without aim, purpose or goal, without the ability to order their own lives. The Army has taken over and provided security and direction, like a strong father imposing his will on immature, disorderly sons, who find it necessary from time to time to fight back and assert their own independence. Prewitt's death as a result of his abortive revolt proves nothing. He is certainly not a tragic hero, nor does Jones appear to present him in that light.

The twin themes of acceptance-rejection of the Army and the soldier's need to assert himself color the pseudo-philosophic haze through which Jones views Army life. With youthful intensity he piles up sordid details and episodes, and they are individually powerful, because he is a talented writer. He has an unerring ear for the common run of everyday Army language. He has an uncanny eye for the minutiae of everyday Army life, and when his soldiers go into town on payday to "assert" themselves nothing is left to a sluggish imagination. But by mere insistent protestation Jones' realism defeats itself. His Army fascinates, but it is the fascination provided by bacilli under a microscope. It is an Army without heart, mind or spirit, and certainly without morality, an Army in which all the soldiers live by a primitive code and fade away in meaningless confusion.

Unlike Mailer or Jones, Irwin Shaw takes a broader and more optimistic view of man in *The Young Lions* (1948), the most ambitious and spacious of the war novels. When Shaw, playwright and short-story writer, set out on his first novel, he aimed at a sort of modern *War and Peace* which would cover both sides of the war in Europe. His technical training in the theater and short story was at once an advantage and a handicap. The novel is enormously readable as superficial narrative, but the contrived over-all structure breaks down into a series of effective single episodes which do not have forward momentum.

The young lions of the title are Christian Diestl, an Austrian

264

Nazi, Michael Whitacre, a Broadway stage manager, and Noah
Ackerman, a sensitive young Jew. Shaw traces their separate
stories from New Year's Eve in 1938 to the end of the war.
In the final pages Noah, walking with Michael through a German wood, is saying, "The human beings are going to be running the world," when he is shot down by Christian, who is
killed in turn by Michael. In conception and scope, this is a
big novel in the old-fashioned sense with three parallel plots
which merge in the final chapters. Unfortunately, both Diestl
and Whitacre are stereotype strawmen, mere excuses for the
profusion of well-managed incident and detail which Shaw
pours into their stories. Only Ackerman comes to life as the
sensitive victim of vicious anti-semitism, and therein probably
lies the major weakness of the book. In his effort to attack the
evil, Shaw has made the war and consequently his novel re-
volve around anti-semitism, and the result of such emphasis
is a feeling of disproportion.

The angriest, the most sensitive and the most sensual of all
the war writers is John Horne Burns (*The Gallery*, 1947).
If it were a real full-scale novel, it might have been one of the
most forceful books to come out of the war. Instead, it is a
collection of eight unrelated portraits or character vignettes
of Army life in Africa and Italy which are loosely draped
about a series of soliloquizing promenades by the narrator in
Casablanca, Fedhala, Algiers and Naples. From the moment
in the very first portrait of Michael Patrick when Burns notes
of the milling GI's in Naples: "They had the ability . . . to
dramatize themselves for the appropriate moment. They
hadn't yet seen the pointlessness of themselves," it is obvious
that he is a powerful, sensitive writer. Michael Patrick sucks
out of his cognac bottle in a box at La Scala and sees

> for the first time in his life that the things which keep the
> world going are not to be bought or sold, that every
> flower grows out of decay, that for all the mud and grief
> there are precious things which make it worthwhile for
> us to leave our mother's womb—if someone shows us
> these priceless things.

In his best moments Burns is a writer of depth and perception. His comments on Americans in contact with alien cultures are among the shrewdest in the whole run of war fiction. His admiration for Italy and the Italians borders on the extravagant and his diatribes on the failure of the ordinary American to appreciate the country and its people are extremely caustic. His problem as an artist is fundamentally one of material and outlook. Much of the time he sounds like an ivory-tower esthete with a hankering for psychiatry coming to grips with life for the first time, and there is more than a hint of the decadence of the early Gide. He favors abnormal people and abnormal situations, though he is capable of quieter, more human interludes, such as his portrait of the two chaplains or his charming study of the very formal courtship of an Italian girl by a middle-aged American officer. But more than half the portraits are decadent or psychiatric, and they give *The Gallery* a destructive, uncontrolled sensual effect.

Burns has the undisciplined instincts and sensibility of a poet, but Alfred Hayes is a professional poet. Hayes' two novels about Rome, *All Thy Conquests* (1946) and *The Girl on the Via Flaminia* (1949), show the discipline of a trained poet and the natural sensitivity of a true artist. *All Thy Conquests* is an episodic, panoramic view of post-liberation Rome. Though Rome itself is the main character, Hayes traces the effect of the liberation on three Italians and two Americans in three-part alternating episodes. Two of the Italians are innocent victims of the liberation and the others, including an epicene Italian aristocrat, are victims of their own corruption and illusions. Like Burns, Hayes ardently admires the Italians and sympathizes with their disillusionment in the liberators. With a keen eye for scene and setting, he can dwell lovingly on the changing moods of the city, without always understanding the rich tradition behind it. Because of its episodic approach, *All Thy Conquests* lacks cumulative power, though individual scenes and episodes are often striking.

The Girl on the Via Flaminia is a tighter and more powerful novel, though Hayes the poet is less evident. It is an extremely simple story of an American soldier and an Italian girl, distinguished for the only three-dimensional portrait of a woman in all the war fiction. Lisa is not a woman of the streets, but she is reluctantly driven by hunger into a liaison of convenience with the American soldier Robert, a callow, all-American type who looks to her for sex, not love. When she becomes involved with the police because of him, she realizes that as a person she means nothing to him. With great dignity she denounces his attitude and deserts him, just as he begins to feel the first touch of real love. He is no longer the liberator who believes that cigarettes and chocolate conquer all: he is a confused young man who has begun to learn something. Within this simple compass Hayes has told a very powerful, moving story.

Tales of the South Pacific (1947), by James A. Michener and *Mister Roberts* (1946), by Thomas Heggen, are also simple in their method and intention, but they are both better known through stage adaptations in which slickness has been substituted for simplicity. The leading male character in the Rodgers and Hammerstein version of *South Pacific* never appears in the original book, which ambles along quietly from one anecdote to another. Some characters appear in several of the episodes, but there are really no main characters. The work is merely a series of impressions of Americans at war connected through a narrator, who seems to be the biggest island-hopper of them all. It has amusing, touching and romantic moments, few of which survive in their natural state in the Broadway version.

Mister Roberts is also little more than a series of anecdotes strung around the memorable title character and his efforts to obtain combat duty. Its greatest asset is an artless simplicity of style and material. Heggen has come upon material he can handle with exactly the right touch. In its slight way, this saga of the good ship *Reluctant* on its regular run from Tedium to Apathy and back is a classic of the war, a minor one perhaps, but one which will outlast the more pretentious efforts of more self-conscious writers. Heggen's characters are completely real, even though they are blown up to a little more than life-size. His simple, basic situations can be recognized and appreciated by almost any civilian and every veteran, Army or Navy, who ever waited in a line or "sweated out" the slow grinding of the vast military machine. He has a natural and universal villain in the Captain, who here stands for all commanding officers and the huge, impersonal machine behind them. In spite of his thin framework, Heggen's touch throughout is right and exact. Even his bawdiness was the result of natural animal spirits and not of the ugly psychoses which become meaningless in *The Naked and The Dead*.

Unlike most of the writers of war fiction, James Gould Cozzens, author of *Guard of Honor* (1948), is a practicing full-time novelist. A solid craftsman of a school now considered old-fashioned, he has consistently matured and consistently been ignored by both readers and critics. *Guard of Honor* was his eleventh novel and the first to bring him any large public recognition. It is the most solid and satisfying of all the novels which deal directly with Americans in war. It covers only three days in September, 1943, at a Florida air base, but indirectly it surveys the whole war and all its complexities in a searching study of the military mind and the military machine in peace and war.

For three days at the air base, Major General "Bus" Beal, the youngest two-star officer in the Army, faces a series of crises. A brilliant combat and operational record behind him, Beal is lost in a maze of administrative problems, local and Army politics, racial squabbles, personal enmities and all the acute tensions of an Army at war. With skillful craftsmanship Cozzens keeps a tight, complicated plot in constant movement. His dialog is intelligent and stimulating. His characterizations are rich, warm and varied. Old Colonel Ross, on whom Beal depends for most of his decisions, is a fine distillation of all the rich practical wisdom of the world, and there are many other portraits of equal depth and understanding. Cozzen's characters are never stereotyped. They are conceived whole, and they live whole. He is not a brilliant or spectacular writer, but rather a conscientious artist who takes a broad, objective view and rejects specious sensational effects. At a time when integrity, technical competence and craftsmanship are at a literary discount, Cozzens stands out among practicing novelists.

The only major novelist to emerge directly out of the war is John Hersey. By training he is a sympathetic reporter whose quiet understanding illumined two major episodes of the war in *Men of Bataan* and *Into the Valley*. These are superior pieces of sensitive reporting, and nothing else. In *Bell for Adano* (1944) he attempted the novel form, remaining close to reporting but achieving a *tour de force* in his study of a small Italian town under American occupation. More than anything else, it showed Hersey's sympathetic understanding of people, both Italian and American. He succeeded completely in assimilating and projecting the mood and spirit of the Italians. There is no sense of the admiring outsider patting them on the head, as there is in Burns and Hayes. Even his transliterations of Italian dialog have an admirable felicity.

Between *Bell for Adano* and *The Wall* Hersey wrote *Hiroshima,* a devastating commentary on the atom bomb, which appeared originally in the *New Yorker* and was later published in book form. Here Hersey the reporter is at his best, restrained but sympathetic, factual but overwhelming in his implications. But his real reputation as a mature writer is established by *The Wall* (1950). Though it does not deal directly with Americans, *The Wall* can be considered the finest American novel to date about the war. Hersey chose one of the great central tragic situations of the war and through it explored the heart and soul of humanity. His Warsaw ghetto is not an isolated place, its destruction not a unique tragedy. The overtones in *The Wall* affect all men, and therein lie its importance and artistry. Just as the bell in *Bell for Adano* is a symbol, so also the wall. Physically, it is the control barrier erected around the ghetto. The barrier thrown up by Jews who turn their backs on the modern, Gentile world and by further extension, it is any barrier laid down between man and man.

The work is not easy to read. Hersey poses as the editor of the papers of Moach Levinson, a meek little Warsaw intellectual who began in 1935 to put down slight notes for a polite Jewish social history with the feeling that events are less important than people's reactions to them. After the arrival of the Germans in 1939 Levinson realized that his notes might be the only human record of life in the ghetto. They became an obsession with him and he went about shamelessly, filling in gaps, collating the various versions of events. Levinson's notes, as allegedly edited by Hersey, provide a day-by-day, circumstantial record of the ghetto up to the moment of its complete destruction. The main characters, sometimes seen from several viewpoints, develop to new heights or depths under the tension. The device does not make for smooth reading, but within the framework of an over-all artistic plan it creates a powerful illusion of documentary truth.

In this study of men, women and children facing spiritual and physical destruction Hersey is concerned with the great human truths, the philosophical postulates like courage, humanity, good and evil which Norman Mailer found it necessary to ignore. He has an acute sense of the continuity of tradition and culture, and his grasp of the spirit and mood of Judaism is deeply impressive. He has no political message and no thesis, except that human dignity exists and sometimes grows more noble in the direst of circumstances. Above anything else, *The Wall* is a great human document.

There have been many other war novels of all types and many more will be written, for five years is a short time for such a vast experience to simmer down into art. Moreover, those five years have shown that World War II was but the dark prelude to a long undeclared war, in which the philosophical postulates so lightly brushed aside by Norman Mailer are a prime issue. The distance from Mailer to Hersey is more than the difference between the most publicized and the most impressive novelist of the war. They represent diametrically opposed conceptions of life. They are the literary representatives of the tug of war which still goes on in American life and the American novel. Taken together, the novels of World War II mirror a tragic state of confusion and contradiction as

America girds once more to defend not only her own freedom but the whole spiritual heritage of the West.

From the evidence in *The Naked and The Dead* and *From Here to Eternity* it would be difficult to believe that Western civilization ever existed, that it ever attained any sort of spiritual achievement. Mailer and Jones, peering at man through high-powered microscopes, find him puny and insignificant, governed by no discernible law except instinct, a mere speck of animated matter struggling for survival. In this they speak for the more obvious materialistic drives of the American character. But the American character also has a less obvious and, in artistic terms, a less sensational side. Cozzens and Hersey, groping for this broader conception, study man within a framework of spiritual values which give him a richer meaning. In between lie all the other war writers, dimly conscious of this basic tug of war between the material and the spiritual, drawn sometimes this way, sometimes that, never certain of solid ground. The religion they most often preach is little more than a glorification of democracy. The values they most often support are pragmatic and hedonistic, though they pay ample lip service to a whole series of watered-down absolutes. They are often at war with themselves and with each other in their efforts to glorify or to vilify the vague American dream.

For five years they have been setting it all down, all about America and the war, as if impelled by some necessity of personal catharsis to tackle the ever-fascinating subject of war. However well the catharsis has succeeded, their efforts have added little to the body of permanent American literature. Like the Great American Novel, the Great American War Novel seems to be a tempting mirage, tantalizing in the distance but never quite attainable.

"*Was All for Naught?*":

Robert Penn Warren and New Directions in the Novel

NICHOLAS JOOST

A HUNDRED years ago, Herman Melville questioned the universe, and nobody minded. Indeed, until recently *Moby Dick* was read not as perhaps the first American novel seriously to doubt the existence of an abiding and universal moral order in which goodness reigns supreme, but as an exciting if somewhat overlong and overwritten boys' adventure story. Today Melville's doubt is a commonplace, in one guise or another calmly accepted by readers and praised by reviewers. The mid-twentieth-century literary vanguard at once shocks us with, and forces us to recognize, another question. In Edward Newhouse's recent novel, *The Hollow of the Wave,* one of the two protagonists "almost savagely" asks at the very end of the novel, "What are we doing here, you and I?" Novelists and their public have come a long way from Ahab's defiance of the white whale when we question, as we apparently do, not the settled conflict of good versus evil, but the very reason of man's place in the cosmic order.

The cosmic order made clear at Hiroshima and Bikini is worse, from one point of view, than mere chaos. Man is superior to chaos, but the distant stars, the indifferent nebulae twinkle on unaffected by what is after all a pinpoint puff of smoke in the vastness of an inhumanly expanding universe. Faced by the vistas and implications of modern physics and astronomy, our most talented new novelists turn to the novel of ideas to express their dismay—indeed, their despair. What are we doing here? they cry. And the most talented of them all, Robert Penn Warren, carries the question a step further. He asks, "Was all for naught?"

The novel of ideas as Warren writes it is not a genre divorced from the main current of American life; this we see in the sales of *All the King's Men* (1946) and *World Enough and Time* (1950). "Writing a best seller," Warren has remarked, "was gratifying. . . . On another side, though, a writer writes to be read, but if he is a writer with any claim to seriousness he writes to be read on his own terms." What are these terms? What is the rapport that Warren has established with his readers?

First of all, he has met a growing taste for conservatism. Indeed, Warren's ideas and their acceptance are characteristics of the new conservatism of America since 1939 or '40, an outlook that, especially in the five years prior to 1950, has gained adherents with increasing impetus. As a representative novelist, Warren is thoroughly traditional in his point of view. His conservatism is reflected not only in his novels but also in his criticism, an adaptation as it is of the Aristotelian bias and method.

Perhaps the roots of Warren's traditionalism lie in his background, the conservative South. He was born in Kentucky and attended Vanderbilt University in Nashville, Tennessee. During his years at Vanderbilt he was a member of the Agrarian group of literary men and economists that based their program on Thomas Jefferson's agrarianism. The literary productions of the group, which included beside Warren such men as Allen Tate, John Crowe Ransom and Merrill Moore, were published in the famous little magazine *The Fugitive*. Warren also contributed to the symposia that reflected Agrarian interests, *I'll Take My Stand* (1930) and *Who Owns America* (1936). Warren's poems, such as "The Ballad of Billie Potts" (1943), and his editorship of the late and still lamented *Southern Review* also reflect his continued interest in the South as a region.

This preoccupation is the wider context of association in which we ought to view Warren's ideas and their fundamentally traditional orientation; this it is which accounts, even in a professedly political novel such as *All the King's Men*, for the absence of "liberal" clichés from the author's vocabulary.

Casually read in their immediate rather than in their wider context, the ideas in Warren's four novels may not seem to carry in them the weight of the past, as assuredly they do. The naturalism of *At Heaven's Gate* (1943) and *All the King's Men* may momentarily deceive us into accepting them as social realism pretty much, except for the Southern locale, in the manner of Dreiser or Steinbeck. But another discipline is present, and it endows these novels with a profundity totally lacking in merely naturalistic works or those written from the standpoint of social realism. As we might expect from what we know of Warren's background and his literary criticism, this latter, more central discipline is that of the humanities.

This it is which gives Warren a truly tragic view of man's estate, a view never degenerating into the futile pessimism of the existentialists, never lapsing into the sentimentalism of Steinbeck. Even at his most somber, Warren seems to cling to the notion that a man has worth, a man has his due place in the universe. Few contemporary novels finish off their casts of characters so relentlessly as does *World Enough and Time;* and yet at the dark and bitter conclusion, when injured and injurer alike have met their violent deaths, Warren refuses to treat them as automata, as mere creatures at the mercy of destinal forces. The protagonist, Jeremiah Beaumont, and men in general may not get the justice they ask for. But the tragedy of this tale results not from the opposition of his characters to a blank and inimical spirit, such as we find in Dreiser and Steinbeck, but from the opposition of men to other men.

Jeremiah Beaumont dies tragically because he allows himself to be influenced by the wrong people and because he uses foul means to try to attain his fair goal. The tragedy of *World Enough and Time* lies precisely in Warren's contemplation of this perversion of the ideal by its contact with the real. He seems to tell us that the most we can hope for in this world is an unthinking peace, inasmuch as we can never attain the truth, swerved aside from it as we are by our concupiscence and the defects of our virtues—the love of justice, of charity. "But men still long for justice," Warren notes; and reflecting on his story, he repeats Jeremiah Beaumont's question, "Was all for naught?"

When the idea comes into conflict with the fact, disaster results. Percy Munn, the tragic hero of *Night Rider* (1939) pursues his ideal of a fairly balanced economy, only to end as an outlaw hunted for a crime he did not commit by the forces of a society he had given his life to improve. Such a view of the conflict between the world and the idea gives rise to Warren's pervasive irony. It is an irony he repeatedly emphasizes in all his novels, the strange and well-nigh inevitable process whereby a man's best intentions somehow perversely produce evil results. Percy Munn becomes a murderer in the course of his attempt to help create a just economy for Kentucky tobacco farmers. In *All the King's Men* Willie Stark becomes a dictator in the process of reforming his state's government in the interests of the common people. Sue Murdock, the heroine of *At Heaven's Gate,* tries to find a viable personal philosophy; but her search for emancipation ends in the most bedraggled sordidness and disaster. Jeremiah Beaumont sees himself as a knight errant in the service of his lady's justice; he ends as a murderer and, ironically, a husband faithless to the very woman to whose cause he has devoted himself.

All these instances exemplify another recurrent idea in Warren's novels; that hidden, dark motives usually underlie our apparently most altruistic deeds. Alone among Warren's important characters, the narrator of *All the King's Men,* Jack Burden, possesses that wary, self-mistrusting consciousness of the complexity of a man's motives which enables him to discern the contrast between the obscure impulses really motivating conduct and those only apparently—to the person himself—motivating conduct. The knowledge of this contrast does not result in a sniggering rationalization of all altruism, all purity of motive and performance. Jack Burden refuses, near the close of the novel, to reveal to his mother the reason for her old lover's (and his own father's) suicide, as doing so would injure her greatly. At the same time, Burden knows himself to have been a factor directly contributing to the suicide, as a member of a political machine that had attempted to coerce the man. To show us the complex motives behind Burden's refusal to tell his mother what actually happened, at the end of the scene, Warren has Burden write:

> Then I thought how maybe I had lied just to cover up myself. "Damn it," I said out loud, savagely, "it wasn't for me, it wasn't." And that was true, it really was true.

The irony is obvious, and Burden, along with the reader, is well aware of the mingling of less admirable, implicit motives and more admirable (because more charitable, more altruistic), explicit motives in making his decision.

The men and women of Warren's novels engage in mortal struggle, yet they fight not against obscure natural forces but against evil. Warren's universe is a moral universe. The conflict is between the real and the apparent, between the world and the idea; however, Warren does not equate the idea—those abstractions, truth and justice, so desired by men—and the real with good, nor does he equate the world and the apparent with evil. The idea is, of course, a good, but evil results when a man deceives himself by insisting on ruthlessly applying the idea without regard for the means used and for its immediate effect on others. The conflict rages between good and evil in man, but between good and evil so inextricably intermingled in man's flesh and soul that the untangling of motive is usually, we learn, impossible.

The extreme to which Warren carries this belief is shown

most clearly in *World Enough and Time*. In one passage Jeremiah Beaumont sees that he has not been vigilant, that he has deceived himself. Thinking the world was a trap, he had taken the sweeter bait of another trap more cunningly set. "And that trap was the 'idea'—the idea itself and pure." He had lived so long with the idea that that alone had seemed real. Because the world had seemed nothing, he lived in the way of the world, feeling safe because he held the idea, "pure, complete, abstract, and self-fulfilling." He had thought that he was redeemed by the idea, that sooner or later the idea would redeem his world. This obvious paraphrase of the Gospel according to St. John ends with Beaumont's coming to believe that "the world must redeem the idea . . . the idea must take on flesh and fact, not to redeem, but to be redeemed." Needless to say, such a reversal of the Christian order does not prevent Beaumont's tragedy; the world's victory, its redemption of the idea, leads straight to tragedy.

The fact is that Warren in none of his novels has presented a definitive solution to this tragic conflict. He sees that there are good and evil but that only ideally, never concretely, do good and evil exist absolutely and purely. Nothing in this moral conflict is ever finally resolved: so muddled are men's motives that the most a man can hope for is the attainment of a "last peace" that is neither happiness nor unhappiness but darkness, "the black inwardness and womb of the quagmire" which is, to Jeremiah Beaumont, the world. Another writer than Warren might call such a state not peace but despair.

This prevailing attitude may seem to be one formulated outside Christianity; and it is true that in *Night Rider, At Heaven's Gate,* and *World Enough and Time* the tragic conflict results not merely in man's defeat but in a conscious refusal to achieve catharsis, or to assert in Christian terms the world's order. In *All the King's Men,* although the protagonist goes down in defeat, the lesser characters, while battered, emerge with a more positive attitude toward themselves and their engagement in the struggle of living. In this novel alone of the four, are characters redeemed, chastened, purified by the conflict in which, as they are born into it, they must engage.

This novel contains both a tragic catharsis and a statement of Christian belief. The narrator Jack Burden and his wife learn how to live because they have observed, and have been caught up in, Willie Stark's tragedy. They are redeemed not by the world that clothes the idea, but by the idea bodied forth in the world, by the Word made Flesh. In the final scene of *All the King's Men* Warren states explicitly that the narrator in his "own way did believe" the version of Christianity formulated by his foster father:

"The creation of man whom God in His foreknowledge knew doomed to sin was the awful index to God's omnipotence. For it would have been a thing of trifling and contemptible ease for Perfection to create mere perfection. To do so would, to speak truth, be not creation but extension. Separateness is identity and the only way for God to create, truly create, man was to make him separate from God Himself, and to be separate from God is to be sinful. The creation of evil is therefore the index of God's glory and His power. That had to be so that the creation of good might be the index of man's glory and power. But by God's help. By His help and in His wisdom."

Such a mingling of Manicheism and Calvinism as this contributes to the well-known "murkiness" of Warren's novels, the darkness and confusion of his universe. If this universe is moral, the morality operating there is based not so much on the traditional Christian ethic as upon a variation which holds the temporal world to be torn between equally powerful antinomies of good and evil, the evil in the world to be a positive force seeking man's destruction, and man to be helplessly doomed to commit sin.

Stemming from these doctrines comes Warren's belief that however much we may think we guide our destinies, in reality we are largely the pawns of others. Man, we have learned, is doomed to sin by the very fact of his creation. He thirsts for truth and justice, but in most cases he does not attain his goal. One of the most interesting aspects of Warren's novels is that he does not excuse the moral failures of his characters as caused by fate or chance or the gods or a blank, inimical universe. The agency of evil is man himself. Not only is Willie Stark—the tragic hero—led astray by his own concupiscence; he is also doomed by other men, much lesser men, squalid little politicians who in turn are the pawns of others.

A similar case is that of Jeremiah Beaumont, at the mercy of his melodramatic, stagy impulses. Despite his ardent yearning for virtue, pride leads him to destroy himself; moreover, so Warren informs the reader, Jeremiah's catastrophe occurs because one person, his best friend Wilkie Barron, consistently betrays that yearning. At every important point in *World Enough and Time*, Wilkie uses Jeremiah to further his own ends, selfish ends that bring on the deaths of the chief actors, Cassius Fort and Jeremiah and Rachel Beaumont, as well as the deaths of several minor characters. Jeremiah finally sees Wilkie as the "mask of the world"—a symbol, no more, of the wrong that men do to men, but nevertheless, a symbol with the power to deceive, to lead astray. Percy Munn of *Night Rider* is also led to self-destruction by his friend and mentor Senator Tolliver, by becoming involved almost unwillingly in the war between the Kentucky tobacco growers and the tobacco buyers around the turn of this century. Willie Stark never learns the extent to which he has been duped—unless we take Willie's dying admission that "it might have been different" to be a recognition of not only his own self-deceit but also the self-deceit of others.

Percy Munn and Jeremiah Beaumont learn explicitly the extent to which they have been duped. Percy Munn intends to murder the man who has duped him and ruined his life, but learning that revenge will not restore the goodness of the past, he gives up the attempt and goes to meet his death. Jeremiah Beaumont of all these tragic heroes is the most articulate, and a large part of *World Enough and Time* is composed of his introspective journal. Here we learn more fully than in any other of Warren's novels what the central figure regards as the solution to the inextricably tangled problem of man on earth: the problem of choice and fate, of good and evil. Warren's tragic hero seems to echo the tragic heroes of Dostoevski's novels, specifically Raskolnikov and Dmitri Karamazov, in his affirmations.

Jeremiah Beaumont believes—we learn from his journal—that there "must be a way, but I may not have it now," whereby the flesh and the word are fused. At present all he has is knowledge of "the terrible logic of life"; he knows that "all the lies, single and particular, will at last speak together in a great chorus of truth in many voices. . . . that is all we need: knowledge. That is not redemption, but it is almost better than redemption. I go home through the wilderness now and know that I may not have redemption. I no longer seek to justify. I seek only to suffer. I will shake the hangman's hand, and will call him my brother, at last."

I seek only to suffer. It is true that we cannot exist in a state of innocence in this world, that knowledge brings sin. Yet it is also true that out of the suffering brought by sin we gain truth; but surely we have a right to ask whether or not suffering is "a way whereby the word becomes flesh." If the suffering does not lead us to redemption, if that suffering does not lead us to a knowledge that we are indeed justified, it will not, cannot, purify us. For himself, Jeremiah Beaumont well may have a way to light; but it is assuredly not a way for others. Suffering without grace means the nameless brutalities of Buchenwald or Siberia; without grace, brutality and wickedness breed only further brutality and wickedness. We need not mere knowledge but justification, redemption.

Beaumont's point of view is typically American in its assertions and its contradictions: the moral fervor; the deep belief combined with a mistrust of institutional religion; the concern with causality as a binding principle of the universe. That a "gratuitous act"—that fascinating invention of André Gide—exists he denies; there is no act uninterested and pure and apart from the world's judgment. A deeply conservative perception, this; but Beaumont's rejection of the gratuitous act does not result in an acceptance of a primal cause. His hero emerges from the black despair; he rejects both extreme idealism and extreme materialism; yet at the end we read that knowledge is almost better than redemption. Knowledge of what? Of life, of the good life. Somehow that knowledge must bring a man communion without contamination, purity without exile. Perhaps; but suffering unilluminated by grace is not, let it be repeated, the way to achieve this goal.

The unqualified, almost terrifying acceptance of the fact that just as all acts have causes, so equally do they have consequences gives an Aeschylean quality to Warren's novels. For him these causes and consequences are moral, and man is inescapably engaged in the moral order. In it he must work out his fate to the bitter end—death for Sue Murdock, Percy Munn, Willie Stark and Jeremiah Beaumont. Only in one novel do we see that not inevitably must a man follow the fatalistic path on which a single act set him. Jack Burden views the tragedy of Willie Stark. Willie needs to be avenged because he has been betrayed; yet Jack Burden knows that Willie died because of his own transgressions as well as because of the transgressions of others and refuses to convey the information which would result in Willie's being avenged— and in the death of Willie's betrayers. If one refuses, as Jack Burden did, to carry out to a logical extreme all the consequences of the action in which he is involved—if a man refuses to act vindictively (or, what is the same, to act according to the world's standards), even if so to act would be to act logically—if a man substitutes charity for this worldly logic—then he may avoid the ultimate catastrophe, which is not death so much as death with the loss of integrity.

Note the fundamental conservatism of this point, the importance of a personal integrity. Thus the seeming rebelliousness of *Night Rider* and *All the King's Men;* the political and personal altruism of *World Enough and Time;* the individual license and irresponsibility of *At Heaven's Gate:* these qualities of Warren's four novels evince his concern not merely with the existence of order but with the justification of order. Like Milton, Warren seeks to show that we cannot escape from the consequences of the past, precisely because we are, whether we like it or not, the point at which all the forces of the past meet, on which they focus. In some ways, Warren's outlook may seem to be an interpretation in modern terms of Aristotelian tragedy, but where Aristotle decreed that the resolution of a tragedy must work an emotional catharsis, Warren's justification of order lacks certitude, and he does not, except in *All the King's Men,* assert the lasting pre-eminence of order. He leaves us with a deep disquiet at the end of *World Enough and Time* when, as we contemplate Jeremiah Beaumont's fate with pity and terror, Warren asks, "Was all for naught?"

We may not see the world as an extension of the dark and bloody ground that is Warren's Kentucky; yet we must admit that with all his darkness of outlook, Warren is representative of America. His outlook is the reverse side of that coin the face of which is the loud and shallow optimism of our booster's clubs. Man's life, he sees, is dark and tragic, but such a point of view is not unique, shared as it has been by Hawthorne, Melville and Twain in the past, by Faulkner, Hemingway, Fitzgerald and Wolfe. Of all his more thoughtful contemporaries, however, Warren gives the most nearly hopeful answer to Jeremiah Beaumont's question: "Oh, was I worth nothing, and my agony? Was all for naught?" Where Faulkner, another Southerner, would shake his head, Warren points out that despite our loss of traditional patterns and belief, "men still long for justice." Almost alone among our thoughtful contemporary novelists, Warren finds meaning in orthodoxy, in the return to and reinterpretation of tradition. Almost alone he presents the past and present as linked not in destructive and irreconcilable opposition, but in an interrelationship that can, by our willing it, be fruitful.

His conservatism represents fairly the most productive trend for American novelists in the future. It is, apparently, the most effective answer to the dissatisfaction, felt for some years now, with the superficiality and the restricted gamut of social realism. For it is not enough that a novel must portray reality truly and that it must portray reality artistically. Neither the well-made novel nor the novel weighted down with symbolism (often Freudianism of the crudest sort, used with neither tact nor understanding) can satisfy man's cry for the profound, the high, the universal in a work of art. Warren's novels satisfy this need. His concern with the American past is as rewarding for our day as was social realism for the 'thirties. His novels, three of which may be classed as historical, possess the chief virtue of such fiction not because they reflect current prosperity and unconcern with social and political problems, but because they seek to interpret the American present as the result of the American past. For the effectiveness of this interpretation we must turn to Warren's point of view. It is tragic; but that very fact implies its ethical quality. His novels are imbued with a strict and grim morality, an almost Puritan regard for causality. Here, too, Warren is a representative American novelist. For our time, he is the foremost bearer of the tradition of Hawthorne and Melville and its freshest interpreter.

II

Unlike Robert Penn Warren, Carson McCullers has not written novels in the classical tradition of Hawthorne and Melville. Neither does she show a sedulous attention to Aristotelian theory. Rather her novels are written in the Flaubertian tradition: short pieces, composed in a cold pure style, the narrative point of view carefully impersonal, with a heavy weight of symbolism—as we see from the titles of her novels, *The Heart Is a Lonely Hunter* (1940), *Reflections in a Golden Eye* (1941—decidedly the most ineffectual, as it is the most immediately attractive, title of all), and *The Member of the Wedding* (1946).

The impersonality of Mrs. McCullers' point of view is maintained only as a narrative technique, however; that she has a bias is obvious from the title of her first published and in many ways most accomplished novel, *The Heart Is a Lonely Hunter*. Ostensibly merely descriptive of what goes on in the human heart, the novel discloses the same Dantean abyss of "blackness, error, and ruin" as do Warren's. And how similar the questioning—and how similar, or simply negative, the answers: ". . . was he a sensible man or was he not? And how could this terror throttle him like this when he didn't even know what caused it? For after all was he a sensible man or was he not? . . . Somehow he remembered that the awning had not yet been raised. As he went to the door his walk gained steadiness. And when at last he was inside again he composed himself soberly to await the morning sun." But the note of optimism that ends the novel is irrelevant, for the morning sun is too vague a symbol to effect a catharsis after the blackness, error and ruin of the previous action.

And what are the reflections in a golden eye? The same blackness, error, and ruin as in the earlier work. Writing of this second novel, Tennessee Williams has understandably identified it with the Gothic School of Southern writing, tales of sensation much like his own plays of sensation. But the novels of Carson McCullers are profoundly unlike the Gothic and Poe-esque fiction which flourishes in the South, literature that titillates without meaning very deeply anything. Here in *Reflections in a Golden Eye* the author is less concerned with ideas as such than in her first novel; but because of the symbolic quality of her characters, a reader understands without being preached at, their wide, bleak implications. Written by a lesser novelist, *Reflections in a Golden Eye* would retain only its surface violence, the violence of rather petty, sordid intrigue and lechery on a Southern Army post in peacetime. Written by Mrs. McCullers, the novel contains depths of meaning of which its violence and grotesquerie are the outward symbols.

Like her other two novels, *The Member of the Wedding* concerns itself with what the author regards as the essential loneliness of the individual man. Here as in her *The Heart Is a Lonely Hunter*, Mrs. McCullers deals with a young girl, an adolescent who must grapple with the spiritual problem of loneliness and love even as she must somehow come to terms with the fact of her maturing. Frankie's development to F. Jasmine and then to Frances means not only the gain of a new peace of mind but also the loss of the old certainties of childhood: a loss of innocence, an agonizing loneliness before the emergence into young womanhood with its acceptance of

285

adult convention. In this latest novel Carson McCullers has not compromised with her vision of individual solitude, but she does seem to suggest that it can be mitigated through the force of human love.

And yet how transient is this linking force! And how indifferent is nature to our gains and losses alike! A small boy dies in the agony of meningitis: "He lay there finally with his head drawn back in a buckled way, and he had lost the strength to scream. He died the Tuesday after the Fair was gone, a golden morning of the most butterflies, the clearest sky." To this writer the sum of our ecstasies and sufferings is something tiny and grotesque, reflected in the immense golden eye of a peacock "of a sort of ghastly green."

With our other rising novelists of ideas, the situations and the images they use to portray their dismay are different, but the central question is the same, the point of view is much the same. Just as Byronism ran much deeper in the Romantic consciousness than mere hero-worship, so in the mid-twentieth-century mind does the cult of dismay run deeper than a fashionable malaise. It is an attitude which affects all the arts. Indeed, one finds the composer Paul Bowles writing *The Sheltering Sky* (1949) rather than composing a tone poem to express his apprehension of man's loneliness and of the black blankness behind the sheltering sky.

Like Warren, Bowles is fascinated by the thought-in-itself— "A gratuitous fact, like a painting of pure design"—but where Warren rejects the possibility of such isolation from context, from past and future and environment and cause and effect, Bowles is just as didactic in insisting on the utter aloneness of his people and of people everywhere. His protagonist, the vehicle of the novel's ideas, dies: "A black star appears, a point of darkness, in the night sky's clarity. Point of darkness and gateway to repose. Reach out, pierce the fine fabric of the sheltering sky." Only the sheltering veneer of civilization protects us from what the existentialist Port Moresby reaches out to grasp, the final blackness.

But what are we to make of a man whose soul only "silences

and emptinesses" can touch? It has been said that the theme of *The Sheltering Sky* is the rapid disintegration of civilized standards once the conventional cultural veneer (that protective sky) is stripped off by a change of environment. The novel seems, rather, to be a moral tale—though not so intended by the author—on the dangers of a life without conviction, without hope, without even much pleasure on the visceral level of existence. Read from this angle, *The Sheltering Sky* turns out to be a pointed tract for the times, one which competently conveys the lessons How Not to Live and What Not to Think.

Much the same nihilism glimmers through the superficially more conventional pages of Edward Newhouse's *The Hollow of the Wave* (1949). Here the twin protagonists do not face the darkness as Port Moresby does out in the Sahara, with no intervening canopy to shelter him from the bitter fact of the universe. They—Larry Holland, the rich man, and Neil Miller, the poor man—must deal with human forces: Communist intrigue, capitalist maneuvering, Freudian analysis of every motive. By the conflicts of these groups Holland and Miller see the world being destroyed; what is more, they cannot ally themselves with "some kind of reasonably harmonious world-view" whose adherents would save the world from those holding another philosophy.

Their not unnatural solution is to retreat into the safety of the peacetime Army. Neil Miller asks only to be alive: "Between spasms [of gratitude for being alive], I sometimes feel I'm in the hollow of a wave and all I want is to ride it out safely." A scientist goes with Holland and Miller to inspect a cave in the Utah desert as a possible site for a World War III factory, or bomb shelter. Struck by the enormity of the spectacle of a culture that in abandoning any rational effort to protect itself returns to prehistoric man's troglodyte pattern, Holland almost savagely asks his friend Miller, "What are we doing here, you and I?" Thus, Melville's doubt has developed into the dreadful question: Has man a place at all in the world that he willfully seeks to destroy?

With his considerable urbanity and a bent more naturally

philosophical than his colleagues' in the field, Lionel Trilling also writes of those lost *per una via oscura* in his novel *In The Middle of the Journey* (1947). Here at last, however, we return full circle to the acceptance of that traditional body of ideas which Robert Penn Warren has sought to relate to the literally overwhelming question, no longer Eliot's "Do I dare?" but the much grimmer "Was all for naught?"

Like Newhouse, Trilling sees the humanistic intelligence as menaced on both sides by absolutisms, the New Orthodoxy that in its return to a refurbished Calvinism seeks to implicate all men in guilt and to hold all men responsible, and the equally absolutist liberalism which preaches the law for the masses, rights and freedom from blame. Unlike Newhouse, however, Trilling does not allow his protagonist, the humanist, John Laskell, to acquiesce in the fact of his own extinction. Harried as he is by friends who try to persuade him to engage himself without scruple on one side in the battle for man's soul, Laskell refuses to throw up his hands in despair. Dismayed he may be, like so many protagonists in so many thoughtful contemporary novels; yet though he is appalled by the sheer ruthlessness of the struggle, Laskell refuses to relinquish his right to discriminate, to judge each problem on its own merits. He accepts his imperfect status, higher than the brute creation, lower than the angels—the man of Pascal, in a universe neither marxist nor existentialist, in which his acts are neither totally determined nor utterly gratuitous.

Warren's Jeremiah Beaumont believed himself committed in the end for all human guilt, apocalyptically saw himself sharing in all of man's degradation; in that realization solely lay his salvation. Carrying on the Great Debate of these postwar years, Bowles and Newhouse envision man as a solitary, cut off from his kind in a brutal struggle against the universe, for individual survival. To ride out the storm, to escape from noise and bustle into the solitude and emptiness of deserts, to deny responsibility: Port Moresby and Larry Holland and Neil Miller ask for no more. Mediating between the extremes, Trilling's scholar, John Laskell, believes that "an absolute freedom from

288

responsibility—that much of a child none of us can be. An absolute responsibility—that much of a divine or metaphysical
essence none of us is." This calm common sense aids us in
answering Warren's query, "Was all for naught?" but it is,
however right, an answer that suffices for the moral, the natural
world and that does not pretend to deal with last things.

Indeed, searching through the pages of postwar American
novels, at least those touted in the great weeklies and the
monthly and quarterly literary periodicals, most readers will
come away empty-handed from their hunt for a positive answer
to that terrible question haunting not Warren alone but all sensitive and many believing men today. The Church has its answer, its store of wisdom in the past, ready for the skeptical,
the despairing, the dismayed; but in America it has lacked a literary voice until these past few years of the nineteen-forties.
Those in search of the answer could go to Dante—in fact, to
all the riches of Christian European culture that include such
novelists as Undset and Waugh and Mauriac—but they would
find no strong voice of their own American culture to tell them:
"This is the way. I have been there and have returned with
my story. Here it is."

Now at last the needed literary voices are speaking and are
being heard. They tell us that the American Catholic is subject
to the same stresses, the same ills that afflict his secularized
brother; but unlike the novelists of despair they tell us that
the answer is not dismay, a negative shrinking away from living
into the emptiness of deserts, the blackness of caves and death.

In Crawford Power's *The Encounter* (1950), Father Cawder,
the cold proud priest, rebels at the horror of life just as deeply
and violently as does Percy Munn, or Neil Miller or Frankie
Addams (of *The Member of the Wedding*). In church after
the police have killed a murderer whom he has harbored, the
distraught priest reflects:

> Beneath this tabernacle it was not required, not con-
> ceivable, to lie—he, it was understoood, did not love God.
> He deferred to His power, respecting the fact of God's
> existence, a fact like gravity or the sun, necessarily as-

sented to, no other course being comprehensible. But it was of no benefit to oneself, it was not pleasing to God, to pretend to love when no such faculty was present. Grinding his teeth together, opening his eyes, Father Cawder knelt erect.

The world is as mysterious to him as it is to Jeremiah Beaumont or Port Moresby, but Father Cawder, despite his own spiritual dryness, affirms the great fact of the universe: "It is immaterial, he said to himself, whether I kneel here or not. Since I am nothing. Since in the face of the mystery which pervades all matter like unconsuming fire I can say only, Lord, I believe that You exist."

In Robert Bowen's *The Weight of the Cross* (1951), Tom Daley, the psychotic sailor, learns—through captivity in the Philippines, loss of his friends, sickness, starvation—the reason for his spiritual illness: ". . . we all run from it . . . Always going farther and farther. . . . In the end you have to stop and face it no matter how far you run or how fast. It's always with you, waiting for you to straighten it out, yourself." A man is very lucky if he can stop and face it before he has "sinned against himself too much. Because when you go against yourself too much . . . you're liable to hand yourself more punishment than a man can take." Like so many men—indeed, all the protagonists of the novels under discussion—Daley had been dying for a long time from aloneness, the American disease. Like Father Cawder, in loss and horror he realized God most strongly; only after tragedy and denial could he "accept the God he had denied through all his lone years," and feel "that he would never be alone again, that he would always be one of many, of all who live and die." And here, at the end of his terrible experience, Daley knows "why he had been psycho." He had denied himself in denying God.

These are two affirmations in reply to the question so desperately posed by Jeremiah Beaumont. They are not doctrinaire; they are grounded fully in experience; they do not negate reality, they face it and affirm it in all its terror and grandeur; above all they insist on the worth of living. If, as

we learn from the history of the world's literatures, the enduring is the true and the good and not merely the immediately
attractive; and if the American art of the novel is to endure;
then surely the affirmations of Father Cawder and Tom Daley
—and how many other affirmations yet unwritten—must be
read when in library stacks the counsels of despair quietly
moulder.

Notes on the Contributors

BRADY, CHARLES A.

Charles A. Brady is Chairman of the English Department at Canisius College, Buffalo, and Saturday Book Columnist for the Buffalo *Evening News*. He was winner of the Archbishop Cushing Award for poetry, is the author of *Cat Royal* and the forthcoming volumes, *Wings over Patmos, Poems 1937-1951* and *Reclaim Imagination: Clive Staples Lewis and Charles Williams* and editor of *A Catholic Reader*. He contributes regularly to *America, Renascence,* the New York *Times Book Review, Thought, Catholic World, Best Sellers, Catholic Library World,* and collaborated in Volume III of *The Great Books: A Christian Appraisal* with the "Song of the Volsungs and the Nibelungs."

CONNOLLY, FRANCIS X.

Francis X. Connolly won his Bachelor and Master degrees and his Doctorate from Fordham University. He is professor of English at Fordham, member of the Editorial Board of the Catholic Book Club and associate editor of *Spirit,* the journal of the Catholic Poetry Society. He served in the Navy from 1943-1946. He is the author of a novel, *Give Beauty Back,* of a critical anthology, *Literature the Channel of Culture,* and has collaborated on several critical studies. He is co-editor with John Gilland Brunini of *Great Catholic Short Stories.* He has contributed to *The Great Books: A Christian Appraisal,* and reviews and lectures extensively.

293

DRUMMOND, EDWARD J., S. J.

The Reverend Edward J. Drummond, S.J., entered the Society of Jesus in 1924 and followed the regular course of studies engaged in by future priests. After his ordination he received his doctoral degree at the University of Iowa; he was appointed Dean of the Graduate School at Marquette University in 1944. He was in charge of the English Department in 1948-1949. He is a member of the Modern Language Society, of the National Council of Teachers in English, of the National Education Association in which, in 1951, he was elected to the planning committee for the National Conference on Higher Education. Other memberships include The National Catholic Educational Association, the Jesuit Educational Association, the Mid-West Conference on Graduate Study and Research.

FREMANTLE, ANNE

English-born Anne Fremantle received her education at Cheltenham Ladies College and at Oxford University where she was, at Lady Margaret Hall, a scholar in Modern Languages. She was assistant editor of the London *Mercury,* fiction reviewer for *The New Statesman* and at various times special dramatic correspondent for the London *Times* in Syracuse, Sicily, in the United States for the WPA Theatre and to the Moscow Theatre Festival. Her published works include a life of George Eliot, *The Wynne Diaries* in three volumes, *Loyal Enemy* (a biography of Marmaduke Pickthall and a history of the Young Turk revolution), *Come to Dust,* a novel, *James and Joan,* an historical novel, *Desert Calling,* a biography of Charles de Foucauld. She has edited a *Commonweal Reader, The Greatest Bible Stories* and *Mothers,* an anthology of stories on the theme of motherhood. She has reviewed extensively in the New York *Times,* the New York *Herald Tribune, Commonweal* and other journals. She is at present assistant professor of creative writing at Fordham University. Her background includes much travel in diplomatic circles, broadcasting during World War II in French and German for the BBC, and special editorial work during the General Assembly of the United Nations.

GARDINER, HAROLD C., S. J.

A native of Washington, D. C., Father Gardiner entered the Society of Jesus in 1922. After classical studies at St. Andrew-on-Hudson, Poughkeepsie, N. Y., philosophical studies at Woodstock College, Woodstock, Md., a period of teaching the classics and English at Canisius College, Buffalo, he returned to Woodstock for theological studies and ordination. A year of ascetical theology in Belgium was followed by his entering Downing College, Cambridge University, for postgraduate work in English. He returned to America at the outbreak of the war, receiving his Ph.D. *in absentia.* In 1940 Father Gardiner was appointed Literary Editor of *America.* He is the author of *Mysteries' End* and *Tenets for Readers and Reviewers* and the editor of the four-volume series *The Great Books: A Christian Appraisal.* He is chairman of the editorial board of The Catholic Book Club.

HEALEY, ROBERT C.

Mr. Healey was educated at La Salle Academy, Providence, R. I. and Providence College. His M.A. was given by the Catholic University of America. During the war he was first attached to the staff of Military Attaché at the American Embassy in London, then later commissioned as a 2nd Lieut., U. S. Army and served in Europe until 1945 with the Historical Section of European Theatre of Operations which was collecting the primary material for the History of the Army in World War II now being issued. He was discharged with the rank of Major, Military Intelligence Reserve. Mr. Healey was executive secretary to U. S. Senator Gerry of R. I. for two years. He has been active in free-lance radio and television writing and in the administration and production of the Blackfriars Guild, New York, since 1940. He adapted *Hoboes in Heaven* from the French of Martens-Obey, and wrote *Shake*

Hands with the Devil, both produced by Blackfriars. He has also conducted a seminar in dramatic writing during 1950-1951 at Seton Hall University. Mr. Healey translated *The Vital Christian* and is the author of a history of P. J. Kenedy & Sons' 125 years of Catholic publishing to appear in the fall, 1951.

HOLLIS, C. CARROLL

C. Carroll Hollis, after graduation from Marquette University, attended the University of Wisconsin for his M.A. He is at present a candidate for the Doctorate at the University of Michigan. His teaching positions have been: graduate fellow at St. Louis University, instructor and assistant professor at the University of Detroit, where he is in charge of graduate and undergraduate programs in American and contemporary literature, chairman of the Arts and Science registration committee, a member of the executive committee of the lay faculty, and faculty moderator of Delta Pi Kappa, a journalist fraternity. He is a member of the Michigan Academy of Arts, Science and Letters. His published works include critical essays in the *South Atlantic Quarterly, Commonweal* and *America.* He is engaged on a study of *The Literary Criticism of Orestes Brownson.*

HUGHES, RILEY

Riley Hughes, a graduate of Providence College, did his graduate work in English at Yale and Brown universities and in philosophy at Georgetown University. He was assistant in English at Brown in 1938-1939. From 1940 to 1942 he was state editor and supervisor of the Connecticut Writers' Project. From 1942 to 1946 he was assistant professor of English and Director of Public Relations at Providence College. Since 1946 he has been Lecturer in English at the School of Foreign Service, Georgetown University. A professional book reviewer for newspapers and magazines since 1932, he is a regular contributor of literary articles and reviews to *America, The Commonweal, Journal of Arts and Letters, The New Scholasticism,*

296

Renascence, The Saturday Review of Literature, The Thomist and *Thought*. A contributor to Volume II of *The Great Books* (1950), he is the author of *Our Coast Guard Academy* (1944).

JOOST, NICHOLAS

A native Floridian, Mr. Joost was educated at Georgetown University and received his M.A. and Ph.D. from the University of North Carolina. He has been instructor in the English departments of the University of Miami and Northwestern University and is now assistant professor in the Department of English at Loyola University, Chicago. He has contributed critical essays to *America, American Literature, Explicator, Modern Language Notes, New Yorker, Notes & Queries* and *Studies in Philology,* and is a member of the Modern Language Association and Augustan Reprint Society.

KENNEDY, JOHN S.

Rev. John S. Kennedy is a priest of the Diocese of Hartford, Conn. He is an associate editor of the *Catholic Transcript* and writes a weekly book column which is syndicated by the NCWC news service. An additional weekly feature on new fiction appears in Catholic newspapers in California. Fr. Kennedy lectures extensively on writing and reading and many articles on the same subjects have appeared in leading Catholic journals. As an interesting footnote he appends the information that he recently "saw a bullfight in Spain without going into a mystical rapture or a paroxysm of disgust."

McLUHAN, HERBERT MARSHALL

Herbert Marshall McLuhan, a native of Edmonton, Canada, received his education at the University of Manitoba and went on for his postgraduate work at the University of Cambridge, where he won his Doctorate. He has held teaching positions at the University of Wisconsin and St. Louis University, and is professor of English at present at the University of Toronto. He is a contributor to such critical reviews as *Kenyon, Sewanee* and *Horizons.*

MOLONEY, MICHAEL F.

Dr. Moloney received his B.A. from the University of Notre Dame, his M.A. from Georgetown University and his Ph.D. from the University of Illinois. At various times he has been a farmer, steel-worker, newspaper man, and for almost two decades a college professor. His teaching experience has included positions in the English departments of the University of Illinois, St. Viator College, Wright City Junior College, Chicago. Since 1944 Mr. Moloney has been in the Department of English, Marquette University, where he has the present rank of associate professor. He is a frequent contributor to *Modern Language Quarterly, Publication of Modern Language Association, Thought, Catholic World* and *America,* and is the author of *John Donne: His Flight from Medievalism,* University of Illinois Studies in Language and Literature.

MONROE, N. ELIZABETH

N. Elizabeth Monroe received her A.B. from Oberlin College in 1919 with Phi Beta Kappa honors, her M.A. from the University of Pennsylvania in 1923, her Ph.D. from the University of Pennsylvania in 1929. She studied journalism in the Columbia School of Journalism, 1929-1930. She taught in public and private high schools for four years and at Temple University for six years. She later became an assistant professor of English at Brooklyn College. Her published works include *Nicholas Breton, Pamphleteer* and *The Novel and Society.* She has contributed many articles and reviews to literary and scholarly journals. She is a member of many learned societies and was chairman of the fiction committee of the Gallery of Living Catholic Authors from 1941 to 1950. Her reviews appear frequently in *America.*

O'MALLEY, FRANK

Frank O'Malley received both his B.A. and M.A. from the University of Notre Dame. He has been a member of the Notre Dame faculty since 1933, at present holding the position of professor of English. Mr. O'Malley has been managing editor of *The Review of Politics* for many years and a writer for various magazines.

SANDEEN, ERNEST

Ernest Sandeen is a graduate of Knox College, Galesburg, Ill., where he also taught from 1935-1937. He is possessor of the B. Litt. degree from Oxford University and of a Doctorate from the State University of Iowa, where he taught from 1937-1943. He is professor in the English Department at the University of Notre Dame.

SLOYAN, GERARD S.

The Rev. Gerard Stephen Sloyan, a priest of the Diocese of Trenton, pursued his college studies at Seton Hall University. He entered the Seminary of the Immaculate Conception at Darlington, N. J. and was ordained from the Theological College, The Catholic University of America, having received there his degree of S.T.L. Graduate courses at Catholic University won him his Doctorate in 1948. His dissertation, "Christian Concepts in the Social Studies in Catholic Schools," was published by the Catholic University Press in 1950. He has been an instructor in the Department of Religious Education at the same University since 1950. He is a member of the American Association of University Professors. His critical ability has found expression in numerous reviews for *America, Orate Fratres* and *The Sign.*

Index to Titles of Novels

BOWEN, Robert	The Weight of the Cross—290
BOWLES, Paul	The Sheltering Sky—286-287
BURNS, John H.	The Gallery—265-266
CATHER, Willa	Death Comes for the Archbishop—82-85
	A Lost Lady—77-78
	My Antonia—75-77
	Obscure Destinies—85
	The Old Beauty—85
	One of Ours—77-78
	O Pioneers—71-72
	The Professor's House—78-81
	Sapphira and the Slave Girl—70; 85
	Shadows on the Rock—85
	The Song of the Lark—78
	Youth and the Bright Medusa—78
COZZENS, James G.	Guard of Honor—268-269
DOS PASSOS, John	Manhattan Transfer—152; 154-155; 162
	One Man's Initiation—152
	Three Soldiers—152
	U. S. A.—152; 157-158; 160-164
DREISER, Theodore	An American Tragedy—43-45
	The Bulwark—45-47
	The Financier—39-40
	The Genius—41-42
	Jenny Gerhardt—38-39
	Sister Carrie—35-36
	The Stoic—46-47
	The Titan—39-40
FARRELL, James T.	Bernard Clare—238
	Father and Son—238; 244-245
	Gas-House McGinty—238; 245-246

302

INDEX TO TITLES OF NOVELS